Grasping for

Grasping for Heaven

Interviews with
North American Mountaineers

FREDERIC HARTEMANN *AND*
ROBERT HAUPTMAN

Foreword by Jan Reynolds

McFarland & Company, Inc., Publishers
Jefferson, North Carolina, and London

Library of Congress Cataloguing-in-Publication Data

Hartemann, Frederic V., 1960–
    Grasping for heaven : interviews with North American
mountaineers / by Frederic V. Hartemann and Robert Hauptman ;
foreword by Jan Reynolds.
        p.   cm.
    Includes bibliographical references and index.

    ISBN 978-0-7864-4202-7
    softcover : 50# alkaline paper ∞

    1. Mountaineers—Interviews.   2. Mountaineering—North
America.   3. Mountaineering—North America—History.
I. Hauptman, Robert, 1941–   II. Title.
GV199.9.H37   2010
796.52'2—dc22   2010036818

British Library cataloguing data are available

Front cover: "Climbers Carrying Loads Below the Northwest Face
of Everest," 1984 (photograph by John Roskelley)

Manufactured in the United States of America

McFarland & Company, Inc., Publishers
  Box 611, Jefferson, North Carolina 28640
  www.mcfarlandpub.com

We dedicate *Grasping for Heaven* to
Norman Vaughan,
who died before we could interview him,
Bradford Washburn,
who became too frail to undertake a discussion,
Christine Boskoff,
who was killed in an avalanche
just a few months after our meeting, and
Charles Houston,
whose recent death greatly diminishes
the number of early 20th century pioneers
among the living.

Table of Contents

Foreword
by Jan Reynolds

When George Leigh Mallory, famed British Himalayan explorer of the early 1900s, was asked after a lecture, for perhaps over the hundredth time, why he wanted to climb Everest and he responded, "Because it's THERE," he wasn't being rude. He wasn't being trite. He wasn't even necessarily frustrated. It was a genuine answer. For Mallory "THERE" had a mystical, magical sense to it. In letters to friends involved in arts and letters, Mallory would comment, you must see this painting, because it is THERE, you must read this piece, because it is THERE.... For Mallory, climbing Everest was a personal, creative form of art; it took him to a place where he felt this wonderful sense of being THERE.

From most accounts it appears that Mallory was misunderstood when he gave his famous answer to this complex question asked of all mountaineers: Why? It has been said that those who need to ask why will never know, and those who know will never need to ask. And yet there are as many reasons to climb mountains as there are mountaineers. It is all so very personal and individual. This is part of the allure of mountaineering. Perhaps it's the peace and simplicity, and the obvious goal of reaching a peak, that draws us to mountaineering. The simple rhythm of *eat, sleep, climb* boils one's world down to its most basic elements. One's connection to nature and other humans is paramount, and life becomes intense. Life is at its fullest, being brought to the brink, making life and death decisions, on a daily basis. This intense focus makes a life feel significant.

Mountaineering is considered an adventure, which an expedition mate defined as "somewhere you are when you wish you weren't, and where you aren't when you wish you were!" An adventure is intangible, indescribable, and that is just what mountaineering is. But perhaps mountaineering satisfies us on an unconscious level, feeding that fire of the mythic quest humans have always longed to go on, much like Jason and the Argonauts, or the challenges found in ancient fairy tales.

But like ballplayers on a field where each person has a different experience of the game, each mountaineer has his or her own personal experience while climbing with others on an expedition. I can only see mountaineering through my own eyes. As a Vermont farm girl, I was first exposed to higher mountains

1

while racing cross country skiing on a national level, and was taken up to a high mountain pass in the Rockies of Colorado as a break in the stress of competition. From that moment on I was hooked! Although I was one of the best skiers in the country, I moved on to spend my time on the rescue squad in Yosemite and Tuolumne Meadows, so I could climb while training, and pursued mountaineering routes in the nearby Palisades.

I also camped at Joshua Tree for bouldering, and lived in friends' garages in Boulder, Colorado, to access rock climbing. Here life's currency wasn't money; none of us had any! It was all about the experiences we had that held value for us in our lives. What route we climbed or designed, how we did it, when and with whom. This was what life was all about, and if we could afford food and drink, life couldn't be better. After savoring the freedom of this life, along with some of the mountaineers interviewed in this book, a door opened to big-game mountaineering, high-profile, sponsored expeditions.

I was sponsored by *National Geographic* magazine, and climbed and skied off the summit of Muztagata in the Chinese Pamirs with Ned Gillette and Galen Rowell, setting the women's high altitude skiing record. I had no idea this record was up for grabs and didn't know I had done so until *National Geographic* researched it as part of the article we wrote for the magazine. Setting records was not my motivation to climb. Ned and Galen had previously set a record, climbing and skiing Denali in one day, so I knew I had strong teammates, and that climbing great gulps of 5,000 feet a day above 20,000 feet, then skiing back down, was normal for those two. My motivation was to experience the joy of the heights ... and not lose sight of those two. Let it suffice to say I was pleased not to be the weakest link. When I threw up on Galen's skis, he gave me the last of his water, and when Galen fell down, I gave him the last of my food. To me, this exchange epitomizes the commitment to each other, and the teamwork demanded to reach the summit. Mountaineering at its best.

When Ned Gillette and I completed the Everest Grand Circle expedition, with a winter ascent of Pumori thrown in, and five passes above 20,000 feet crossed all on one expedition, I was launched into the world of news and press conferences, interviews with the likes of Tom Brokaw on the *Today Show* and Joan Lunden of *Good Morning America*. The line blurred between being a professional mountaineer and a professional writer and photographer, much like some of the interviewees of this book. Just what was I? I experienced the loss of close friends in the mountains. I reflected on the cost of high-profile, high-altitude mountaineering, and all the responsibility that came with it, and the statistic of one in eight not coming home.

My response to this was to make the U.S. Biathlon Team. Here I learned to take the previously adrenaline-induced focus of climbing, and access this focus at will, while calm, and on the run, or ski I should say, and hit a thumbnail-sized target with five bullets at 50 meters. Time seemed to stop, my heart was pounding, and I was shooting. I loved it. But the mountains never left me alone. I returned to the Himalaya to do perhaps the most dangerous expedition of my life. I took a hot-air balloon over Everest with some British and Australian pilots and mountaineers, and crashed. The expedition did, however, set a record, and became an award-winning film.

But I also continued to design and organize more personal experiences in the mountains, soloing over the Himalaya near Cho Oyu, to document what was left of the ancient salt trade, climbing and skiing 26,000 vertical feet of Mount Ararat in one day, by mistake! Doing the first ski descent of Otgon Tenger in Mongolia, skiing Mera peak in the Himalaya on cross country skating skis. Many of those interviewed here in this book have done similar creative explorations, and have an array of experiences under their belts, while some are more focused, and have stuck solely to particular disciplines. Most of those interviewed in this book are acquaintances, friends, or intimate buddies of mine. Many have families as I do, and juggle the balance of life.

My balance was to spend time with the indigenous people living in these mountain environments around the world. They had a reverence for the peaks that I felt should be shared. I wrote and photographed a book series entitled *Vanishing Cultures*. These people taught me that a young child could be wrapped in a carpet, tied on the back of a yak, and crossed over a crevasse-ridden 20,000-foot pass in the Himalaya: no problem. A baby could be tied on his mother's back and cross the Sahara on camelback; a baby could be born in an igloo. They inspired me to cross a portion of the Sahara while in early pregnancy, climb and snowboard Toubkal in the Atlas Mountains while six months pregnant, and shoot video in the Himalaya until my eighth month, while my climbing friends demanded I go home! Despite my protest that babies are born in Namche Bazaar in the Khumbu all the time, and despite my Sherpani friend delivering her baby days before I left, I agreed to go home to my midwife and my home birth in Vermont.

I have come full circle, back to Vermont farm country and our charming Green Mountains. My boys hike and ski our mountains regularly as a way of life. Soon we'll be skiing hut to hut in the Alps and exploring trekking peaks of the Himalaya as a family. Some of the interviewees in this book have done the same. It is enough for me to share the joy of the simple heights with my loved ones, there are no expectations to go further. Like George Leigh Mallory, I can only hope that my family will find joy, high on a mountain "because it's THERE."

Jan Reynolds is an author and mountaineer. She has been a member of expeditions to China, Tibet, Nepal, New Zealand, Australia, Lapland, Amazon Basin, Canadian Arctic, Mongolia, and the Sahara. She also set the women's high altitude skiing record on an expedition sponsored by *National Geographic*.

Preface

Some years ago, the authors of this collection of interviews, Frederic Hartemann and Robert Hauptman, who for more than 15 years had climbed together in various parts of the world, published *The Mountain Encyclopedia*, an enormous compilation of terms, people, and ideas related to the world's mountains; it contains more than 2,300 entries and some 500 images, 400 in color. We were so inspired by this work that we decided to seek out some of the premier mountaineers whom we had included in order to interview them. We proceeded to contact people and get permission to visit them; Hauptman read some apposite material and constructed a set of questions tailored precisely to each individual. We then flew to their cities and met with them either at their homes or in motel rooms. Hauptman posed the questions and Hartemann recorded each interview in high definition video and on a digital audio device, and then took some still photographs. Hauptman transcribed the CDs that Hartemann made from his recordings. We then supplemented these with a number of additional in-person interviews and others done either through electronic mail or telephonically. An introduction and glossary were added. When we were done and the manuscript was ready, we contacted all of the interviewees and requested appropriate photographic images. These all arrived electronically. Hartemann arranged, collated, and transferred them to a disk. The result is a collection of mountaineering interviews unlike any other; earlier book length collections that do exist are now extremely dated.

The interviews are very lightly edited transcriptions of the recordings. When something was impossible to decipher, ellipses indicate that it is missing, at the beginning or in the middle of a sentence thus: ... but if the hiatus comes at the end of a sentence then a fourth period is added: .... Whenever a speaker breaks off and does not complete a thought, and then recommences, a dash is used, e.g., In 1967, I climbed a lot in—and I was very successful. If it is necessary to intercalate a word in order to make matters clear, then square brackets are used: Once, on Denali, I dropped my [ax] and I could not go on alone. The editors silently expunged words or phrases that are repeated frequently but have little meaning, e.g., you know, obviously, certainly, well.

The many trips that one or both of us took to San Francisco, Seattle, Spokane, Golden, Aspen, Lexington, and other locations were especially enjoyable because we were able to spend time with each other and we often began or ended with some climbs. It was also an extremely rewarding privilege to speak with these glorious people, many of whom not only climb but give of themselves in their quest to help others, e.g., those Nepalese who have vision problems or the poorer peoples in the Himalaya.

Introduction

Mountains allure, seduce, and demand, though this was not always the case. Indeed, in the past, they repelled because of real and imaginary dangers, but during the past 300 years, they have worked their magic on an ever-increasingly large group of climbers, people who often seem to have little choice: they see a geophysical extrusion and they are compelled to clamber or climb or claw or crawl their way up in order to stand on the summit.

Taxonomies of climbing can be constructed in various ways, but the simplest is the most effective: One either climbs sheer, vertical rock (from small boulders to 3,000 foot big walls) using one's hands and feet, with few accouterments other than a bag of chalk; or one does the same thing on vertical ice (frozen waterfalls) using crampons and small ice axes; or one climbs big mountains (peaks in ranges and free-standing volcanoes) sometimes alone or with a partner, sometimes as part of an enormous expedition or more recently in a guided group, many of whose members are ill-prepared for the demands that even a smaller peak places on them. Those who venture into the Alaskan wilds, the Andes, the Himalaya, or the Karakorum should spend years honing their skills. Lamentably, many people fail to serve their apprenticeships; even when they do, tragedy can strike because it is impossible to predict who will succumb to poor decisions, tiny mistakes with devastating consequences, acute mountain sickness, bad weather, vicious storms, or avalanches.

A taxonomy of climbers is also a simple matter. One may climb professionally, under sponsorship; one may climb in order to write, photograph, or film; one may climb as a guide; or one may climb purely for pleasure and often pay a hefty monetary price for his or her amateur status ($60,000 for a guided Everest attempt). It is also possible for a professional to have other occupational affiliations, and many fanatically devoted mountaineers earn a primary or secondary living as builders, physicists, lawyers, doctors, or scientific researchers.

Certain points and ideas, including dangers, the use of oxygen, environmental pollution, and gender discrimination, come up with some frequency. This last has had an impact on some of the interviewed women, whereas others felt they were accepted by their male counterparts. This is partially due to a change in attitude on the part of male climbers. It is interesting to look back at Arlene Blume's experience in the late '60s and early '70s. (She is not one of the interviewees.) Those in charge at the time often refused to take her on expeditions or even to allow her to climb simply because she was a woman and women are weaker than men. As it turns out, women are sometimes stronger, acclimate better, and reach the summit while their male counterparts retreat to the safety of a tent. Attitudes toward many (though not all) other recurrent themes have also changed for the better during the past hundred years.

Finally, one of the truly positive results of the mountaineering life is that many committed people realize that though climbing is personally and even socially rewarding (it brings work and revenue to a diverse group of people in many parts of the world), there can be something more: In visiting third world countries these people discover for themselves that life can be difficult even in Chile, let alone in Nepal (one of the poorest countries in the world). Taking their lead from Sir Edmund Hillary, who eventually devoted his life to helping the Sherpa, many of the interviewees in this collection have transcended what some outsiders erroneously view as a selfish and unnecessarily dangerous pursuit, and give of themselves in the most altruistic of ways. For example, Dr. Kenneth Kamler provides medical assistance to people he encounters in many different environments. Pete Athans ("Mr. Everest") assists Dr. Geoffrey Tabin in Nepal in his work for the Himalayan Cataract Project. Erik Weihenmayer advocates for the blind and aids the disabled. Rick Ridgeway, as a Patagonia executive (vice-president for marketing and the environment), helps to protect the environment. And Brent Bishop cleaned up much of the trash left behind high in the Himalaya and Karakorum. For all of this and so much more, we give thanks.

PART I.
MOUNTAINEERS

The first section of this collection consists of interviews with well-known North American mountaineers, some with important first ascents. We have tried to strike a balance among many different variables and so we have included older, seasoned climbers and younger people who are still actively making history; professionals and amateurs; men and women; those with one truly outstanding achievement and others who have had many conquests. Some of these wonderful people have passed away. We are grateful to all of our interviewees for inviting us into their homes, coming to us in out-of-the-way locations, and spending time talking or corresponding via electronic mail. We would also like to thank Greg Glade, owner of Top of the World books, for his frequent invaluable help.

Stacy Allison

(October 18, 1958–)
Mountaineer, motivational speaker, builder

Date of interview: July 5, 2006. *Location:* Clackamas, OR. *Interviewer:* Robert Hauptman. *Method:* In person: taped and videotaped. *Videographer:* Frederic Hartemann.

Stacy Allison, the first American woman to stand on Everest's summit, has been called "America's premier female climber." She led a K2 expedition and summited Ama Dablam on an all-women's climb.

> The climbing community has never had a lot of patience with women.
> —Stacy Allison

RH: Thank you for agreeing to talk with us. It was a most enjoyable experience reading Beyond the Limits; *your extraordinary exploits are overpowering and extremely inspirational.*

SA: Well, thank you.

You have been called "America's premier female climber." Do you do any climbing or mountaineering now?

I am no longer climbing big, dangerous mountains. I have two children and right now it's not about me, it's about my children, and raising my two sons to be healthy, productive, kind, caring male adults.

In Jon Krakauer's Into Thin Air, *Scott Fischer is depicted in what one might consider an unflattering light. He appears much more human in your memoir, although even you admit that he was a risk-taker. At one point you wonder: "...Was Scott ever going to wield his authority to bring us together?" How would you describe him in retrospect?*

Scott was a very charismatic person. He was like the older brother that I never had: very supportive of me personally. I had a lot of respect for Scott. He was a risk-taker and when I made that statement what I really meant by that is that he was not a leader. He was able to organize people, get them to come together around his vision of climbing, his vision of an expedition, but once that expedition was underway, he was not the person to lead [it] and our expedition should actually have been led by someone else.

In 1987, after months of hard work, you failed to reach the summit of Everest. Instead of giving up, you continued to climb and then returned once again to Everest. You really wanted to summit and, at one time, to become the first American woman to achieve this honor. Most people do not have such a strong drive. Is that one of the main differences between those who succeed generally and in the high mountains and those who fail?

I believe having a strong drive is certainly how you make it to the tops of mountains. If you don't have that strong drive, you'll give up part way because it's tough. The physical, the mental, the emotional demands that are put upon you in order to reach the summits of most mountains is tremendous. If you don't have that drive you probably won't be willing to put out the energy that it takes to get there. And for me, it wasn't about—what I realized after failing on the first expedition—it wasn't about being the first American woman to reach the top. It was more about, was I physically, mentally, emotionally capa-

Looking down Everest North Face, Cho Oyo in the background (photograph by Stacy Allison).

ble of climbing Mount Everest. What would it be like to stand on top of the world's highest mountain? And I'm very driven; if I don't reach a goal the first time and I fail, it's, what can I learn from that failure, and then I go back and I try it again.

If you were in a different position today, do you think both that you would be interested in climbing big mountains and capable of climbing them?

If I did not have children, absolutely. I'd still be climbing big mountains. ... Climbing is my passion. I miss being in the mountains; I miss standing on those big mountains. And, yes, if I didn't have children, I'd still be climbing.

An interesting sociological phenomenon is the way in which male athletes react to and treat their female peers. Here, I do not mean a male baseball player's attitude toward players on an all-women's team. Rather, I wonder how, for example, the Yankees' Mickey Mantle would have reacted to a talented women playing alongside him in left field. Have things changed in the last decade? Can the great male mountaineers cope with female success? Can they admit that a 100-pound woman may be stronger and more talented than they are? (Sexism is reflected in the building trades, where men discriminated against you.)

Yes, first of all, I look at myself as being a person first and I just happen to be a woman and so I never think of being a woman and doing the things that I do. I just choose my hobbies; I choose my career and that's who I am and that's what I'm about. I am not a threat to the men that I climb with. I'm not a threat to my subcontractors or other contractors because I'm not out there trying to prove that a woman can do it. They're not threatened by it. Therefore, I tend to have great support with the men that I climb with and the men that I work with. Only one time in my life did I ever run up against a problem in the construction company. ... I will never be as strong down here at sea level as someone who is 50 to 60 pounds heavier than I am, but when you climb at high elevation you tend to level out, and the higher I go in elevation the stronger I get.

Stacy Allison (photograph by Fred Hartemann).

And that's not true of some of the men you climbed with [on Everest]. Did you do the last 4,000 feet on your own?

The last 1,000 feet. My two fellow climbers who turned around were healthy. They weren't ill; they didn't need my help going down and one of us was going to go; and in the lottery I won the oxygen bottle. And I did it!

Some years after Arlene Blum's all-women's team succeeded on Annapurna (despite two deaths), you managed to reach the summit of Ama Dablam as part of an all-women's expedition. Was climbing without men different in any meaningful way?

No, it wasn't; actually, I suppose it was in that I think women..., I would like to think that women are very supportive when they do activities together, but my experience is that when you get very competent, capable, competitive women together, they are incredibly competitive with one another. And that's how it was on our all-female climb of Ama Dablam. We were supportive, yet there was that underlying tension and competitiveness. Certainly, all of us wanted to reach the top; we all did reach the top in the end but you never know when you climb at high elevations who's going to get there, who's not going to get there. So it was very competitive and not as supportive and nurturing as you would probably think or hope.

You say that "Climbing teaches you how to think." Is that really true? I find that many climbers, especially high altitude hikers and mountaineers, do not think at all. They just act, often foolishly and dangerously. I could offer many examples, but I am certain that you have seen many unpleasant things.

I have. When I made that statement, where that was coming from is I think you learn how to be very resourceful; I think you look at your environment; you assess it; you figure out what needs to be done, what tools you need, what skills you're going to need, the route you're going to take. You have to constantly be thinking; you have to constantly be paying attention and when you're not thinking you make foolish mistakes. We all get into bad habits like that. So, yes, I absolutely do think it teaches you how to think; it teaches you how to be on your toes; it teaches you to definitely pay attention and, again, resourcefulness: When you run out of rope and you still have a thousand feet to go, how are you going to get from here to there safely? You have to be creative. You often use your tools in ways they were never meant to be used, because you have to. ... The whole sport of climbing, I believe, demands respect. Can I get off on a tangent? You see climbers going up and down Everest now all the time. They're hiring someone to compensate for their lack of skills, knowledge, experience, judgment. Someone else has that; they don't. People think, I can get a guide; I don't know anything; and I can climb these big mountains. Well, you can't. If your guide gets hurt, you better darn well

Broken spectre on Nuptse (photograph by Don Goodman; courtesy of Stacy Allison).

make sure that you have the skills to be on the mountain, the experience to get yourself down or up, and the judgment to be safe. And if you don't know how to think for yourself, if you hired someone else to think for you, then you can't expect climb after climb after climb to be successful or alive.

Jamling Tenzing Norgay said the same thing, that climbers today lack respect or they don't have the respect that they did have in the past.

This is, I think, very specific to Mount Everest, that self-aggrandizement. We're taking our satellite phones; we're taking our computers, so that we can email every day: Look at me, look at me. Well, where's the climbing in that experience? Are you really there to climb the mountain, to be a part of the mountain for that very short period of time or are you there to show your friends, to show the world who you are or who you would like to be?

In Alaska, on peak 12,380, you were caught up in an avalanche: you rolled along with the snow and through the air. You purposely tossed your ice ax away.

Temple in Kathmandu, where climbers often visit for a puja ceremony prior to climbing with sherpas (photograph by Stacy Allison).

Didn't this experience terrify you? Most people who survived would never return to the high mountains during avalanche season.

It was terrifying, but I have to say that that was an experience very early on in my climbing career and I learned a whole lot from it. The first thing I learned is how to cross an avalanche slope properly and the second thing I learned is that you never throw your ice ax away. Obviously, I survived; I didn't get hurt. It was a failure, but it was something to learn from. And when I left the Alaska Range that summer, I left knowing what I needed to do, if I wanted to climb big mountains. One of them was to certainly learn the skills and better prepare myself for doing any sort of snow and ice climbing. It was peak 12,380 that we got caught in the avalanche on, but we tried to climb Mount Huntington by a new route. I had never been on a peak like that in my life. It required a lot of very technical, very steep ice climbing, the route that we did, and I was absolutely physically unprepared for that. ... I think that I'm fairly cautious; certainly, as I get older, I tend to be more cautious; certainly now that I have children, I'm very cautious but I was willing to take some risks back in my younger years and I'm very fortunate that I've not ever been hurt and that I'm still alive. I've seen a lot of my friends die. ... I was willing to take the risk in order to pursue my passion and to be in the mountains.

When I was at Canada's Mount Robson, I learned that a climb (including the approach) could take five days. You tried for the summit (after the approach) in one. You were caught in a bad blizzard with no food or water and little protection. It was so horrific that for a brief moment you even considered suicide.

Well, we were in very good climbing shape and we were trying to climb very fast. We did our route in good time; we reached the top of the mountain; it was absolutely crystal clear. We decided to spend the night on top and that's when the storm moved in. We woke up to a raging blizzard. It took us almost three days to get off the mountain. We didn't have tents, food, fuel, sleeping bags, anything. Coming down it was very cold. I climbed down and then my climbing partner was climbing down above me; he broke his ice ax; he was trying to get his ax planted into the ice and it kept knocking down these huge chunks right on top of me and it hurt. I was exhausted at that point and I thought death—if I cut the rope now—death would be so much easier, the pain would be gone. I wasn't serious but thoughts go through your head and it was then that I realized something that has made the difference between survival and death in many of the climbs that I have been on. I realized at that point why many people die in the mountains. It's because they cross that line, they give up, they sit down, and they die. It would have been easy to give up. Surviving is the hard part. Surviving is when you have to go through all the pain of getting off the mountain. I knew that wasn't for me. I wanted to live. I didn't want to die. ... If you want to survive in the mountains you keep going; when you're exhausted, it doesn't matter, you keep going: one foot in front of the other until you reach a safe spot.

You progressed so quickly. I would be happy to be helicoptered to the top of Denali. When you decided to do Denali early in your career, instead of climbing the West Buttress route, you chose the much more difficult and challenging Cassin Ridge, and you succeeded!

Yes. I'll be darned. I was very fortunate early on in my climbing career: I had a climbing partner, Curt Haire, and we did a lot of fairly challenging technical climbs together. Curt and I wanted to go climb Denali. We didn't want to do the West Buttress because it was so crowded and so we started looking at other options and the Cassin Ridge seemed like, to us at the time, the most logical thing to do: steep ice, steep rock. It is a fabulous route; it was a very good climb. Now, what happened with us is that we thought it would take six days to climb the Cassin, so we only brought six days of food and fuel. It took us 11 days, I believe, so we had to start rationing fairly early on. ...

An unidentified person seeking inspiration and good fortune from Buddha (photograph by Stacy Allison).

Because of climbing the Cassin Ridge—that's why I was invited to go to Ama Dablam the following year.

You are extremely strong physically, mentally, and emotionally. Of the second Everest expedition you say "In terms of strength, climbing ability, hauling capacity, and altitude reached, I matched anyone in the group, man or woman." Nevertheless, you had some unpleasant personal problems that could have resulted in terrible harm. I understand if you prefer not to comment on those.

...On the first climb of Mount Everest, we were actually all friends and by the time we left the mountain many of us were not speaking to one another because of various things that happened and unresolved issues. I think ultimately it was a lack of leadership. On the second Everest expedition, I think the main challenge was that we had three women, and I made it to the top of the mountain and Peggy Luce made it to the top and Peggy was not really a strong climber; she had very little climbing experience at all. Diana Daily did not make it to the top and she was a woman who had tremendous amounts of climbing experience. And because she didn't make it to the top it really created some conflict amongst the three of us. [Now Diana is okay with this.] And

Top: Q. Belk and Stacy Allison celebrating her 28th birthday on the North Face (photograph by Scott Fischer; courtesy of Stacy Allison). *Above:* The bent ladder shows that icefall moves fast! (photograph by Don Goodman; courtesy of Stacy Allison).

that was very unfortunate. You have to expect on these big mountains, even though you have the will and the drive, your chances really are so low that it has to be okay if you don't make it to the top. ... There were some small issues with other people. ...

On Pik Kommunizma, Maggie broke her leg and Fredo [two of the expedition climbers] simply died. How do you deal with such tragedies and still go on climbing?

Well, again, I think you know what the risks are before you go. ... It's always sad when you lose a climber. The last climb I did [of a] big mountain was K2. I led that expedition, and we lost a climber. It is tragic. ... With Fredo ... what can you learn from the experience? He was suffering from high altitude hypoxia from below 19,000 feet and he wrote it in his journal. ... Yet he didn't share that with any of us. I think if you are going to be in the mountains, you have to be candid with yourself and you have to be candid with your teammates....

You briefly discuss the garbage problem on Everest. In America, the National Park Service now insists that backcountry adventurers leave no trace, and this entails

Stacy, carrying a big load! (photograph by Don Goodman; courtesy of Stacy Allison).

The early part of the trek to Everest base camp, which can take several days (photograph by Stacy Allison).

hauling even one's bodily refuse out. But what can those concerned do if neither the Mexican government, for example, nor Mexican climbers nor the large body of international mountaineers who visit the volcanoes simply do not care? No one, for example, has bothered to erect a small outhouse on Orizaba, a simple but effective solution to the excrement that litters the area around the refuge. On the Aiguille du Tour, near Chamonix, I was horrified to see that the refuge's toilet empties directly onto the snow-and-ice-covered rock face. Besides cleaning up, as you did on Everest, what can the climbing community do to stop people from sullying and polluting the environment they claim to love?

Well, I think it's getting to the point where you've just stated that it is a concern to many, many people. I think probably local climbing clubs are going to have to band together and say, look, we're going to put the money up, we're going to put the manpower up (the people power up) to erect latrines, to erect bins to dump your garbage in, and we're going to haul the waste out because it's important to us. You can't depend on the government; it's not worth it to them. So it will be up to the people who use those environments to come up with the solutions for those problems. ... What really surprises me is—we do a lot of hiking and river running here in Oregon—you get out into

Top: A typical Everest expedition requires many tons of supplies, even when only four or five Westerners are involved (photograph by Don Goodman; courtesy of Stacy Allison). *Right:* Stacy and her leech bite (photograph by Steve Ruoss; courtesy of Stacy Allison).

these pristine environments and there are people who care ... but how many people still litter in these pristine environments? You go out to a pristine environment and you litter. ... People are still going to litter, if it's not important to them.

You supported your own upper camps in your first (1987) Everest attempt. Do you think that not having Sherpa help diminishes the chances for success in the high mountains?

No. I think Sherpa support certainly makes it much easier, but no. I think you can be just as successful without Sherpa support. On K2 we didn't have Sherpa support and we got three people to the top. Most people on K2 do not have that help. You have to climb fast; you're not stocking as much stuff; it was a smaller group of people. But I think even on large expeditions—I believe that on that first climb, if we had not had so many conflicts, if we had been working effectively as a team, we would have made it to the top....

You were still stocking camps in early September. Isn't this quite late in the season? Do you think that early spring climbs in the Himalaya are preferable?

Back row: Charlie Shertz, three unidentified Sherpas; front: Dawa, Geoff Tabin, Steve Ruoss, Stacy (photograph by Dave Hambly; courtesy of Stacy Allison).

I like climbing in the fall in the Himalaya. There's more snow; I guess you have to watch out for avalanches. I think climbing in the fall is quite nice. ... You have cold days but I think either spring or fall is fine....

I have read hundreds of climbing accounts. I do not recall ever encountering a physical fight before [reading] your book; and Bob McConnell punched a Chinese official. Could you all have been arrested?

I forgot about that. ... We were horrified when it happened. The Chinese official was so pompous and Bob got angry and just lost it. ... That was really very unfortunate.

You were trapped in a snow cave for many days during the worst storm in 40 years; and ultimately you failed to reach the summit, but you were back in 1988.

At that time in my life, I didn't have children; I didn't have something else that was driving me to then go to. I had the opportunity; it's now in my life that I can go back to Everest and I still want to reach the top. So now, let's take what we learned and accomplish that.

A puja ceremony is performed prior to a climb either in a temple, lamasery or at the base of a mountain. Westerners take part out of respect for Buddhist sherpas (photograph by Stacy Allison).

Twice, group members went off, leaving you on your own, which forced you to rush to catch up. Why do people do this?

I was physically healthy; there was really no reason why they should have waited. I knew that I could catch up. It was my own anxieties. When I wrote that in the book it was me thinking, why am I so slow? They are going to leave me. How can I catch up? When in reality, it was not really an issue at all. ... However, you're right; you do want to always be watching out for one another. ... When our Sherpas—when we were going up, and they were fiddling around with their oxygen, I was the one who stayed behind and went down and tried to help them with it. ... Should we have all been climbing together as a close-knit group? I don't know. If you have to stop and wait for someone, you risk

The Khumbu Icefall (photograph by Scott Fischer; courtesy of Stacy Allison).

cooling down and getting cold. That last 3,000 feet, you really are on your own. You have to move at your own pace; you've got to move as fast as you can just to get up and back down safely. I think we all knew that; we discussed it before we went. It's a team effort up to 26,000 feet; we're all working together fixing the route, setting up those intermediate camps, but the team can only take you so far and that last 3,000 feet, you're on your own. Now, that is not to say, and I want to make this real clear, that if one of us was having a problem, we would not have all turned around to help get that person down, because that's what you do. You don't continue on to the summit while someone else is dying....

Although 40 people just did that twice.

And that's atrocious. I think that's absolutely atrocious....

Not too far from the summit, two Sherpas inexplicably turned around, taking most of your oxygen canisters with them. Four of you continued but then decided that it was impossible without oxygen. You were randomly chosen to continue with a Sherpa and the little oxygen you had. But didn't it surprise you that Jim Frush

The seracs of the Khumbu Icefall—note climber at upper left (photograph by Scott Fischer; courtesy of Stacy Allison).

and Steve Ruoss turned back so close to the top? And then you made it: The first American woman to summit Everest!

If I had lost the lottery, I would have gone on. I would have chosen to go to the top. That I know. I was there to climb the mountain. We were so close. That's the choice I would have made. ... Yes, it surprised me a little bit. They probably thought that they would get another opportunity to try for the top.

You climb for different reasons and these change over time, but your mother said that "climbing is how you express yourself." Can you explain that?

It's my passion; it's where my spirit soars; it's where I feel truly connected to this earth. When I'm climbing, I feel like it's where I belong and it allows me to use my physical body, to use my mind, to push myself beyond what I should be able to do. It makes me think....

Have you done any major climbs recently? What do you have planned for the future?

Well, I haven't done any major climbs recently and for the future, I don't know. If I choose to go back to climbing big mountains, when is the right

Steve Ruoss crossing a large crevasse in the Khumbu Icefall (photograph by Stacy Allison).

Pink flamingos at base camp (photograph by Stacy Allison).

Pasang Gaylsen and Stacy Allison on summit (photograph by Stacy Allison).

time? How old do my children need to be before I feel comfortable and before they would feel comfortable letting go?

When you do your motivational speaking does it revolve around mountaineering?

Yes, I use climbing as my metaphor. I tell stories. Every story has a point depending on the group, what their focus is, and what they want me to talk about. ... I feel very fortunate that I have had an opportunity ... to discover my passion and pursue my passion....

Thank you so much for sharing your thoughts with us. We really appreciate it.

Well, thank you.

BIBLIOGRAPHY

Allison, Stacy. *Many Mountains to Climb: Reflections on Competence, Courage, and Commitment.* Wilsonville, OR: BookPartners, 1999.
_____ with Peter Carlin. *Beyond the Limits: A Woman's Triumph on Everest.* Boston: Little, Brown, 1993.
Netzley, Patricia D. "Allison, Stacy." *The Encyclopedia of Women's Travel and Exploration.* Westport, CT: Oryx Press, 2001 (13–14.).

Peter (Pete) Athans

(March 1, 1957–)
Mountaineer, guide, cinematographer,
motivational speaker

Date of interview: June 30, 2008. *Location:* Bainbridge Island, WA.
Interviewer: Robert Hauptman. *Method:* In person: taped and
videotaped. *Videographer:* Frederic Hartemann.

Peter Athans is a mountaineer and guide, the only non–Sherpa to climb
Everest 16 times. He continues to visit Nepal and he often works with Geoffrey
Tabin, who performs free cataract surgery on Nepalese people who would otherwise have little or no access to such medical procedures. He helped rescue
survivors of the 1996 Everest tragedy.

~

*RH: We know that you are busy so we thank you for spending some time with
us.*

PA: It's my pleasure.

*You've climbed Everest 16 times and reached the summit on seven occasions, a
record for Westerners. Don't those three month-long expeditions become difficult and
tiring, especially since one does not merely miss the comforts of home, but often eats
poorly, gets ill, finds others annoying or disagreeable, and so on?*

Just to clarify the record, I think now that Dave Hahn has climbed Everest
10 times, so as far as any Westerner holding any type of record for summiting
Everest, I think he probably pretty clearly [would] be the that record holder.
... And as for the time we spend away on expeditions, it's difficult. In recent
years, I've been able to do expeditions, not to Everest specifically, but to other
places where I've taken my family with me. My wife is a film producer and
did several Everest projects for Nova, when we were living back in the Boston
area. And she's an avid climber and my kids are learning climbing. My son
and my daughter came with us up to Camp Muir [on Rainier] last summer,
so I'm hoping that my son will climb Rainier this summer. And certainly the
privations of living at Everest base camp become difficult, but I've always found

Mount Everest is the highest mountain in the world at 29,035 feet. Nuptse is a smaller satellite of Everest.

myself remarkably adaptable with local food and with the altitude; I speak the language, so it really almost feels like a second home to me. I don't feel like there are really any privations in being at Everest base camp. We usually have a Sherpa cook; we usually have people who help us do all of the basic things, so we can focus fairly intently on climbing the mountain. There's some suffering sometimes; I think that's what mountaineering is all about. It's about transcending that. But generally for me living on the mountain is pretty inspiring and I enjoy being in those high places for long periods of time. The mountain requires that you adapt yourself to the environment and that you obviously deign to respect the mountain and to live with that environment that you can't have any control over. The thing that you can control—you can control your emotions, you can control how you respond to the challenge, and you can approach that with equanimity or you can be frustrated by it. You know, it's your choice.

You've done this so frequently that I presume that you acclimate very easily.

It didn't start that way, but more so about ten years into Himalayan climbing; and at that time I was also living in Leadville, Colorado, which is at about 10,000 feet, so making a fairly rapid transition from 10,000 feet to Everest base camp at 17,500 is something I have been able to do quite readily. And I think most of the people studying high altitude medicine now, while there's no testing for it and there's certainly no established fact, most people are finding that there is actually the ability or kind of a physiological plasticity to be able to make those rapid metabolic changes. So I found that's definitely operative in me and people like Ed Viesturs and Dave Hahn and people who go repeatedly. I think we find that to be true.

You have also climbed Annapurna South, Pumori, and other Himalayan giants as well as K2 in Alpine style. Did you have any support on these speed ascents?

On peaks like Annpurna South and Ama Dablam, are they pure solo speed ascents? Well, if you're going to be using a piece of fixed line that's in place that was put there by somebody else, how do you call that a solo ascent? How do you call that an unsupported ascent?

What I meant was do you have a large cadre of porters carrying things in or do you do most of your own hauling?

I've done my own generally. We just came back from doing a first ascent in the kingdom of Mustang in a completely unclimbed range, unexplored range, and I was just there with one other person. So, we were just taking all our own things; we didn't have any local support; we didn't have pack animals with us. We just set out from the last village and started walking. And five days later we were back.

In a previous interview, you mention that fear is a factor in your work. Often, mountaineers do not make decisions based on fear or danger. Ed Viesturs is different: he turns back when things appear extremely unstable. How do you react?

I don't think that that's necessarily fear. That's something that we all deal with just respective to wanting to succeed but obviously tempering that with what's more important is returning and certainly in my situation, and Ed's is quite similar, in that we have little kids at home, and they rely on us coming back. It's more out of love and concern for the people who are back here rather than fear for ourselves that we make those decisions. Fear does come into play, obviously, but not in those situations specifically like the one you talked about Ed responding to. I'm not so sure it's as much fear. Transcending fear is at the heart of the mountaineering experience and obviously it's what we deal with, whether you go on or you go back. And ultimately we try to answer to that time after time because we want to stretch ourselves and we want to achieve a greater type of awareness; we want to achieve a greater sense of self-actualization as people. So constantly we push ourselves in that direction.

During the 1996 debacle on Everest, you climbed high on the mountain and rescued two people including Beck Weathers. Was his appearance in camp after being left for dead a life-altering experience for you and for others? You also helped with Makalu Gau. For these selfless acts, you received the Sowles medal.

What affected me was how surreal it was and the fact that on two occasions prior to our seeing him, people had said, He's already expired; he's near to death; he's comfortable; you don't need to do anything. And our situation was, we had more than a dozen people who were right in front of us on the South Col, many of whom had been without water, had been without food, certainly had been without oxygen and they required a lot of attention as well. So we really tried to deal with the people who were right in front of us when we got there. One life-altering thing for me is to not accept someone's diagnosis of a situation until I've actually checked it myself. Because I had climbed with Beck Weathers in Antarctica, I know he's not terribly experienced as a climber but he has remarkable resilience and is very strong, in his own way, and for me to see him come walking in wasn't that surprising. But to have had the corroboration of other people saying he was dead and then having him come walk in was very surprising. So for me personally, what I learned from that and what was transforming about it is don't accept the fact that if someone's dead or close to death—you don't have to accept somebody's word for it. You can go out and check. ... What was more surreal about it was that he was in remarkably good shape given that he had lain out on the South Col for 20 hours or whatever it was. He just has great mental toughness. ... He got up and walked into the South Col and that's where Todd Burleson and I were, so we were able to work with him and obviously get him down.

Weathers's strength, fortitude, will to live, and courage, both then and now, are beyond my ability to grasp. It is as if he has some super-human attributes that carry him forward in the face of insurmountable misery. This is especially evident when one considers that Charlotte Fox reached a point, suffering so much from the cold, at which she wished to die.

Well, I think that also there's in Beck's case the will to survive.... There's something very primitive about that urge and primordial about that urge in the sense that there's something beyond what one is, beyond one's own identity. It's something of your own family and the people you wish to have the same opportunity that you've had and obviously not to abandon them at a time when they're very vulnerable.

Are your children quite young?

Two and five.

Oh my god. Wait a minute. Didn't you say you wanted to take your children up on Rainier?

My son's been to Camp Muir [at 10,000 feet]. He hiked almost all the snow field. He's a pretty tough kid....

*You insist that a leader must adhere to "a non-negotiable turn around time."
But what if one is just ten minutes from the summit of a major peak and has paid
in physical deprivation, emotional exhaustion, and lots of money? How about 15
minutes? How about 20 minutes?*

I think that that's what makes guiding on Everest difficult. It's the crux
of being able to evaluate the condition of the people that are with you and
knowing what they have still left in the tank to get all the way back down, let
alone finish the 20 minutes to get to the top or the ten minutes or the five
minutes or whatever it is. And that's what goes through the mind of a guide,
when he's with a client. Obviously, yes, if they are really close at that point
and they've spent all this time, all this money, committed all these resources
to get to this place and fulfilling that is something that will give them quite a
bit. But ultimately where they are, the type of risk that a guide is willing to
accept—it's for the round trip; it's not just getting to the top. People can't just
collapse and get down. There's no way people can really be responsible for getting somebody off the mountain like that. People like Rob Hall tried to do
that and everyone knows where he is, and he will be there for eternity. That
was one of the reasons why I stopped guiding in '96. I felt like there is only a
rare combination in partnership of novice climber and guide that really makes
climbing Everest safe. I think I did have a couple of good years where I summited with some novice climbers or people who weren't that experienced. But
also there's going to be the risk for not coming back, and being pushed because
people who have committed so [many] resources to that want to be successful.
... You can't judge an entire expedition by what happens on summit day. Unfortunately, people do: Whether you get to the top of the mountain is judged a
success or failure. ... That's certainly what guiding Everest was all about: being
in the game for the round trip. ... Having people for the round trip ... is obviously the ethic for most guides.

*That brings up what would seem to be an ancillary question but it's pertinent
to the structure of the entire book: ... Do you think that Anatoli Boukreev acted hon-
orably?*

Maybe my opinion is somewhat different: Anatoli came from such a different cultural milieu that I think that there was such a lack of his responding
to the ethic of full service, western Everest guiding, which means that you'll
do everything from starting your people on oxygen at Camp 3, short-roping
them—but you're with them all the time. Anatoli's background was much
more—the Master of Sport category that one achieves in Russia through climbing and through mentoring climbers is very different because you're much
more like a coach and an athlete. You're not there as a coach to be on the field
of play with your athlete; you're there to prepare them; in this case, you're there
to prepare the route, to do whatever you can to make their climb their own.
But ultimately for you to short-rope them, to carry their oxygen with a long

tube, that kind of thing would taint that athlete's ascent of the mountain. So, Anatoli felt like he had fulfilled his contract with those clients and with Scott Fischer, who, I'll say, Scott having been there—I saw how hard Scott was working that year and the fact that he probably did two or three round trips on the mountain getting close to the top before actually going on his summit bid. He had been to the Col at least two or three times by that point and when he took someone down on a summit attempt, he really rushed to get himself back up. I think he was very tired and he might have been a little sick; he might have had an upper respiratory infection. And he was behind the entire team at that point, so really a lot of the decision making, the leadership, fell to Anatoli and to Neal Beidelman. And Neal did a wonderful job getting people out of that desperate situation. I think that most people recognize the fact that Neal did not have that much experience on Everest prior to going there, so what he was able to achieve was remarkable. And the fact that Anatoli, given the restrictions of physiology, not having oxygen—he stayed on the South Col; I was with him on the South Col. We went back up to get Scott Fischer and that's when Makalu Gau came down and I elected to stay with Makalu Gau because he was right there in front of me. Having spoken to a couple of the Sherpas who had seen Scott, made it pretty clear he wasn't breathing any longer. However, Anatoli decided he wanted to go and be sure for himself. I was fine with that. I was there with the guy whose hands and feet were terribly frost-bitten. None of his teammates were with him. There were several Sherpa who were with him; I wanted to be sure he had care because I thought he could survive. But the long and short of all of this is, I think Anatoli's role is very poorly understood. I think people don't understand the distinction. I know that Jon didn't appreciate the distinction of Anatoli's background. Jon [Krakauer's] feeling was that if you're going to guide on Everest, you're going to use oxygen, because there's really no medical support for saying you're going to climb better without the use of supplemental oxygen. Jon's point is very well taken: That if you're going to guide on Everest, you need to stack the deck in your favor; you need to be at your very best; you need to be making the best possible decisions. To do all that you need to be using supplemental oxygen....

You are usually associated with the Himalaya; indeed, you are sometimes called "Mr. Everest." But you have also done impressive climbs in other parts of the world. Your Alpine-style assault on Mount Hunter, as recounted in Glenn Randall's Breaking Point, *is one of the most harrowing, nerve-wracking accounts I have ever read. You had bad ice, some unbelayed climbing, vicious storms, all on very difficult terrain. At one point, I think you mentioned that you were scared.*

Probably to this day, I haven't done anything as committing as Mount Hunter was. And getting into that situation with Mount Hunter—it was a little bit as a result of being a novice alpinist. I had spent a fair amount of time in South America and also in the Western Alps and felt like, okay, so this is a six, seven-thousand-foot route; we were doing 2,000, 3,000 foot routes there; throw in a day for bad weather; throw in a day for harder technical climbing and you're off in four to six days. The truth of the matter was we weren't off until the thirteenth day. And my friend, Pete Metcalf, had climbed in Alaska, quite a few expeditions, actually, and he really possessed this route; he wanted to go back to this route. And I did a number of expeditions with him in Europe, South America, and a variety of places before we went there. And Glenn Randall is another great friend from Colorado, and our team, I felt, was incredibly strong and very well prepared and obviously we all got through. It was a really supreme test of the strength of that team and the fact that together we were able to pull it off in very difficult conditions. I think the route has been done one or two more times now in the last few years. But not in really appreciably different times....

The dangers, the near misses, the storms never seemed to end. Was this climb more stressful and difficult than your Everest climbs?

Absolutely. It was completely committing. We just had our own resources, what we had on our backs, whereas on Everest, there are other people around; you have Sherpa support; the teams are bigger. Oftentimes, though, on Everest, there isn't really security in numbers, and I think people sometimes think that and that gets people in trouble. But by the same token, within your own team, you have a lot more resources available.

Do you think that Randall was too hard on you? You were cautious and that is how lives are saved.

I'm a pretty conservative climber. I've always been that way. Glenn's still around and Pete Metcalf's still around too. I think that I've always had a very, let's just say, spacious approach to mountaineering. I've always seen it that the summit's very important but the process is more important and returning from the process is really the success. Whether the summit's involved or not, that's one part of the equation. And it's great to summit, don't get me wrong. But by the same token, just being out there in the elements, being part of the natural world and allowing yourself to transcend what we feel is a very comfortable life and putting yourself out in those trying, challenging situations are what allows us to achieve a greater self-actualization....

At one difficult point you fell through a cornice. What was that like, since you were dangling over open space? Was that very scary or difficult? How did you bring yourself back up?

By that point I just felt like an idiot because I knew there a was a cornice there, but I also knew that it would be faster for me to get on the lower angle terrain right on the back side of the cornice, because this was about day nine into the expedition and we were very close to the summit plateau at that point, so I wanted to finish the pitch and get Peter and Glenn up there. I just felt like an idiot. At that point the emotions of fear were much less trenchant, much less powerful than they had been earlier and lower down because every day was like that and [I] became somewhat inured to it. And just getting back on—I had some big wall tools and had my jumars and just jumared back up the static rope and got back on and finished the pitch and Peter and Glenn came up and we just carried on....

Randall lost some parts of his fingers. Did you come away physically unscathed?
Physically fine. No problem there.

Did you spend much time with Bradford Washburn?
I did. One of the great privileges of having climbed on Everest was being able to be with Brad, not so much on the mountain but to work with him doing GPS-related studies on Everest and we finished in—I guess it was 1999; we were able to run five machines synchronously to be able to bring back the most accurate data for the current maps that are available now. But even before that, taking laser prisms up to the summit and having Brad actually down, several villages below Everest base camp and knowing that he was there and knowing that he was with us in spirit—he's such an iconic figure and such an inspiring figure, from his very early years climbing in the Alps to his remarkable legacy of what he did in Alaska and the photographs that he brought back and that record that he brought back—just such an incredible person to have influenced [us].

Are you continuing with your goal of reaching the summits of the 14 8,000-meter peaks? How many have you done thus far?
I've really only done a couple. To the summit, I've only done Everest and Cho Oyo. And I never really had the goal of climbing all of them; especially once I turned about 45, I made a pretty strategic shift in my career and realized that although that's a remarkable achievement, I felt like I wanted to do something more transcendent and I got more involved with development in Nepal and got more involved with organizations like the Himalayan Cataract Project that provides eye care for people who suffer from cataract blindness. My wife and I started the Magic Yeti Libraries, which are a system of libraries that started in the Khumbu Valley, and we're going to take it into other parts of Nepal. We bring illustrated textbooks, books that are trilingual—they're in Nepalese, English, and in some cases Tibetan—for young children who are just about to enter school because there's such a great tradition of oral story-telling in these places but not necessarily a literate one; so for kids to learn from books is something that's a much greater step for them when they get older and they're in school. So our idea was to try go over with these illustrated texts, [to] try to show the kids that education is something that can be fun....

So we have two libraries already up and operational and plans to start two more. And this is a family type of project. We work with the Alex Lowe Charitable Foundation....

There is one thing that truly differentiates you from virtually all other visitors to the Himalaya. You are not only an extraordinary mountaineer, you also speak Nepali. How did this occur and do all Sherpas speak Nepali or are some only fluent in their Tibetan dialect?

I speak Nepali because I applied myself to it; I went to the point of taking language lessons and realized very early on that if I wanted to be an efficient and, I think, a great expedition leader, I needed to be able to converse with the local people. I needed to be able do everything from my own logistics— buying food, procuring everything I needed, and it also made it a lot easier, having the doors thrown open for me when I went into places like the Khumbu Valley. For most Sherpa, their second language is probably Nepali. They speak Sherpa [which] is essentially a Western Tibetan dialect, as you mention. It's not a written language. Many Sherpa, while they may not have the capacity to read or write, they may be conversant in five or six languages. They're remarkable people that way, and very inspiring. So, being able to at least address them in Nepali, I felt was a very basic requirement that I expected of myself....

Mountaineers are sometimes considered foolhardy egotists, risking their lives for no real purpose. Thus, that you work with Geoffrey Tabin and the Himalayan Cataract Project, as you mentioned, helping to restore the sight of Nepalese people who often have no medical care let alone access to an ophthalmologist, is extremely praiseworthy. Thank you very much for doing that. People who care about other people are grateful for the contributions that you make, you and Sir Edmund Hillary, who, in part, devoted his life to helping the Sherpa people.

I think Sir Edmund Hillary left a great legacy and provided, along with Tenzing, the greatest role model any of us could have: to take the mountaineering experience and for it to be transcendent in our culture. I think you need to go beyond.... I think that you need to move beyond the more selfish aspects of the sport, which it is, and be able to deliver something back to the people who, in some ways, make it all possible, certainly in the case of the Sherpa. And to recognize [that] these beautiful mountains, from which we take such great inspiration, [are] the home of probably some of the most underserved populations in the world. What's great about that project is that not only do people have their eyesight restored, but they're able to do it at such a high rate and I think [with] such a great quality of medical care and also at such low cost, because now, per patient, we spend about $16 to restore their eyesight, because the interocular lenses are now created in a small factory in Kathmandu, very close to Tilganga Eye Center, where the hospital is. So, the price of the surgery and the price of ... the ongoing care has just dropped tremendously....

You have been involved in many ways with film production both as an advisor and as the talent. What was it like working on Seven Years in Tibet*? Was Heinrich Harrer involved at all? Were other well-known mountaineers?*

No. Heinrich Harrer was not involved. He might have been in the writing of it but I wasn't part of that. I was just doing second unit work in Tibet. It was fun; it was really fun. It was the first time I had a chance to get out into far western Tibet and to see Mount Kailash....

The Dark Side of Everest *is an unusual film, because it is interested in the ethical aspects of mountaineering. Can you tell us something about it?*

I haven't seen that film in a while; I think they did that about ten years ago. I think that was an interesting premise upon which to do a film, and it's something that we all wrestle with: Where do your responsibilities end as a fellow climber or as a part of the climbing community on a mountain like Everest? If someone gets in trouble, do you have to go and rescue somebody, especially if perhaps your team isn't capable of doing it. Is it requisite that you do that? And it's an interesting question to explore, and it's one that people deal with on a day to day basis now, when they're on Everest in the spring because there are teams of people there, hundreds of people there; people they never even meet even at Everest base camp. Should all those mountaineers be responsible for all those people who are there to climb Everest? Should all the guides be responsible for the novice climbers who sign up on an à la carte expedition where they choose whatever services they want and try to come in at the lowest price they can [find]? Are the people who are part of the bigger expeditions that are better organized or better led, are they responsible for the ones who go there obviously much less well prepared? These are [the] kinds of questions that everyone deals with now. I don't pretend to have any answers to them. I also know that I don't ever want to go back to Everest as a guide again because I think it puts people like the guides at the greatest risk because our first instinct is to try to help. And that was certainly my first instinct when Beck Weathers and Makalu Gau and everyone else were in [a] terrible situation up there. But today, I don't know if I would have been so quick to go and do that, given the fact that I have two kids at home who require my attention and have great need for my continued existence in this world. I don't know if I would have been as quick to pull the trigger on that decision. I know I would have done whatever I could have done to preserve my own safety. In any case, I think it's more a difficult question now than it was for me ten years ago.

You sometimes lend your name to commercial advertisements, in Esquire *posing for clothing or for North Face, for example. Is this something you enjoy doing?*

... I think I don't necessarily enjoy doing it. It's not really my—I don't feel any need for the recognition of that; it's really more to make some of the other things that I do possible: working with the Himalayan Cataract Project, The Magic Yeti Library, and also the Khumbu Climbing School, where we teach young Sherpa climbers on Everest and other places safe guiding techniques, avalanche awareness types of techniques, and avalanche prediction, medical skills, those kinds of things. Being involved with the North Face, I think it's a powerhouse of a brand; it also has ... a great conscience in supporting all of those projects as well. So, if we have to sell a few fleece jackets to make that all possible, bring it on.

So, the implication is that you continue to go back and forth to Nepal to do some of these things. Is that true?

Definitely. We're still very active. We came back after three and a half months in early May and we're getting ready to go back in August....

Is there anything else you would like to add?

No. Thank you for your time. I think ultimately you guys are crafting an important [book] and what will be, I hope, fun for people to read. It will give people some insight into why we're motivated to do what we do but as importantly to look to the great examples of our sport like Sir Edmund Hillary and Tenzing Norgay. What did they do after their ascents? Sir Edmund Hillary— one of the last things—when I spoke with him, he said, "Yes. I want to be remembered, or what I want on my tombstone, kind of down in the footnotes section, would be, 'Oh yes, he climbed Everest too.'" Because he wanted to be remembered for doing philanthropic, humanitarian work. And I think, in some ways, he was so well loved and lionized and sanctified by the people who live in the Everest region. ... He probably was the best known person in the world....

Thank you so much for your time.

Sure. My pleasure. Let me know if I can be of further assistance.

AWARDS

David A. Sowles Memorial Award: American Alpine Club
Tenzing Norgay Award: The Explorers Club

BIBLIOGRAPHY

Childs, Greg, with Peter Athans. "Peter Athans: Athlete-to-Athlete Interview." The North Face. <www.the northface.com/na/athletes/athletes-PA.html>.
Coburn, Broughton. *Everest: Mountain Without Mercy.* [Washington, D.C.:] National Geographic Society, 1997.
The Dark Side of Everest. [Film.] Great Northern Productions (This is one of many films by or about Athans.)

Heil, Nick. "Light of Seven Mountain Suns." *Outside*, December 2005: 110 ff.

"Interview with Pete Athans." Nova Online: Alive on Everest, 1997? <www.pbs.org/wgbh/nova/everest/expeditions/97/team/athans.html>.

Randall, Glenn. *Breaking Point: Challenge on Alaska's Mount Hunter*. Denver: Chockstone, 1984.

Brent Bishop

(July 17, 1966–)
Mountaineer, guide, environmentalist,
motivational speaker

Date of interview: July 2, 2007. *Location:* Seattle, WA. *Interviewer:*
Robert Hauptman. *Method:* In person: taped and videotaped.
Videographer: Frederic Hartemann.

Brent Bishop is the son of the legendary climber Barry Bishop. In addition
to his own mountaineering and guiding achievements on five of the seven continents, he organized the ongoing removal of oxygen canisters and trash in the
high Himalaya and Karakorum. He is one of only seven father-son pairs to
reach the summit of Everest. Interestingly, his brother-in-law is Greg Morten-
son, author of *Three Cups of Tea* and executive director of the Central Asia
Institute.

*RH: Thanks for having us visit for the interview. You first came to the moun-
tains as a young child with your dad, Barry Bishop. Was it intimidating to climb
with such a well-known and successful climber or did you just consider him your
father?*

BB: I was exposed to climbing from a very young age. My father, of
course, had done a lot of notable ascents in Alaska and the Himalaya, and he
worked for National Geographic and I remember, growing up as a kid, that
we were always surrounded by images of the mountains and it was the who's
who of friends visiting D.C.: We would have people like Jim Whittaker stay
at the house, Lute Jersted, all these notable climbers from the sixties. Reinhold
Messner—these people passed through the door; we had dinner with them.
So, to me, this was all pretty normal, which in retrospect, as I've gotten older,
it certainly was not normal to be exposed to those types of climbers. I think
what it did as a young boy, it shaped [to] me what adventure was about. Adventure lived in the high mountains. It certainly influenced me at a very young
age.

Did you start out with simple rock climbing or did you actually head right up into the high mountains?

Well, we lived in D.C. ... and there's good rock climbing close to D.C. and there's good rock climbing in West Virginia, so as a young boy, we were always going off to climb, pretty simple stuff, and then we took family trips out to the Tetons and climbed in the bigger mountains there. But I remember, as a young boy, climbing terrified me. I really was scared of it; the height scared me. I remember on one hand wanting to go in the direction of adventure and please my father and at the same time being terrified. I think what happened was just being in D.C., the avenues to climb weren't there on a continuous basis.... I certainly followed the path of a more traditional athlete as a soccer player, a wrestler, and a lacrosse player and it wasn't until college that I started focusing back on climbing and focusing on it very hard

Your dad climbed Everest and then you did too, thus becoming the first of the [seven] father-son pairs to accomplish this feat. Isn't it rather interesting that no father-daughter nor mother-daughter triumphs have occurred? By the way, we have also interviewed Jamling Tenzing Norgay [and John Roskelley], of other father-son pairs.

In '94 was my first trip to Everest and it was a small team of climbers from Montana and Wyoming (all of us were professional climbing guides) and we pretty much begged, borrowed, and stole to get there. This was before the

Brent Bishop (photograph by Fred Hartemann).

tragedy of '96 and Jon Krakauer's book [*Into Thin Air*] which really introduced climbing to the consciousness of America. So we go off on this trip and we climb Everest; four out of five of us summit. We bring 5,000 pounds of trash off the mountain (we can get into that later). We got back and our friends and family were pleased that we had climbed and that we were alive and it was on to the next project. There was no fanfare; nobody was asking us to give lectures or speeches. I don't think we thought too much of it at that point. I was young at that point; I was 27, and I shared that period with my father. I remember he was quite pleased that I climbed Everest; we talked about it a little bit but there were other things to move on to. Tragically, three and a half months after I climbed Everest, he was killed in a car accident. So, there really wasn't this time to reflect. It's only as time and space have come between those events that I look back on the significance of it: of really being able to follow in my father's footsteps, and the connection there. I'm just sorry that there wasn't more time to share that.

I don't know what the statistics were at that time, but just a few years earlier [in 1953], the first people had summited Everest. Do you know how many people summited this year? I think the figure is, incomprehensibly, 500. It's unbelievable.

I summited in '94. We were in, I think, the 600s for all those years. ... Climbing Everest via the north or south side has changed totally. It is not a true climbing experience. It's amazingly significant on a personal level for all those people that do that but in terms of climbing, does it hold any significance? Absolutely not. By no means is it easy, but I think that the real change occurred after '94, when you see a lot more of the commercial guiding and full scale efforts.

Could you remind readers of your legendary father's accomplishments?

My father was a climber; he started at a very young age climbing in Estes Park; he went to the YMCA camp there, and climbed there and then climbed in the Tetons and went to Dartmouth for his undergraduate work. And he came up with the idea that he was going to climb Mount McKinley, or Denali, as we refer to it now. And he and his climbing partner wrote a gentleman named Bradford Washburn to get some photos and to get some insight into climbing Denali. Well, Brad Washburn looked at the photos that he sent them and their idea and basically joined the trip, and in a way, took over the trip. And that turned out, in 1951, to be the first ascent of the West Buttress of Denali. Where the impetus for that trip and the driving force were early on, two 19 year olds. And that was my father and his climbing partner. ... And then he did a bunch of other climbing around the states and in Europe and then in 1961–62 was in Nepal again with Sir Edmund Hillary doing research for high altitude physiology, which came to be known as the Silver Hut Expedition. A number of scientists stayed over at basically eighteen, nineteen thousand feet on the flanks of Ama Dablam and conducted high altitude physiological research, and this really became the foundation for what we know about altitude. And at the end of that trip, he and three other members of the climbing team did the first ascent of Ama Dablam. They had a permit to go anywhere in that drainage system and they surmised that the drainage system started at the top of Ama Dablam, so off they went, and they climbed the southeast route on Ama Dablam, which is a beautiful route and now it gets a tremendous amount of traffic with guiding. It's very technical. I climbed, well, I guided it in 2003, and to me it's the finest moderate Alpine route that I've done; and I was very pleased to once again be able to follow in his footsteps.

But have you found sufficient challenges in the U.S., in the Rockies or Cascades, for example? And then also, of course, in Alaska?

Certainly. There is so much climbing to do in your backyard. The only limitation to climbing is a person's vision, strength, and commitment. In many ways, there's no reason to ever leave the U.S. or Alaska or Canada. There are lifetimes of new route possibilities, and that just really boils down to how good are you? how tough are you? what's your vision? I think the public looks at Everest as the beginning and end of climbing and in reality it's not. ... Of course, more people are interested in mountaineering and climbing than they ever have been, but if you want solitude, you can certainly find it. You just have to work a little harder.

Everest naturally is dangerous, as are other Himalayan peaks, but the Alpine Eiger scares me more. Was it extremely trying for you, especially since on Everest there are often many other climbers nearby, whereas on the Eiger, you were basically alone?

Well, I've tried the Eiger twice and I've retreated off of it twice. So I have not been successful on it. I will go back and certainly get back on that face. The Eiger is a storybook climb—the history, of course, with Heinrich Harrer and the '38 ascent and what led up to that. It looks like what a climb should look like to me: It's hard, it's committing, it's long, it's got rock difficulties, ice difficulties, and it's beautiful. It looks like a climb should look. Does it scare me? Certainly. All sorts of climbing scares me; even on a big mountain that's relatively benign, you've got to still contend with the objective dangers of avalanche. I don't know if scared is the right word. You just have to understand the risks and be able to weigh them and act accordingly.

You've climbed both Everest and Lhotse. Do you plan to climb any more of the 8,000-meter peaks?

I do. There are a few lines that look very interesting to me. I am more interested in smaller teams and the lighter style, and the west pillar of Makalu is fascinating—the way it cuts the mountain and it has a direct line—[it]is something that I would be very interested in climbing. I am not interested in hiking up any more snowy things. ... I am only interested in climbing things that have technical challenges for me. ...Everybody has their own technical benchmark and everybody gets the same feelings and satisfaction at those benchmarks. One of the best all-around Alpine climbers in the world, Steve House—his benchmark is just higher. The things he feels are the same things that other climbers feel at their benchmarks. You can climb your whole life and the experiences you get can be significant at every stage in your life and you might not be climbing as hard as you were before or at the top of the field ... but the personal satisfaction and the exploration that you have internally is always there. I think that's what holds climbers: People that are really interested; it's part of them.

What was it like climbing with Scott Fischer?

Scott was a lot of fun to climb with. Scott was kind of wild and he was strong and he was tough and he had fun wherever he went. You could walk around the block with him and have fun and he took that attitude into the mountains. We climbed a bunch of rock locally; we always had a good time. He was amazingly strong in the Himalaya. My contention with Scott is if he had been a little more cerebral in his approach to climbing, certainly in the Himalaya, I think he had the potential to be the most prolific and significant Himalayan climber of the late '80s and early '90s from the U.S. But he had a family and a business to run. Genetically he was gifted, and he was technically strong and he was very bold. So, all those things could have come together for some more significant climbing than he accomplished, not to diminish what he did, but he had that potential. He was just stronger than pretty much everybody else out there....

I've always loved mountains, not only because I ski and climb and observe animals, birds, and plants but also because they are part of nature and esthetically magnificent. So, of course, I care about the exploits of the great explorers, mountaineers, and skiers, but you're like Michael Jordan—in a class of your own because you not only enjoy and respect the mountain environment, you did something to clean it up, for which we thank you. ... Could you tell us about the Sagarmatha Environmental Expedition and what your organization does.

This all started in '94. I joined this team of four other climbers to go to Everest and it was at a point where there was some bad press about trash on Mount Everest. So, someone came up with the idea that—and the Ministry of Tourism in Nepal adopted it: the idea was that they would limit one expedition per season per route. Basically there would be only one team on a route per season. And then they realized that these expeditions that pay $50,000 for the peak fee are funding the motorcades and lining the Ministry of Tourism's pockets because not much of the money that goes into these expedition fees gets anywhere near the mountains. It's a pretty corrupt environment over there. That's an understatement. They realized that we've shot ourselves in the foot: instead of giving away ten permits a season and getting $500,000 into the coffers, they give away one or two. They couldn't change the rules because at the time Nepal was a constitutional monarchy where the communists controlled the parliament. So if you figure out that anything can be done in that system, it can't. The Ministry of Tourism wrote an addendum to the rules and regulations that said that at his discretion, he [a minister] can give away an environmental permit, and the environmental permit, of course, had no stipulations. It was simply an environmental permit and you paid your fee just like everybody else. So, we had an environmental permit. But we thought, All right, we're going to do something, because all the other four climbers had been connected with NOLS, the National Outdoor Leadership School, which has great ethics about leave no trace in the mountains and hard skills; so, we decided that we were going to do something: clean up some trash on the mountain. The year before, I had been sitting in grad school and I did a dual degree: a master's in business and a master's in environmental management, and we talked about incentives: how do you get things done? Well, you can't rewire a culture's value systems but you can change incentives. If you look at aluminum cans in the U.S., there's a five-cent deposit on most of them and you'll never see one lying around. So, right out of the classroom where I was probably staying asleep, I came up with the idea that we'll just put a bounty on the oxygen bottles up high. [On] a big mountain like Everest, it takes a month to acclimate and put the higher camps in; you're basically building a logistical pyramid; you're climbing up and down, up and down for about a month until you're finally ready to climb, and every time you come down, you come down empty as do the Sherpas for that month. So, it is pretty easy to look at this and go, well, there's a lot of manpower on the mountain. We came up with the idea of a deposit on the bottles and all of a sudden, they started coming down off the mountain, and we started collecting trash from different trash dumps. In the end, we had four out of five of us summit and we brought down over 5,000 pounds of trash. This little group of climbers that was woefully funded was able to go there, climb the mountain—because we were all first and foremost climbers—and make a significant mark environmentally. And that redefined the expedition paradigm: You can be an environmentalist and at the same time you can be a serious climber. Where we really got our manpower for this was that—because we only had two climbing Sherpas with us, that wasn't very much, and the five climbers, so seven of us—I used the commercial teams of Rob Hall with Adventure Consultants and Todd Burleson from Alpine Ascents International. ... Each of them had 10 or 15 Sherpas. ... We came back and the American Alpine Club looked at what we had done and they awarded us the David Brower Conservation Award, which was quite an honor. And then I was able to get funding and Nike came on board and they said, Look, this is a valuable endeavor you're pursuing and we'll fund it and we're interested in the outdoors because we've got our ACG division, our All Conditions Gear division, which makes outdoor products; so, all of a sudden after '94, I had the funding to be able to go back and make sure the clean-up effort was working. Every year, I'd go back or someone would go back and we'd coordinate all the Sherpa teams on the mountain and trash would come off. And over the years, between 25 and 30,000 pounds of trash had been brought off the mountain. And in essence it's clean. In 2002, when I was up at the South Col, there weren't any old bottles to bring down; they were all gone. ... The new bottles can be recycled; they're worth about $50 empty anyway, so you'll never see a new bottle left up there. It looks clean. I just wish I had saved more of the bottles because we just recycled them in Kathmandu and now they are memorabilia.

Paying local inhabitants on the spot to remove rubbish from the high Himalaya is a brilliant and beneficial idea. It is the type of project to which many caring people might like to contribute. Do you want to mention the name and address of the organization?

You know, I don't, and this is why. Because the trash was a problem that climbers produced; we came up with the idea of how to get it cleaned off and it's been done. It took really very little money to do. There's so many other things that need to be addressed. ... There are amazing organizations out there. The Z Foundation, for one, does a lot of work with women, with girls in Nepal; the Central Asia Institute, which is run by my brother-in-law, builds schools in Pakistan for women. Those are the organizations that need funding.... [Now] climbers have changed their behavior, and it seems as though the approach is different. People are bringing out all of the trash that they take [in]. ...

What do you think of the paved road the Chinese are building to the north side of Everest base camp?

Well, I think there's a road that goes pretty close anyway. The Chinese aren't the most environmentally friendly [people]; they do a lot of things that don't benefit the Tibetan culture or the environment, and this is just another brick in the wall. I think it'll bring some more tourists to base camp but as far as climbing on the north side, it won't alter it at all.

Was it very rewarding to participate, along with Peter Hillary and Jamling Tenzing Norgay, in the making of Everest: 50 Years on the Mountain?

It was a tremendous experience. When you go on expeditions, there's a certain pressure involved...that accelerates the social interaction and so you either become very good friends with people...or you leave an expedition and then you're never going to talk to someone again. Just because these expeditions are stressful. They wear on you, physically, mentally, emotionally. I can say that being with Peter and Jamling was a delight. Those two are wonderful

Brent Bishop (photograph by Fred Hartemann).

men; they're good climbers; they're fun to be with and I'm sorry I'm not able to spend more time with them. But I had met them before we all rendezvoused in Kathmandu; so here we are in Kathmandu and here's this guy that I'm going to climb with and spend the next two months with, and be in a stressful and dangerous situation, and Peter and I got along quite well. I count him as one of my friends.

Just a year ago, we interviewed Christine Boskoff, not far from where we're sitting. Her recent death in China was a big shock because she was such an excellent mountaineer and such a lovely person. Did you enjoy climbing with her? I had asked her about your little accident: you struck some black ice with your ice ax and it bounced back and hit you in the head. Was this very painful?

Hitting myself in the head with an ice ax was strictly user error on my part. I was just coming out of this serac hauling loads between camps—I think it was captured on film and it was kind of funny. Christine [was an] amazingly strong woman, very focused. What I liked about Christine is that she was amazingly modest, and I don't think she spent too much time looking in the rear view mirror. She was a woman that just wanted to climb and she climbed season in, season out. I don't think she realized that she was as good as she was. She didn't care about press; she didn't care about notoriety. At least, that was my perception of her. I felt like the press that she received was because there were people around her that wanted to get notoriety for their own reasons and she was an avenue for that, which ... was all complimentary to Christine. She just wanted to climb. She didn't care if it was on a big peak or something very difficult, with her partner Charlie, that really no one would know about or even understand. And it's a tragedy that she and Charlie were killed. But that type of climbing and that type of commitment level—it's part of the landscape.

Do you have any plans for the near future, anything coming up that would be of interest?

Well, I was supposed to be on a plane to the Eiger last week ... [but this] being the modern era, they've got the Eiger webcam and I could look at the weather and I could look at the face and it was a disaster; so I cancelled the trip and I went rock climbing in Idaho instead.

So, you were planning to do the Eiger about now?

I would have been back by now. It was last week. My climbing partner was in Switzerland with his wife, and so the plan was, if the Eiger was in condition, I was flying to Zurich and a day later I would have been up on the north face. So, that's sort of modern Alpinism: fly, and climb and get back in four or five days.

You're always acclimatized?

Living here at sea level, you're not acclimated to anything, but I climb all the time and I train all the time. Like I said to you before, there are parts to climbing the big snowy things that I like but I'd much rather go out and rock climb. ... I'm always doing something and ready to go.

I think I've come to the end of my questions. Thank you. Thank you very much for the interview.

I hope you got some things that are useful.

AWARDS

David Brower Conservation Award (1994)
Lowell Thomas Award (2003)

BIBLIOGRAPHY

"Brent Bishop: Climber, Environmentalist, and Businessman." www.everestspeakers bureau.com/brentbishop.htm.
Everest: 50 Years on the Mountain. [DVD]. Dir. Liesl Clark [Washington, D.C.:] National Geographic Television and Film, 2003.
Potterfield, Peter. "Cleaning Up Everest: Brent Bishop and the Buy Back Program." <classic.mountainzone.com/everest/98/bishop.html>.
Potterfield, Peter. "The Eiger Nordwand." <classic.mountainzone.com/climbing/eiger>.

Christine Boskoff

(September 7, 1967–November 2006)
Electrical engineer, mountaineer, guide,
owner of Mountain Madness

Date of Interview: July 7, 2006. *Location:* Seattle, Mountain Madness headquarters. *Interviewer:* Robert Hauptman. *Method:* In person: taped and videotaped. *Videographer:* Frederic Hartemann.

*We dedicate this interview to Christine and
to Charlie Fowler, her climbing partner,
who, in late November 2006, were lost in China.*

Christine Boskoff began climbing relatively late, but when she did, she found her calling and dedicated herself so fully that in little more than a decade her résumé compared favorably with those of professionals who had been going on expeditions for half a century. After Scott Fischer lost his life on Everest, Boskoff purchased Mountain Madness. In 2006, she was lost in an avalanche in China. The body of her climbing partner, Charlie Fowler, was soon found, but Boskoff's body was not discovered until the following year. She was a lovely person and was considered by some to be the greatest female mountaineer ever.

> "What do you do for a living?" one [climber] asked her as she limbered up a 5.10 line. "Oh," said Boskoff, who had recently topped out on Mount Blanc and the Matterhorn, "I run a travel business."
>
> —Bruce Barcott

RH: Thank you for talking with us; we appreciate it. I know something about mountaineering: its practice, practitioners, and history. I am stunned by your accomplishments. You began climbing just a few years ago, and someone recently called you the greatest female mountaineer ever. Another commentator insists that you are "One of the greatest mountaineers of all time." How did you manage this extraordinary feat?

CB: Well I started climbing in 1992 and I think what it was, I found my passion in life and I think what you are going to see with all of these people you interview is that we all have a passion for climbing, the outdoors, adventure, and once you find your passion, you become driven, you become focused and that's all you want to do.... I took a two-day rock course and when I climbed to the top I just knew that this is what I want to do for the rest of my life. And now I just love every aspect of climbing, and every day I go out, I try to improve, I try to get more experience and for me it's not even just the summit or to climb real difficult peaks but it's the people I get to climb with, and just the whole experience of culture when you go to a different country. And then when you just love a sport so much or a lifestyle like this, you try to be the best, and I am a very driven person and I put everything into it. There are some things that I do better than others, for example, high altitude mountaineering; I am very strong at [it], because my body adjusts very quickly, so I was able to progress really quickly versus something like ice climbing; I am not as strong as I am with maybe rock climbing. But it is mainly finding your passion and when you find your passion, you become good at it.

But you also have to have an inherent skill; my passion might be mountaineering, but I don't have the ability; I could never do what you have done at the lowest level....

Well, I think my success is because—and if you ask my mother she would say I am hardheaded—when it came to mountaineering I knew I had to train a lot; I'm really driven when it comes to exercising. When I trained my first time I went to Everest, I would get up at three o'clock in the morning and drive up to one of the local hills just outside of Seattle [in the] pouring rain; I would be carrying a heavy pack and I would do it three or four times, with a 10,000-foot elevation gain, or I would run up Mount Sy—it's a three- or four-mile run—and I'd do it three times. You're looking at ... 18 miles for a workout. ... I really work at it. And it's not like it just comes naturally: [as if] I roll off the couch and go and climb. I put a lot of time and dedication into it, and a lot of pain, just having the discipline to get out of bed at three and go and train.

You are the first American woman to reach the summits of six of the world's 14 8,000-meter peaks (Everest, Lhotse, Cho Oyu, Broad Peak, Shishapangma, and Gasherbrum II). It took Ed Viesturs 14 years to complete the cycle. Do you plan to continue to do more than one expedition per year?

Well, my goal isn't to climb all 8,000-meter peaks, all 14 8,000-meter peaks. For me, climbing is challenging my own self; and I don't like checklists; I don't like saying I climbed all the Seven Summits or I climbed all the 14 8,000-meter peaks. For me it's picking a route and challenging myself. It might not be the highest peak and it might not be the hardest peak but it's a good challenge for [me], and even though I love 8,000-meter peaks—I love it because you are gone for so long, you get to know everybody on your expedition, and

Christine Boskoff (photograph by Fred Hartemann).

I enjoy it and I still want to go out and do more—I don't want that as my goal, because I think climbing means something else to me than that.

You own Mountain Madness, the company that Scott Fischer founded. How is the business doing? In addition to your own expeditions, do you also guide clients?

Yes, I do. First of all, Mountain Madness is doing great. We have been growing regularly for the last several years. When I first took it over in '97, the company was pretty much going out of business, so it's been very hard. I've had a lot of personal and business challenges in my life, so it's been over-coming those hurdles, and now the business—we have a great group of people here at Mountain Madness and with everybody working together, we are doing a great job. It's not just me; it's everyone [who] works there. Everybody puts their hundred percent into the business and we love what we do, and it's going really well.

On your Gasherbrum II climb, you employed 200 Baltis to haul your equipment. Do you plan to try to do some of the other 8,000-meter peaks in Alpine style, or any other mountains that require, or at least in the past have required, some kind of help—Baltis or Sherpas—and do you think that expeditionary climbing will even-tually go out of style?

Well, let's go back. The Gasherbrum II expedition, we hired 225 Balti porters, but that was just to get to base camp. And it's pretty much, anybody that climbs that way, tries to get into these mountains, you have to hire help to carry all of your stuff in. On the mountain itself, we didn't use any porters; it was just all of us. For most of the climbs that I have done, I've always carried my own stuff up and down except for Cho Oyo and Lhotse. We had like maybe one Sherpa to help to carry a few loads; I prefer doing it myself. When I guide 8,000-meter peaks, we have Sherpa support. I'm not against having people help me. First of all, they're working, they're getting paid, it's part of their income, they bring it back home to their families. It helps people to be successful. Not everybody wants to be the Ed Viesturs or the Doug Scotts. For them, it's a personal challenge of summiting Everest, and if we can make it easier for them to reach their personal goal, I'm for it. Most people, when they go to Everest, they're not getting sponsorship, but it's a personal challenge; it's like running a marathon.

I guess that's a kind of ticklish question for a person who owns a guiding service. I think that some of the individualistic mountaineers like Messner or Viesturs or Steve House would probably conclude that ultimately expeditionary type of climbing would go out of business, but that would be a hard thing for you to say because, in

Christine Boskoff (middle row, second from right) and team at Gasherbrum base camp. Scott Fischer is in the middle row, second from left, wearing a tank top (photograph courtesy Mountain Madness).

a certain sense, you're a part of that: you guide and in guiding you have larger groups and sometimes you would certainly need help because some young person who is attempting to climb a high peak can't do what you can do, so he or she would need help carrying tents and food.... So that turns out to be a leading question; I didn't mean it to be....

Everybody has their opinion and their style to climb a mountain and I look at it as, nobody's right or wrong; it's their opinion. When you climb Everest, do you use oxygen, do you not use oxygen? It's your personal choice. ... Of course, if somebody's going to become sponsored, you don't want the person being guided or you don't want the person to use oxygen. You want to take the elitest, the top one percent, and those people get sponsored. Most people these days that climb Everest are your normal Joe Blow; they work 80 hours a week and they're going on vacation, and I'd much rather see them climbing Everest or climbing Rainier or climbing Baker than going on a cruise. ... I love it when people get outside; they get athletic; they're not overweight; and they try to push their personal physical goals that way....

In Ascent on G2, *the wonderful film that traces your climb of Gasherbrum II, you speak briefly with Alex Lowe, considered, before his untimely death, the best all-around climber in the world. What was he like? And did you climb with him?*

I didn't climb with Alex Lowe. My climbing partner has quite a bit and the things I've heard about Alex—he was a very nice person. I just met him for a minute; we did an interview together, but he was a very nice person. I've always heard good things about him.

Someone in the film speaks of the pain involved in climbing. Have you suffered much physically or psychologically in the mountains? Peter Habeler remarked that you suffer quietly, without complaining. Just knowing Lowe briefly and then learning of his death is a painful experience, is it not? And every other woman who has tried the 14 8,000-meter peaks has died. This too must be painful and frightening.

You do suffer a lot. I think some of us—that's why we're in the sport, especially high altitude mountaineering: it's cold; sometimes you have a headache. It's not a very pleasant experience versus rock climbing on a sunny crag. But I think that's why a lot of us are drawn to it. I enjoy that hardship, the physical challenge; the more I push myself and the more I have the pain, I enjoy it, and when I look back at it, I feel like I really accomplished something. And that's me.

That's amazing. You quote a Japanese climber who exclaims, "Either summit or die!" How do you feel about this attitude?

That came from one of our Mexican ... a really good climber, Hector Ponce de Leon; and he said that once on Aconcagua: This Japanese climber [in a] storm, and they said, you better turn around and the Japanese climber looked at him and said "summit or die." So that was always kind of an ongoing joke that we used on that expedition. But for me personally, I think everybody in the mountains, they have to take responsibility for their actions, and when people push themselves so much, you kind of sit there and go OK, I might not come back, and that's your preference but when you bring other people into the picture for a rescue, I think that's very selfish. These other people might get hurt because you're up there at 8,000 meters needing help. So I think ... when you climb you need to take responsibility for your actions.

I am sure you know that in certain cases, especially with Japanese and Korean climbers, they set out with the a priori supposition that we will *get somebody to the summit of our group and if someone dies that's a sacrifice we're willing to make, whereas for the most part European and American climbers do not set out with that; they would say, we'd love to get someone to the summit but if it's a matter of someone dying, we, I hope, would stop and rescue the person, despite what just happened on Everest, which was quite horrible.*

Yes, I see that with the Korean culture. We've helped out Koreans on Makalu.... I think some of that is starting to change. [That] is what I've heard, that they're getting a lot better trained and more experienced when they go to the mountains, but I am not sure where that all stands anymore.... I've seen it with inexperienced Europeans, Americans too. So it's not just one country.

Well, we have a mountaineering ethic obligation and we also have a human obligation to help people who are in trouble. Fred [co-author], when he climbed in the Alps, 20, 25 years ago, told me that guides in the Alps from Chamonix have an obligation, even when they are guiding, to stop, have their clients stand still, while they climb down and rescue a person who is calling for help. And I think that that's a good attitude even though the client might suffer, maybe not make the summit, but it seems horrible to let someone purposely die when you could help. Sometimes you can't, and I don't know what the outcome would have been on Everest, if some of those 40 people had stopped and tried to help, but that's a very unpleasant situation. For people who aren't mountaineers, it gives them a bad perspective on what we do.

I don't know all the circumstances on this last Everest thing so it's hard for me to speculate, but I have helped people already and have had to put my clients ... and tie them off on something and help somebody else that was in trouble, but that's just part of the game. As a guide, you're a role model, and you need to show your clients the proper etiquette when you're in the mountains. And, of course, not just for the clients; you should help other people....

Brent Bishop (who is one of the few son-father pairs to summit Everest) was one of your fellow climbers on G2. What was it like climbing with him? I was amazed that he tore his head open with an ice ax.

Well, Brent is a character for sure. Really, the only time I ever climbed with Brent was on the Gasherbrum II expedition. He's a funny guy; he's very nice.

What happened with his head?

I think what he was doing was he put his ice ax into a serac to push himself up and it popped out and hit him in the head.

Was it bad?

It wasn't bad, he didn't need stitches or anything like that.

Once you reached base camp, the climbers did the entire route to the summit without any aid from high altitude porters. In the film, I noticed some fixed ropes. Did you put all those up before the filming began? What was it like climbing and setting up camps completely unaided?

It's a lot of hard work. On that expedition, I was telling you, we didn't have any porter support and so a few of us ended up doing most of the work.... The fixed lines were already up. There were a few expeditions that had already been there before us and they already had rope up earlier that season so we just used it. We might have put in some extra rope in certain sections. God, that's a long time ago, in 1999.

On summit day, you had a long, difficult climb to a tent that someone had left high on the mountain. Then you continued without a rest to the summit. The narrator mentions that you still had eight hours to go. And of course you had to get back down. Can a person who has never done this sort of thing (at 26,000 feet) really comprehend what it feels like?

No. That summit day was probably the hardest summit day I have ever had in the mountains. I was completely exhausted. I remember, we started out at nine, ten o'clock at night and we climbed up all throughout the night, and before that we had already attempted the summit twice before, so we were pretty tired. The expedition was now well over 60 days, and we were ready to go home, so it was really hard for us. And I remember getting up to a point and I could kind of see the summit, and I said, We'll be up there in an hour, and this was eight o'clock in the morning, and it wasn't until one we topped out and it was so hard, and then we had to get all the way back down again. I think we got back down to camp by five. And that day was probably the hardest day I ever had in the mountains.

It was amazing.

It was amazing, yes.

Weren't you truly astonished to learn that while you were high up on the dangerous mountain, an avalanche inundated base camp far below, wreaking destruc-

tion, and forcing you, as expedition leader, to return briefly to assess the damage? Normally, you would think the avalanche would happen up high....

We had so many things happen to us on that expedition. We had our base camp wiped out by an avalanche; and thank god all the local staff went down to Concordia to visit some other friends, just by chance. I think they were playing cards down there. So it was lucky for us nobody was hurt, but our kitchen tent, everything, was wiped out. We lost several tents. And what had happened was some freak avalanche from the mountain about half a mile across the glacier—a huge serac came down and just went all the way across that glacier and wiped out our camp, and the Korean camp got wiped out and one other camp.

That's so unusual. Normally base camps are safe from those types of inundations.

Yes, you would assume. In this case, it was just a freak occurrence. And then on top of it we had several big storms hit us that completely—we had snow and snow and it collapsed our kitchen tent again.

Was the base camp at around 18,000 feet?

It was 5,000 meters, 5,200 meters [ca. 17,000 feet].

The narrator in Ascent on G2 *says that mountaineering is a solo sport? Is this true?*

On the bigger peaks, it's probably, in some ways, solo, because if there's fixed line you're moving independently. However, it's a team effort. And a lot of times in the mountains it's just you and another buddy, and it's you two. It's not a solo sport.

In 1995, on the descent from Broad Peak's summit, you got disoriented in a blizzard. Were you alone? How did you find your way back to camp? During this same storm, the great British climber Alison Hargreaves was killed nearby on K2.

Yes, that was a big experience for me. That was after I summited my first eight thousander. That's when I first met Scott Fischer. He had his own expedition that was on the mountain at the same time. What had happened was I was the only person in my expedition (there were four of us ...) who went to the summit that day, and when I was coming down, I was kind of following Scott Fischer's group. They were about an hour in front of me. And that's when that huge storm came out from the north, from China, and as I got further away from the mountain, the winds picked up, and I couldn't see their tracks anymore. The sun was just going down and all I kind of remembered is the contour of the glacier and I was trying to remember that from the way I came up; I was actually heading right off a cliff, and for a brief second, the wind let up and the sun was in between the clouds and it came out just for a brief second and I saw a dark patch and I said, That's Camp 3, and I headed right towards it. I was so happy to be at camp, because I looked and I was headed right off that ice cliff....

I am happy for you. It' such a horrible feeling to not know where to go, get a little lost....

You can get lost anywhere in the mountains; it's not just the big peaks. Yes, to spend a night alone or out alone....

Were you prepared to bivouac?

I had a sleeping bag with me.

It would have been unpleasant.

It would have been unpleasant. ... I would have survived the night, probably. The next day it was a beautiful blue day, crystal blue day. We didn't hear about the K2 incident until we got back down to base camp. There was a Canadian team there and they were listening to the dispatches on K2, with Jeff Lakes trying to make it down; Peter Hillary was talking on the radio, saying, You're almost there, Jeff, you're almost there. Then we went over to Scott's camp and they had this huge telescope and they were watching what was going on in the mountain and that's when we realized Jeff must have died because they were digging a grave for him; it was really sad; and we heard about Alison and Rob Slater and all those folks, and it was really sad. It was the first time that I experienced so much death in the mountains. I never thought of mountaineering as—somebody could die. For me, in that way, it was a good lesson to be learned that day.

A hard lesson.

A hard lesson, yes.

You have made 12 attempts on 8,000-meter peaks, with six successes. How many of them were done without oxygen?

Seven. I did Everest twice. No, no. Out of those, Everest I did with oxygen both times, and then I used oxygen on Lhotse. So, I don't know what that is; so four of them I did without oxygen.

Very impressive. When they first started this business back around 1950 and a little before, they didn't imagine that it could be done without oxygen. It was incomprehensible that it could be done without oxygen. Now, as a matter of course, strong people do it without oxygen and choose to and they have been doing it without oxygen probably since the middle '70s. I am a rank amateur, but I manage to do 20 little climbs a season, so it is reasonable that a professional would do many more small mountains as well as some large expeditions. Nevertheless, when I read through your climbing résumé, I am simply floored: You have guided on five continents and six of the Seven Summits, climbed a panoply of high Asian and South American peaks, and established innumerable new rock routes in Colorado. How do you do this? Do you go directly from one big climb or expedition into another? How do you deal with the austerities of three months in a tent over and over again?

You just love what you do. I climb at least four times a week. I go to the rock gym, I train, ... I go rock climbing, I climb mountains all the time. I'm constantly in the mountains.

And being in Nepal for three months, coming home, and then going right back somewhere else doesn't bother you? You enjoy sleeping in the tent, waking up, and eating the breakfast they prepare, and so on. That's a good thing for you.

That's a good thing for me. I love it.

Boy, that's hard.

You look tired just talking to me.

It's not so much being tired. It's the fact that you have lost not merely the luxuries of modern life, but it's so austere—bathroom facilities, showering, lack of specific types of food like fresh fruit, and on and on through a broad array of things that one sacrifices in order to be on a three-month expedition in Antarctica, for example. That's just difficult for most people; you've found your chosen profession because you actually enjoy it.

I love what I do, but I think [in] our culture, we're so used to having a toilet, running water, and all that kind of stuff, but if you look around, and the more you travel, you see people without those frilly little things in life, and they're happy. I think it's really your frame of mind....

It's not a sacrifice sleeping in a tent for you.

No, it's beautiful. Look at the things you wake up to....

You are an extraordinary woman: an electrical engineer, an entrepreneur, an excellent rock climber, and the premier female mountaineer in the world. I recall that John Roskelley got angry on a climb and said that he would never again climb with women. Have you ever experienced discrimination in mountaineering because of your gender?

You do. The thing is you have to understand.... When I do climb with men, I try to understand them and I try to get a sense of who they are. Some guys, they don't want any interaction with women and some do. Some are fine with it. So I try to get that kind of sense; especially with my guiding, I have to be real sensitive to their needs. So I try to balance that out versus my climbing partner; I said before, I wouldn't go climbing with John, if he doesn't want to be with a woman. I want to be with climbers that want my company; my climbing partner, [whom] I climb with all the time, has 30 years of experience, a lot more than I do, and we make a good climbing pair. But you do run into that and it is a delicate way of handling those situations. Like I said, everybody has their own opinion and everybody's been brought up differently.

I have never used a guide in my life for virtually all the different things I've done, not just mountaineering; I've traveled very extensively, and only when I was forced to because of legal necessities have I taken a tour.... But if I were to use a mountaineering guide, I would much prefer a woman because, I would presume, she wouldn't be as strong-willed and macho and tough....

I think all professional guides, if they are good guides, they are not going to use their ego or machoness to go and plow [into a storm] and make the summit even though it's bad weather or conditions aren't right. Women might be a little more motherly; but there's a lot of our guides that are men who also are very motherly and very good as caretakers.

What do you have planned for the future and do you have anything else to add?

I am just building a great company and making it better; that's my number one plan, and continuing to challenge myself in the mountains and doing what I love which is running a guiding company and climbing. I love it all, and every day I go in the office and I'm happy and I never say, Oh, I got to go to work today. I'm the luckiest person in the world....

Thank you so much for sharing all of this with us. Thank you.
You bet.

BIBLIOGRAPHY

Ascent on G2: One Woman's Journey to the Top. [Videocassette.] Dir. Robert Yuhas. n.p.: Robert Yuhas productions/Travel Channel, 1999.
Calhoun, Joshua. "Boskoff Sizes Up K2." *Outside Online* <http://outside.away.com/out side/news/headlines/20020719_1.html>.
Dappen, Andy. "The Great Unknown." *Rock & Ice* 130 (January 2004): 60–63, 88.
Lambert, Pam, et al. "Aiming High." *People* 52.22 (December 6, 1999).
<www.mountainmadness.com>.

Carlos Buhler

(October 17, 1954–)
Mountaineer, motivational speaker

Date of Interview: January 11, 2010. *Location:* South Burlington, VT, and Canmore, Alberta, Canada. *Interviewer:* Robert Hauptman. *Method:* Taped telephonically.

"Carlos Buhler is one of the most accomplished mountain climbers in the world. His climbing career spans thirty-nine years with major ascents on five continents. He draws from experience gained on forty-six expeditions to Canada, Alaska, Ecuador, Peru, Chile, Bolivia, Argentina, Uganda, Kenya, India, Pakistan, Nepal, China, Kyrgyzstan, Tajikistan, Kazakhstan, Russia, and Tibet. In 1983, he climbed to the summit of Mount Everest with the American team that made the first ascent of the Kangshung (East) Face from Tibet. It was Everest's last unclimbed face and its ascent established the mountain's most technically demanding route. Their climb has never been repeated."

RH: I recall the first time that I read through Christine Boskoff's climbing résumé. It seemed impossible that someone could have done so many climbs in so many parts of the world in such a short period of time. Your achievement is similar. In 1970, you did one small Wyoming peak. A year later, you spent 35 days on an Alaskan expedition, and in 1972, you managed Monte Rosa, the Eiger, and many other European peaks. How did it come about that you made such a full commitment to mountaineering so quickly?

CB: In the early years, Bob, I was being introduced to all the different aspects of the mountain environment, the out of doors, and I had no idea or plans to make mountaineering a centerpiece of my life; I was just trying to burn off some energy, I guess. My father passed away; my mother had as much to do with my going to that Wyoming peak in the summer of 1970 as I did because, of course, I had to ask her. That was also a NOLS [National Outdoor Leadership School] course, and NOLS really introduced me to the world of mountains. And that 1971 trip to Alaska was a kayaking trip to Prince William Sound. However, we did some small amount of mountaineering, because we were near the ice fields that fell directly into the sea. In any event, we were learning how to survive in inhospitable places. Alaska in August is inhospitable [because] there are so many mosquitoes. The end result was that in 1972, although I had only been climbing for a couple of years, I joined this team of American high school students in northern Italy; I was somewhat more experienced than most of the people there and that was due to those two 35-day NOLS courses, which in total were 70 days in the wilderness.

Hmm.

We established our little base camp in northern Italy; the teacher who organized this outing—[it] was called the Rum Doodle Expedition. There were about a dozen of us that came and went during the summer and probably seven or eight of us stayed the whole summer. It was a fairly long, from June to August kind of gathering. I, for the first time during the summer of '72, felt like I was given the opportunity to create my own destiny. Those NOLS courses couldn't allow that. But in 1972—the man was named Peter Shreiber and Peter came with his wife and their two children and led this group of high school students. He was a private school instructor ... in Vermont....

Hmm.

He normally took a group of students out to British Columbia every summer. But this year, he decided to change his venue and he went to Europe.... The end result was that Peter asked me if I would be in charge of the group, so to speak, while he had to drive some of the students to the airport in Paris.... We were above [a] town on a ski slope where we had built our little base camp in a herder's hut, one of these cabins that's a thousand meters above the valley floor. That was an astounding directive to me, because at the time I was 17 years old and nobody had ever put me in charge like that in real life. NOLS had kind of feigned it but this was real life. And he said, I'll meet you guys in Germany somewhere, because we were driving up to Norway.

Yes.

The reality was that I got a huge charge out of this responsibility. I realized that I could actually make decisions in the mountains that would prove whether I was alive or dead the next day. That was a watershed for me. We spent that summer doing nothing but hikes and climbs and Peter introduced us to a lot of modern climbing techniques which I hadn't learned at NOLS. For example, I was introduced to crampons. ... The question is, How did you manage to climb so much? In those early years, I wasn't really trying to climb a lot but I had these blocks of time where I was able to do nothing else than climb, which was an incredible opportunity given to me by my mother. But that autumn, the autumn of '72, I really found that I was thinking about climbing a lot. [Then] I went to Spain to study.

Gee.

And I join[ed] a club there and I realized now that this was going to be a real part of my life. And although I could only dream about going out to the crags on the weekends from Barcelona, where I was studying, it really occupied a lot of my thoughts. When I look back, I remember thinking, I'm a really lucky person ... because I don't have to struggle for my meals every day. ... So I tried to utilize every moment I could get and I kept thinking to myself over the next few years, There will be a time when I can't do this. ... So every moment I [could], I tried to climb. ... It wasn't until I got out of university in 1978, that I was finally able to say, Now I've got a decision to make: Am I going to go to grad school, get a job, or am I going to climb? I knew at that point, it was important to understand the doors that were going to close. ... If I was going to climb, I owed it to myself ... [that] I should really climb and not just dabble in it. So I went to work right out of school, guiding. ... I was offered this job to guide in Latin America. ... Latin America was becoming a kind of adventure/tourism Mecca.... I spoke Spanish and I was a climber, so I had those jobs offered to me. So every moment I got, I went climbing in addition to taking people on an extraordinary holiday....

Dr. Louis F. Reichardt, one of the four first Americans to climb K2, observes that you are "arguably the best American Himalayan climber there is. Nobody has had such a long and distinguished career" as you have. Ed Viesturs may be better known because he set himself the goal of climbing the 14 8,000-meter peaks without oxygen, and he has gotten a great deal of press exposure. Do you think that the general press has slighted your many achievements?

On the contrary, I never felt that the media slighted me. ... I never had that impression. ... Pretty quickly I realized a couple of things about the media, and one of those things was that they were in the business to sell something, whether it was [PBS] *NewsHour* or *Time* magazine or *Sports Illustrated* or *Climbing* or whatever it was; they were under an obligation ... and I certainly understood why they existed. So it never felt to me as if I was overlooked or slighted. I never expected the media to follow the mountaineering world. You place yourself back in the '70s: there were no professional climbers. Climbing was a very private kind of community of people that all had other jobs ... and climbed as kind of a pastime. In those years, although I dreamed of climbing in all the great ranges of the world, I never really felt like the media owed any obligation to paying attention to it. When I first got a little bit of recognition—I'll just make an example: it was about 1978 and I was selected for that team that was going to climb with a Soviet team on an international exchange.

Yes.

Just the fact that I got selected for that team in 1978—[it] had nothing to do with the media—was overwhelmingly positive for me. It was the first

time that an official body, a committee in the American Alpine Club, had said
to me, All that time you've spent climbing is worth something....

Was that in the Pamirs?
That was in the Pamirs.

Yes. That's the famous debacle where those eight women were killed, I guess.
When the eight women were killed, [that] was on the first exchange in
1974. And that exchange began when they invited six Americans ... to climb
on Pik Lenin. In 1975, we reciprocated and invited a team of Soviets to the
United States. [In] '76, they brought a team over to Russia again, and in '77,
we took a team of Russians or Soviets to Alaska. They reciprocated in 1978:
It was the third group of Americans that was going to join a team of Soviets
for a climbing trip in the Soviet Union. And we were fully expecting to invite
a team back in 1979, but they invaded Afghanistan. ... When I got that telegram
that I'd been selected, I can tell you—I was up here in the Canadian Rockies;
I'll remember it for the rest of my life—I was just amazed.... I was just blown
away. ... What I am trying to say with all this is that the media, when they
covered something about me, I was astounded. Later on in life, when professional mountaineering became more common in the '90s, then I was forced to
fight for and compete for media attention. It was what allowed people to func-
tion as professionals in a very small and competitive world, where sponsors
relied on pairs of eyes who saw their logos. And so, if you weren't getting
media attention, you weren't displaying a logos. ... Long before Ed Viesturs
came along in the late '80s, I had received enough media attention that I was
well-known in the climbing community....

It has been said that you have "spent the last quarter century amassing a record
of ascents and attempts that rivals anyone, anywhere. A vigorous proponent and
practitioner of the small and self-sufficient expedition, [you have] pushed the edge
of the alpinism envelope as aggressively as any climber in the world..." [Telluride's
annual 2003 Mountain Film Festival catalog of events]. Ted Mischaikov echoes
this: "He is a leader in converting the sport of alpine climbing from an assault men-
tality to one of group centered, strategic planning; mutual respect between climbers
and sherpas; use of high tech gear; and best environmental practices." Messner
switched to Alpine methods in the Himalaya quite early and Steve House also strongly
advocates non-expeditionary methods. Do you think that the big 19th-century,
1,000-porter expedition, or even a more delimited endeavor but still with many
climbers and attendants is no longer tenable? Do you think that it is unethical to
overwhelm the economy, environment, and the mountain itself with hundreds of
people and their accouterments? But doesn't this occur no matter what we do, since
even 100 small groups (on Denali, for example) are equal to one or two enormous
ones?

... That depends on how you look at the world, I suppose. I could make arguments on both sides. It has become very stylish to do small two-person expeditions, for example. What is it that irritates people about big expeditions? Is it really the environmental impact? Is it the style issue that's going on there? You know, the expedition style of climbing with fixed ropes and camps. ... Does it really make any difference if you have twelve two-person expeditions or one 24-member expedition? And the reality of that, Bob, is that, yes, it's much better to have everybody in a 24-member expedition, environmentally speaking, than having, I think, 12 two-member expeditions off to different areas. Each one of those two-member expeditions has to hire porters and travel to Nepal or Pakistan or wherever they're going. It's much more efficient, if you put them all together and drive one bus to the roadhead, right? ... It wasn't merely the size of an expedition that was causing problems, it was the way that the mountain was approached as well.

Well, that leads to the next question, which is, At a time when a truly over-whelming number of sometimes inexperienced people are interested in local and for-eign mountaineering and trekking (I once climbed Colorado's Bierstadt and was accompanied by a literal parade of hundreds of people, including a four-year-old girl; for some, this not only harms the environment but also spoils the pleasure), should organizations and/or governmental bodies attempt to more fully control access to the high peaks?

By necessity, we have limited amounts of wilderness. This comes back to the question of wilderness and ethics. Do we value the fact that we can save a little bit of wilderness, say, on Mount Katahdin? That is a tough question, because in Europe, wilderness is seen very differently, for example, than it is in the United States. They behave very differently, with a series of huts and téléfériques and ski lifts that give access to the high mountains for an enor-mously large segment of the population; in the United States we have a problem with [this]. Nobody has a téléférique [in] the Grand Teton National Park. We just don't like that. It goes against our wilderness ethic. In terms of limiting the numbers, it depends on how much wilderness (and how you define wil-derness) you want to keep. My sense is that the problem is not merely about wilderness. It's about overpopulation on the planet—you point that out—it's about agriculture; it's about the destruction of the oceans with garbage; it's everywhere. And I must say, I find it a bit controversial to make a very firm stand on limiting the number of tourists that can sleep on the lower saddle in the Grand Teton [National Park] every night, and then sending 100,000 troops to Afghanistan.

Or even more oppressive is the fact that when you go to Katahdin, if you don't get there before the last of the 30 people, they simply don't let you in the park at all. We found that quite offensive.

The parks are trying to respond to a wilderness ethic that has somehow been created in our national park system. And I'm not saying that it's wrong. Our national park system is one of the great legacies of some very innovative thinkers and people have copied it all over the world. ... These are very tough questions. I can't really answer. All I can tell you is that there are good arguments on both sides, ... It doesn't only have to do with mountaineering. As a matter of fact, mountaineering is one of the tiniest ... most insignificant activities in this. Much more important are game parks in Africa. ... How we limit people to access these areas—these are huge questions and have to be decided by countries in their own ways. ...

Lorenzo Ortas has observed that "If I had to emphasize one thing about Carlos, it is his capacity to know when to turn around, however close he may be to the summit, if the act of continuing on goes against his strict set of requisites for prudence." In this you are similar to Viesturs who is famous for turning back where almost all other serious professionals would continue. This indeed is why the 1996 Everest debacle occurred. No one was willing to turn back. Is it difficult for you to call a halt or do you know that you must because a summit is not worth a life?

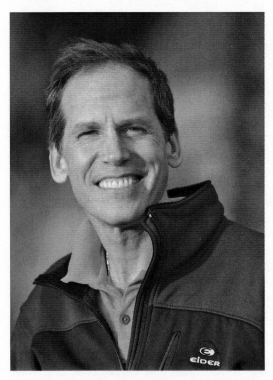

Carlos Buhler (photograph by Beto Santillan; courtesy of Carlos Buhler).

... The analysis of risk plays a very prominent role in those decisions. You examine why different people go forward and different people turn back and there is every imaginable place on that spectrum, [every] type of person and character on that spectrum. As a matter of fact, the same person shifts on that spectrum not only on a short term basis but on a long term basis. So from day to day, you can accept or not accept risk more or less. ... I think that this ability that Lorenzo speaks about to turn around is in some way available to me because I felt as though it was never my last opportunity. I climb with people sometimes who have the sense that where they are in that moment has taken so much that their opportunity to return there is almost infinitesimal.... So if they're 400 meters from the summit of K2, they can't imagine ever getting back. Fortunately for me, after many expeditions to the mountain areas—in the beginning I thought, I'll never get back here and then I would get back there to the Andes or some place in the Himalaya. ... If I played it right, I could go back as many times as I want to the Himalaya. ... Since I didn't have a kind of tick list ... what I was really trying to do was kind of an inner journey. It didn't really matter where the stage was, what mountain I was on, in other words. [What was] important [was] what was happening inside me. I knew that if I turned around at one point, within nine or ten months I'd probably be back on that stage again able to examine everything I wanted to look at....

Yes.

... It wasn't such a big deal to turn around. Now I'm not saying it was easy. When I turned around from going to the summit of Makalu in 1984, it was extraordinarily emotionally painful for the next ten years. But at the moment I needed to make that decision. I think I could see, hey, whoa, someone could get killed here....

One day, your mother turned up at Everest base camp. This was an astounding surprise for you. Subsequently, she visited with you on many of your climbs, trekking long distances to base camps. How did you react to these most unusual experiences?

Well, very positively. My mom did surprise me coming in to Everest base camp. I had no idea that she was going to come. My step-dad ... said, Go. She decided to come after I had left for ... Everest. When I realized how much she enjoyed the experience—and my mother was an anthropologist by studies—I invited her on all of my trips and we kind of became a fund-raising team because she could lead a trek to base camp and we could find people who would be willing to come in to base camp and make a small donation to the cost of the expedition in addition. And this led to a great ... teamwork thing and it helped raise money for these trips. It gave my mother joy because she was going on these amazing journeys to these countries she had always wanted to travel in and it gave me great satisfaction to have her coming in. She began to understand everything about Himalayan and Asian mountaineering.... I was amazed that she loved it so much and glad she could take part. She did until just before she died.

Stephen Venables insists that "The American climber Carlos Buhler is one of the world's most successful expeditioners. Over the last 25 years he has been at the forefront of exploratory mountaineering, with many first ascents in Peru, Alaska and the Himalaya. High altitude successes include alpine ascents of K2 North Ridge with the Russians, Kangchenjunga North Face with Peter Habeler and the first ascent of Everest's Kangshung Face. However, it is on the more elegant, 6000ers and 7000ers that he has really made his mark, most notably on Changabang's North Face Direct and, this year, the first ascent of Sepu Kangri." How important are first ascents for you? [Do you think they are significant?]

If you look at what the definition of first ascent is, and I'm going to define it as exploration, the answer is, yes, I do, because what I was after was personal growth and for me to achieve the most personal growth possible, I wanted to challenge myself by going to places where there was a minimum of information; it is part of what I was looking for through climbing. First ascents are the result of a successful exploration of some place. There were many trips I did that didn't result in a success or reaching the summit. ... [I] appreciate a great route that someone else had done, and I repeated hundreds of routes, but I wanted to maximize my time and my growth as a person. I tried to go where people hadn't been. But it took 20 years of learning.... It wasn't easy to just do that from the beginning ... [to] try new stuff.

In 1994, you stopped just 100 feet below the K2 summit? This must have been a difficult decision. In retrospect, do you think that it was the correct one?

Yes. It was the correct decision given the information that we had at the time. ... I would have made that same decision today.

Did you ever summit K2 subsequently?

Yes. But here's the thing. If you ask yourself (and this I wondered about many times), did I take more risk in turning around in 1994 100 feet from the top (it was actually less than 100 feet from the summit of K2) and again have to return for another full expedition, there are 100 things that can go wrong that lead up to a summit day, and I felt as though I wasn't sure because if you just had stretched that last hour—it actually turned out to be 20 minutes but we didn't know that at the time; Rob Hall knew it; they got it and won a gamble because Rob Hall was with us and he went to the summit and the four of us turned around. ... But here I had to go back two years later and endure an enormously stressful expedition in which I did summit K2 but my partner died on the descent with me. And I realized that it easily could have been me....

In 1988, you became the first American to reach the summit of Kangchenjunga, and in 1990, you became the first North American to summit four 8,000-meter peaks. Do you intend to continue with the quest to do all 14 of these?

No. Climbing [to] the summits of the 8,000-meter peaks is a wonderful experience, but what I learned rather early on, fortunately, was that there is a recipe for success: If you wish to climb all the 14 8,000-meter peaks by roughly the easier routes on them, and that's what most people tend to do, you'll learn how to do them. And you can obtain a fairly high probability of success on every expedition, not a hundred percent.... There's so much known about these

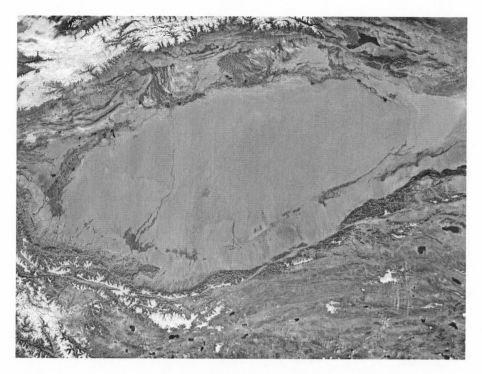

Taklimakan K2

mountains now, you're leaving little up to chance. That didn't interest me because I wasn't growing at that point, when I climbed four or five of them ... and certainly that was quite extraordinary for me. Kanchenjunga was with a very small team, when we repeated the north face. It wasn't the normal route and we almost died on that mountain. On K2, again, I succeeded on the north ridge, a very difficult route on the mountain and one that hadn't been climbed very often. I don't know how many people have climbed it, about 20. When I looked at [how] many people have climbed the three highest peaks on the planet by routes other than the normal route, it's a pretty small group of people. ... To do another eight of them was for the outside world, it was for the money, it was for the power, it was for the prestige. That was important but it wasn't important enough for me to give up the exploration, which was where I was growing internally.

In 1999, you did Siula Grande. Was this an eerie experience? I believe you were the first person to repeat this infamous climb described in Joe Simpson's extraordinary book and film, Touching the Void.

Yes, it was an eerie experience. When we went there, nobody had gone back to that face. I said to Mark, somebody's going to have to go back to this face. It's kind of haunted. We should go and look at it. The book had come out in 1987—I guess they were there in '85—and this was 1999, 14 years later. It was bizarre and when we climbed it ... we had the book in base camp; we had Joe Simpson's book, *Touching the Void*, in base camp, but we wouldn't read it; I hadn't read it yet; I didn't want to read it; I didn't want to know all of the horrible experiences that these boys had had until we were done with the climb. We did a line that led up to what we considered the summit of the peak, which was very similar in altitude to what Joe and Simon thought was the summit, but about 200 yards farther along the ridge. In any event, we ended up going over to their summit as well, just to make sure we'd climbed both of them.... And I thought, if anything screws up—because in any of these climbs something can happen: a serac can break, you can take a fall—...if something happens to us on this climb, this is going to make Siula Grande a cursed mountain. ... I was certainly aware when I was leading these pitches that if I fell and I broke my ankle, ... we were going to be really scrutinized.

Then when you read the book, did that really affect you? I thought that was a fantastic book.

It was. It was a fantastic book. I know Simon personally and I don't know Joe but I know Simon pretty well. The big problem was the descent. We finally had done the face—it took us four days...—and when we were descending, it was difficult because there was a lot of soft snow and it's a very exposed knife-edge ridge with big cornices on it. And I said to Mark, we're just begging for disaster here, because the mountain is cursed, in a sense. Let's just rappel the face. So what we did was, we gathered all of our loose cord and we set off down the face 200 yards, 300 meters before the ridge ended, somewhere in the middle of the ridge, but those two or 300 yards of corniced ridge were what Simon and Joe had had to negotiate, and I could certainly understand how he broke his leg going down those cornices. He wasn't as experienced as I was. Those boys were on their first foreign expedition. They'd never climbed outside the Alps, so they weren't experienced in Andean snow conditions and so forth, and they made some huge mistakes and that's why he broke his leg. But given all that, it could have easily happened to me too. I was just glad we got to the bottom of the face and nothing had happened. I looked at that crevasse where Joe entered, where the rope was cut, I looked at that big crevasse—because, of course, we had to rappel over it, maybe a hundred yards further to the right—but it was pretty spooky.

You've had so many extraordinary experiences, have you thought of writing a comprehensive account, a book, like Steve House just did?

Yes. I'm working on one. I'm working on finding a publisher. I'm open to suggestions.

Thank you very much for your time.

My pleasure, Bob.

AWARDS

"In 2003 Buhler received the Distinguished Alumni Award from Western Washington University for his work leading lightweight, international teams facing extraordinary challenges."

BIBLIOGRAPHY

Klepinin, Liana. "At Home Among Foreigners: A Foreigner Among His Own: Carlos Buhler/The Best Mountaineer of the Century About Himself and America. *Risk Online* (hard copy edition), 2002/3 (4).
vanNoordennen, Pieter. "Buhler's Monster Mountain." *Outside Online.* <http://outside. away.com/outside/destinations/200311/200311_monster_mountain.html>.
<http://www.carlosbuhler.com>.

Charlotte Fox

(May 10, 1957–)
Mountaineer, ski patroller

Date of Interview: March 7, 2007. *Location:* Aspen, CO. *Interviewer:* Robert Hauptman. *Method:* In person: taped and videotaped. *Videographer:* Frederic Hartemann.

Charlotte Fox was one of the small group of climbers stranded just short of high camp during the fateful 1996 descent of Everest. Like Beck Weathers, she survived, and continues to work as a ski patroller in Aspen. Fox is the only American woman to have climbed three 8,000-meter peaks.

RH: Thank you for agreeing to talk with us. I know that you sometimes prefer to stay in the background. So many of the people involved in the horrible 1996 Everest disaster have become household names, even those who were killed. Many of the others have written accounts of their experiences, but you seem happy to remain unheralded. The strange and ironic fact is that sometimes those in the background may be more involved and may have insights to offer that elude those in the spotlight.

CF: I didn't go to Everest because I wanted to tick off an accomplishment. Of course, I wanted to summit but I climb on a regular basis and that was my third 8,000-meter peak, and I have probably been over 18,000 feet 13, 14, 15 times before that. So I feel that I had worked my way up the ladder and had gotten some mileage and I had a true love for the sport more than being a dilettante. And so to me it's more important to be accepted among my peers, not the general public, for the general accomplishment and in fact it's a little embarrassing to be involved in the greatest mountain tragedy ever. So I can understand how people confuse the two teams and thought that most people were just guided clients when, in fact, Scott Fischer put together a team of climbers who needed a leader and had us on our own much of the climb on a schedule and the fact that we had to think for ourselves ended up helping out greatly when the evening of May tenth came.

If you thought about writing a short or longer account, do you think you might have some insights that other people who were involved in a very different way would not have? You are very different than the other folks because you were not involved in the negative things, the really bad things that happened

I was out in the huddle for a long time! Well, I wrote the account of the trip for the *American Alpine Club Journal.* ... I was very honored to be able to do that and summarize my version [for my peers]. But otherwise, I just wanted to come home and go climbing. As I said, I just got home from ice climbing a few minutes ago. It's what I love to do.

Were you an avid skier and then a professional ski patroller before you became interested in mountaineering? Do you still enjoy downhill skiing?

I moved to Aspen from North Carolina right out of college, when I was 22, for a summer. I already had a love for the mountains. Moving to the Colorado Rockies was remarkable. I started climbing fourteeners and that took me around the state and to some beautiful places. And it wasn't very technical. It seemed that after the fourteeners, I ended up going internationally and climbing at altitude on very simple routes on peaks around the world. Then I developed into a more technical climber. I've stayed home more the last few years just because that's where life has pointed me. I've been doing more technical climbing closer to home than international travel but I am getting back out there in the last year and I am really excited about it. And I still enjoy downhill skiing. I don't know that if I retired I would just go skiing nine hours a day, five days a week like I do now. I am really fortunate: I love my job. But on my days off, I either go ice climbing, which is most of the time; to get away from work, I go backcountry skiing. I would be tired [of skiing] if I were not working at it. You engage your mind with avalanche control work and medical situations and just generally running the mountain. I would be bored without that.

Do you run into a lot of major accidents in which you have to help?

Definitely. Our number one priority is medical. On the mountain we have mostly intermediate skiers at Snowmass who ski once a year or so; they are not really strong folks. We get very interesting medical trauma wrecks, accidents, up there. I do avalanche control work; I help train the avalanche dogs; and I am an emergency medical technician. [On the slope I] stabilize and transport. Every day is different, with the weather and the people. That's what's exciting about it. It's a lot of fun.

Is there a strong connection between the two activities, mountaineering and ice climbing and skiing? Surprisingly, some, though not all, people only like the one or the other. But for you it's all kind of interconnected.

It is. I am jack of all trades and master of none. I just love to keep up the enthusiasm and with the change of seasons, you're doing something different for half the year than the other half. When you switch over from winter into summer or fall into spring, it's starting over again; it's really exciting to get into shape and ramp up your skills. ... The really good climbers are hardly skiers, I find, or really good rock climbers just rock climb. There are a few who are crossovers with ice, more in Europe, but they are not so much mountaineers either; hence, they don't ski. I love the connection. ... Technical, rock, and ice climbing are just a classroom version of what you are going to get in the greater ranges. I'm lucky, because many mornings I skin up before work and I can test my equipment and know what foods work for me and what drinks and how often I need them and all that, so that when I'm on an Alpine climb I already know what works and how my body speaks to me.

You mentioned you are, additionally, an emergency medical technician. Has this skill come in handy during mountaineering expeditions?

It has, less often than one would imagine, luckily. Just assessing mountain sickness or minor injuries ... you have the confidence and the know-how to recognize or deal with certain medical problems or injuries.

I am sure you are well aware and remember that two medical doctors checked Beck Weathers and said that basically he was dead. And then 18 hours later he got up.

He is the miracle man. It is astonishing and good for him.

Do you keep in touch with some of the other people?

Not so much anymore. I think people just want to go on with their lives. But when we are at the same place at the same time, we try and get together. But I don't even run into Neil Beidelman and Tim Manson anymore.

You were the first American woman to reach the summits of three 8,000-meter peaks. Are you still pursuing these high Himalayan mountains?

I went in the fall of 1998 to the south face of Annapurna I and it's true: that mountain is falling apart. We spent two and a half months trying to climb and it was horrifically dangerous. We ended up backing off after all that time, and it was a good thing, without loss of life. ... I also went to a sub–7,000-meter peak, Dorje Latka, in 2000 with a group from Aspen. It's more important to me now to go someplace and have fun with whomever I'm with....

You are okay being in a tent for four to six weeks?

Yes. I'm fine with it. You just get your system down, as long as the food is good. I have been very fortunate. I seem to do okay on these trips [not getting ill]. ... I remember after five weeks being on the mountain deciding I was going down to base camp by myself and eating a good dinner and a good breakfast and having a shower and I'd be back.

You also have managed five of the Seven Summits (the high points of the seven continents)? Would you like to complete this cycle by climbing Carstens and Elbrus?

Six now! ... I might go to Elbrus this summer, might not. I am planning to go to Pakistan. I might not fit it in. I am not just driven to complete them; they were never a big goal; it's just kind of happened over the years....

On Everest, you shared a tent with Scott Fischer, and you have indicated that he did not appear to be sick prior to the summit attempt. Do you think that things fell apart because he was ill and weak? We should not forget that Rob Hall was not ill, but he too could not get down. I realize that this is a difficult question and calls for some conjecture on your part.

Well, there's a lot of speculation and none of us will ever know. What is important is that he did not indicate that he was tired and weak. And maybe he wasn't until he got to the summit. He did comment, I remember, that he was tired on the summit. But altitude is so tricky; you don't know if it was something that had come on that day or if he was tired or weak or sick from the previous days....

You injected Sandy Pittman with dexamethasone. If others were in dire straits, why did they not do the same thing?

The others were not in such dire straits. [Pittman] was ataxic and aphasic [before the huddle]. I was having a hard time talking her down. ... She snapped right around after she got the injection, and maybe that helped her get through the night.

Would you mind commenting on Pittman? She has gotten such bad press, but what many critics fail to take into account is that she did suffer, she did risk her life many times, and she did reach the Seven Summits.

I think Sandy took an unusually heavy hit because of her social standing and she did sometimes mix up her social life with her climbing life, but the fact is Sandy didn't kill anybody, and she's a strong girl and she did climb that peak on her own. I don't know anything about the short-roping; whether [she was] short-roped or not, I don't care. She made the footsteps to the summit and back. And she has been treated pretty harshly, and I think she went underground after that and is now married to a non-climber named Tom Ditmar and they are very happy and they do other things....

Do you ever think about what might have occurred if Anatoli Boukreev had not found you and the others huddled together in the vicious storm? Krakauer quotes you as follows: "By then the cold had about finished me off. My eyes were frozen. I didn't see how we were going to get out of it alive. The cold was so painful, I didn't think I could endure it anymore. I just curled up in a ball and hoped death would come quickly."

There you have it! Probably would have frozen to death. Got lucky on this one....

Krakauer states that Boukreev saved your life, so I do not want to put you in an awkward position, but do you have anything to add concerning the events on Everest? The Krakauer and Boukreev accounts differ in a number of important ways. Are there factual inconsistencies or are these merely differences in perspective or opinion?

I never read Anatoli's book. Jon was nice enough to give us copies of his book. Anatoli didn't do that and by then everything I read except for Jon's book made me so mad I was just over it, particularly the magazine articles. They all had an angle, and they quoted people out of context and [it was] very, very frustrating. I just feel that Anatoli could have done his team better by at least giving us his book....

Did you sustain any permanent damage from frostbite?
No. I'm so lucky....

How did the Everest tragedy affect you and your desire to climb, and especially to pursue high peaks?

It didn't take away my desire. It took me a couple of months to recover completely from the frostbite. I still worked that winter and still climb. ... I just haven't been back to the Himalaya but two times beyond that. ... I ended up marrying ... and then I lost my husband ... in a paragliding accident.

I am so sorry. Do you think that the intense media coverage did more harm than good?

Yes. Definitely. I hope that [my experience on Everest during the 1996 tragedy] is not the defining moment of my life.

How did your experiences on the other 8,000-meter peaks compare with the Everest climb?

Not nearly so hard and cold. Cho Oyo—I remember when I summited I thought, well, Everest is only 2,000 feet higher than this. I felt really good today. How much harder could it be? It was a lot harder. ... Fortunately, having climbed at altitude a bit, you kind of recognize how your body is going to be and how to think when you are not thinking at altitude in a way: Let's check the harness three times, let's look at this, let's look at that. You can somewhat motivate yourself to think safely because you are used to being hypoxic....

You have summited all 54 of Colorado's 14,000-foot mountains. Could you place that achievement in the perspective of European, South American, and Himalayan climbing?

The fourteeners in Colorado are in general not that difficult, maybe somewhat exposed. I just cut my teeth young doing that; that was where my enthusiasm lay. And a lot of people have done that. But I've also skied a lot of them. I think I am the only woman to ski the north face of North Maroon Peak. That was a big day; that's for sure. I enjoyed that.

Has your gender ever played a negative role in your work in skiing and mountaineering?

Oh, yes. Not in mountaineering, but in ski patrolling, yes; it's a boys' club. One would hope so [that I am accepted], but as politics are going this winter I would say not. And so I am going to Telluride next winter, with my dog, after 24 years on the patrol here [at Aspen's Snowmass]. ... Well, women in an expedition atmosphere change the way things are; it used to be all men and now when women go, it just changes the feel and many of those men are boys' boys. I found that the Canadian women that I've spoken with, who are guides up there, don't have any problems; they are treated as equals.

Could you tell us about your work with the Access Fund?

... I was on their board for six years and then on a membership committee for a year after that. They're in the business of saving climbing areas; they're a non-profit; they work with land owners and government officials to keep

Charlotte Fox (photograph by Fred Hartemann).

properties open for climbing. And they also build trails. ... They try to be proactive in a lot of things instead of just reactive. More and more [they work with other organizations]. And the American Alpine Club (I am now a board member)—we are taking steps to be more involved in conservation on a world-wide budget. ... We need as many people out there as possible to save our environment.

Is there anything else you would like to add?

My project this summer is through the American Alpine Club and the Alpine Club of Pakistan. Six of us women—two are a photographer and a filmmaker—are going to Pakistan and we are going to teach Pakistani women how to climb, and at the end of three weeks, attempt a 6,000-meter peak with those women. The first lady of Pakistan may be our patroness. She's very interested in this. Because a Pakistani woman has not yet climbed a big mountain; they are interested in empowering these women....

Thank you very, very much for your time and good words.

Thank you for inviting me. It's been fun.

BIBLIOGRAPHY

Boukreev, Anatoli, and G. Weston DeWalt. *The Climb: Tragic Ambitions on Everest.* New York: St. Martin's, 1998.

Krakauer, Jon. *Into Thin Air: A Personal Account of the Mount Everest Disaster.* New York: Villard, 1998.

<www.everestnews.com/history/climbers/charlottefox.htm>.

<www.nationalgeographic.com/adventure/0304/field.html>.

Charles S. Houston

(August 24, 1913–September 27, 2009)
Mountaineer, medical doctor, researcher, professor

Date of interview: March 24, 2008. *Location:* Burlington, VT. *Interviewer:* Robert Hauptman. *Method:* In person: taped.

Until his recent death at 96, Charles S. Houston, along with Cassin and Herzog, was one of the grand old men of mountaineering. A medical doctor and researcher and first head of the Peace Corps in India, Dr. Houston led two early important assaults on K2. His book *K2: The Savage Mountain* is a classic account of triumph and tragedy. Although toward the end of his life, his sight was extremely limited, he nevertheless managed to edit the awe-inspiring films he shot on the 1938 and 1953 K2 expeditions. This film is included on a DVD that accompanies Bernadette McDonald's biography of Houston (noted in the bibliography below).

RH: Thank you for agreeing to speak with us. I know that your time is precious so we appreciate this very much.

CH: My time is not precious at all [laughing]....

You are undoubtedly our most extraordinary interviewee. You are, naturally, well-known for your role in the famous 1953 expedition and the classic account, K2: The Savage Mountain, *that you and Robert Bates wrote about it. But there is so much more. You are a medical doctor, a researcher, a professor, and a prolific author. Do you think of yourself primarily as a doctor or something else?*

Oh, I am primarily a doctor.

Many expeditions include medical practitioners and for good reason. Sickness and accidents occur with horrifying frequency. But most of these men and women are general practitioners; a few, however, are of especial interest. Kenneth Kamler specializes in extreme medicine. Peter Hacket and you are concerned with the effects of altitude on physiology and other biological functions. Was this the case when you first began climbing?

No. I got interested in altitude after I went to Nanda Devi in 1936. And that led me into the navy as a flight surgeon when the war began.

During the Second World War, you did some groundbreaking experiments in altitude adjustment using a decompression chamber. What practical applications, especially for mountaineering, grew out of this work?

Well, it was something of a scam, I suppose, because I had read so many accounts that a man would die if he stood on the top of Everest without oxygen, and I didn't quite believe it. So after the war, as the war ended, the decompression chambers lay empty. I told the chief flight surgeon of the navy that we should study the effects of extreme altitude on pilots because at that point airplanes could go higher than pilots could tolerate even with oxygen. So the plan was to see whether acclimatizing people to altitude would give them [ability to reach] a greater altitude while they were breathing oxygen. That was the goal and that's actually what turned out to be the main thing. For my own personal interest, it was to prove that you could stand on top of Everest without dying. From the navy's point of view, it was to see whether acclimatizing at lower altitudes would enable you to fly higher than the enemy could fly, and that turned out to be true.

You were the first person to investigate the possibility of climbing Everest using the now popular south route. How far up did you get?

We didn't go anywhere. We went to the base of Everest in 1950 and looked up at the South Col, the West Cym, and from Kala Patar decided that that was the route to go, Bill Tilman and I; and we came home with pictures and descriptions of the south side, because no Westerner had ever been there before, and so we didn't discover any route. Well, we pointed out the best route because we stood at the bottom of it. We didn't do any climbing.

How far would you say were you from base camp, the typical base camp today at Khumbu?

We were at just about the level of base camp.

You climbed with Bob Bates, Bradford Washburn, and Bill Tilman. As early as 1934, you did the first ascent of Alaska's Mount Foraker and in 1936, you climbed Nanda Devi, at that time the highest summit reached. Would you comment on that?

Nanda Devi was probably the most wonderful expedition that anybody could ever have. Four young Americans and four distinguished British mountaineers got together and successfully climbed a very high mountain. And found a way, and came home devoted friends and remained friends for the rest of our lives.

Did everyone summit?

No. Only two, Odell and Tilman. Tilman wrote a marvelous book about it, a wonderful book. The last paragraph says something to the effect that we were two countries separated by a common language but we seemed to pull together rather well in important things like war or climbing. And he said we had a very good time together because the game is more than the players of the game and the ship is more than the crew. But it's a fantastic book; it's one of the best mountaineering books I know.

One of the most amazing things about your 1953 K2 climb is that everybody got along; there seemed to be no disagreements, let alone animosity, anger, or fighting. This also appeared to be the case on the expedition led by Maurice Herzog (who, like you, represents the last of the early 8,000-meter pioneers).

No, unfortunately that's not true. They ended up bitter.

Oh, I know. When David Roberts recently went back and examined matters, he discovered that things were not as rosy as Herzog depicted them in his famous mountaineering memoir, Annapurna: The First Eight Thousander. *Were you really such a cohesive and agreeable group of people? You got along really well?*

Oh, yes. That's the whole theme of my film, *Brotherhood of the Rope.*

Yes, I watched it again today. It is awe-inspiring to see these things. How many cameras did you people carry with you?

I just had one.

And color film?

Yes, early. We didn't have a lot. It's a very good film. I am very proud of that.

When Arthur Gilkey became ill, all seven of you attempted to evacuate him. If the weather had been absolutely perfect rather than horrific, it would have been extremely difficult to get him down safely. And yet, even in the fierce storm you almost succeeded. Had an avalanche not carried him away, you might have pulled off the greatest rescue in history.

I doubt it.

9,000 feet to base camp on one of the world's most unforgiving peaks. You don't think you would have made it down?

I don't think we could have made it down.

I think it would have been very difficult but if you had, do you think he would have been okay going down with the thrombosis caused by altitude?

Yes, the thrombosis was caused by altitude and staying too long immobile; and it was likely that he would have had more emboli. He might not have survived even if we had gotten down. There was nothing else to do; there was no choice; we had to take him down; we never even considered leaving him.

When climbers somehow ended up tumbling uncontrollably down a steep slope, Pete Schoening managed to hold all six of you on an ice ax jammed behind a rock frozen into the ice. This improbable miracle is known simply as "The Belay." Do you sometimes think back to this and how you were seriously injured but nevertheless were able to make it back down?

Nope. That was yesterday.

You don't spend time reminiscing?

No. I did the film; I did the book; I've given several, many, talks about it; we read each other frequently; we talk quite often, the survivors, and it's still a band of brothers.

The equipment used in the eighteenth and nineteenth centuries was primitive and often ineffective. (The tragic debacle on the Matterhorn occurred because a rope broke.) But even 50 years ago, equipment did not serve as well as one might have hoped. When I look at photographs of your pup tents set up at 25,000 feet, I become queasy. How these flimsy nylon units managed to protect you is a real mystery. And the best clothing of the time is not nearly as good as the coats and boots students wear to school today. Do you think you might have fared better or had an easier time on your early climbs if you had had contemporary equipment?

Not at all. Our equipment was perfectly adequate. The boots were bad, yes; they had nails in them; they had nails in the soles. We had beautifully woven Shetland underwear made for us by a women's sewing circle in the Shetland Islands and each of us had three or four beautifully woven sweaters in the same Shetland wool, and they were different sizes so we could wear one over the other. So we usually wore the underwear and then two sweaters, a flannel shirt, heavy wool trousers, and windproofs because there is no doubt that the windproofs were perfectly adequate. We all got some frostbite on K2, on the second expedition (George Gill lost a tiny piece of his little toe, and that was all). And actually, I would say that our clothing was perfectly adequate and nothing like as bad as people think it was. The best clothing you could get.

Today, climbers above 25,000 feet often do use oxygen, which you decided against. Could its use have made a difference?

I doubt it. We probably would not have taken it; we didn't want the weight. And it wasn't quite an ethical matter, but people were convinced you could climb it without and so we did.

At one point you note that "rush tactics" are dangerous in the higher peaks. But today, there is, at least for some, a desire to avoid big expeditions. Gören Kropp climbed Everest unaided and Steve House and his partner often do Alpine ascents in the Himalaya. Do you think that this is a good trend or is it foolish to depend only upon oneself, in case of emergency, the kind of horror so powerfully depicted in Joe Simpson's Touching the Void?

Well, I think solo climbing of high mountains is ridiculous.

How about people like Messner and Habeler doing it together?

Well, that's a pair.

Do you still feel that you failed on K2? That you did not reach the summit was due to being trapped in an unceasingly vicious storm and bad luck that caused clots to form in Art Gilkey's legs. Otherwise, you might have made it.

Not at all. I think Messner said, "They failed in the most beautiful way you can imagine." And I think that's exactly the way all of us feel.

How does your research on hypoxia connect with your mountaineering experiences? And what practical results emerged from your High Altitude Physiology Study, which went on for many years, near Mount Logan?

Well, that's still going on in a big way; there's an Altitude Research Institute in Colorado named after me. [The study results] allow you to predict who will and won't get sick; they allow you to estimate the blood gases with great accuracy; oh, yes, they have a lot of applications to mountaineering but they have even more applications to people who get sick at altitude from other diseases or even people who go to altitude with a neurological problem that is made worse by hypoxia. So the practical applications of hypoxia research extend far beyond climbing.

You were the first Peace Corps director in India. Did you visit the northern mountains and do some climbing?

No. I was working too hard.

Just a few years ago, you edited the film from your early climbs; you then produced a cohesive DVD that is included with Brotherhood of the Rope, *the biography of your life that Bernadette McDonald wrote. It is simply awe-inspiring to see extensive original footage of one of the most famous mountaineering events of the twentieth century.*

I don't think it was the most famous mountaineering ascent [but] it was an extraordinary event. The film, I am very proud of the film; it was a lot of effort. I had only a small hand-held Bell and Howell camera for most of the climb. I used a beautiful Bolex for distant shots from base camp, but climbing I had just the small hand-held cassette-loading Bell and Howell camera, which I had to keep in my sleeping bag at night, of course.

What percentage of the film that you shot ended up in the final version?
A quarter.

I would like to thank you so much for your kindness. It is a true honor to have spoken with you.

Well, it's a pleasure and I hope you [give] an honest report. Bernadette wrote a very open, frank picture of me and parts of it are painful to see how other people saw me but other parts are very good. ... We talked for endless hours and she read lots of my private papers. Well, it's a very good book....

AWARDS

King Albert Medal of Merit, 1996

BIBLIOGRAPHY

Houston, Charles S. *Going Higher: The Story of Man and Altitude.* (Rev. ed.) Boston: Little, Brown, 1987.

Houston, Charles, and Robert H. Bates. *Five Miles High.* New York: Dodd, Mead & Co., 1939. Reprint, New York: The Lyons Press, 2000.

Houston, Charles S., and Robert H. Bates. *K2: The Savage Mountain.* New York: McGraw-Hill, 1954. Reprint, Seattle: The Mountaineers, 1979.

Houston, Charles S., and Geoffrey Coates, eds. *Hypoxia: Women at Altitude.* (Proceedings.) Burlington, VT: Charles S. Houston, 1997. (Dr. Houston edited at least five volumes that deal with hypoxia, of which this is one example.)

McDonald, Bernadette. *Brotherhood of the Rope: The Biography of Charles Houston.* Seattle: The Mountaineers Books, 2007.

Kenneth Kamler

(October 4, 1947–)
Mountaineer, explorer, doctor (extreme medicine),
surgeon, motivational speaker

Date of interview: January 10, 2010. *Location:* South Burlington, VT, and New Hyde Park, New York. *Interviewer:* Robert Hauptman. *Method:* Electronic mail.

Kenneth Kamler is a doctor who specializes in hand surgery, a mountaineer, and an explorer. He has been an expedition doctor on Everest many times. In 2002, *New York* magazine included him in a list of New York City's best doctors.

RH: I would like to thank you for taking the time to talk with me today.

KK: Thanks, Bob. I always enjoy talking about climbing, especially with another climber.

Many mountaineers are obsessed with climbing, and at least the professionals devote their lives exclusively to this pursuit; amateurs have additional lives and work as lawyers, professors, or clerks. But there is a small group of people who pursue the world's high peaks and bring some related interest to climbing: explorers, cartographers, and geologists come immediately to mind. For me, the most fascinating dual career here is the medical doctor, especially one who becomes an expert in high altitude, or as you put it, extreme medicine. How has this added burden enhanced your life?

It's not a burden. It's a responsibility, but it's an opportunity and it's a privilege. We climb mountains to challenge ourselves, to bring out the best we have within us. Being a doctor on the mountain adds to the challenge and gives me the chance to do something beyond myself. The first big mountain I ever climbed was Yanapacha, a 19,000-foot peak in the Peruvian Andes. Before we even got to the mountain, a truck loaded with villagers, livestock, and produce passed us and toppled off a cliff right before our eyes. A dozen injured people were strewn along a ravine. There were some serious injuries but with help from my teammates, I was able to stabilize everyone and evacuate them in our truck to a remote clinic and eventually to Lima. We then went on to climb Yanapacha. Reaching the summit was thrilling, but I realized even then that helping to save those people was a higher summit.

Thank you! As a medical practitioner, do you see and experience the climb and your fellow climbers differently than I might?

I'm always aware of my added responsibility. I make it a rule that all climbers have to come out for breakfast every morning. By the way they eat and talk, I can casually assess their general health and spirit. And I try to make myself easy to talk to. Climbers will often come to me at odd moments to privately share their health problems or even their fears about their climbing abilities.

In the past, some expeditions purposely did not bring a doctor along. Do you think that other expedition doctors take their roles as seriously as you do? Do they worry and prepare, study and discuss, and manage to purchase all of the necessary medical materials?

A lot of expeditions do not bring doctors along, and of those that do, some of the doctors are not trained or supplied well enough. A doctor is not essential. A well-trained nurse or EMT would be preferable to a doctor who only knows his limited specialty. Unfortunately, climbers from many countries do not have the resources to come adequately prepared medically. And some expeditions, I have to say, take advantage of the well-prepared ones, knowing that a doctor will never turn away a sick or injured climber because he's not on their team.

Do you think that your surgical training gives you a medical edge on a long Himalayan expedition?

Training in surgical trauma is very useful but certainly not enough, especially in remote settings where you're going to be the only doctor for a long time. There's no residency in expedition medicine. Doctors who do this work must develop competency in all the other relevant areas outside their formal training. This has become a lot easier to do in recent years now that there are wilderness medicine journals and courses. On a remote expedition, it's not enough to know what to do until help arrives. You have to know what to do when help isn't coming.

Are you able to emotionally and psychologically deal with your normal Long Island patients (some of whom, to be sure, are suffering dramatically, but who have different and perhaps unreasonable expectations) after meeting someone like Nima Tashi, who hobbled around on a broken ankle for a year, and then once it was fused, went back to high altitude climbing, though you thought that would be impossible?

Ken Kamler on Mt Washington (photograph by Granis Stewart; courtesy of Ken Kamler).

I consider that I practice in two distinct locations, each with an endemic population. I'm not sure which environment is the more extreme. My upscale suburban New York practice will include teenage girls brought by their mothers for second opinions on hangnails. My practice in the wilderness includes people like Nima Tashi, a mountain guide in Nepal who fracture-dislocated his ankle, and for two years couldn't even hobble on it well enough to plant potatoes to feed his family. I brought him to the U.S., fused his ankle and told him, with luck, he'll be pain free and able to plant potatoes, but he'll never climb again. He said "Yes, Doctor Ken," went back to Nepal, and since then has climbed Everest ten times. Both my practices are very rewarding. The combination gives me the chance to use the most modern medical technology available and also to use my most basic medical skills to help people improve the quality of their lives.

A mere mortal (such as this interviewer) can do little except thank you for bringing him to the U.S. for life-enhancing surgery. It is gratifying that people like you (and Tabin, who performs cataract surgery in Nepal) are willing to give of yourselves in this way. So thanks!

Thank you. It is gratifying to see that what you do has an absolute positive value to others. Patients on opposite sides of the world can inspire each other too. I have X-rays of Nima Tashi that I show to my patients when they need motivation to recover. I tell them "This guy climbed Mount Everest on this ankle. You can climb your own Mount Everest."

Some well-meaning people criticize mountaineers and rock climbers for being self-indulgent and risking their lives for little apparent reason. But a climbing doctor palliates, succors, cures, and saves lives. Additionally, you help the local people with their problems. When your efforts, despite your extreme exhaustion, save a life (such as Koncha's), do you feel that your participation in the climb is especially rewarding?

Participation in any sport can be seen as self-indulgent, but climbing adds the element of controlled risk. The risk brings intensity to the sport and to our lives, but also danger. When we win, it's exhilarating. When we lose, it can be devastating. If I can mitigate the consequences of losing, it of course adds to the rewards of climbing. There's also the great satisfaction of helping the local people along the way. It's frustrating, though, to see people who could have been helped by simple treatments had they been seen earlier in their lives, and others who could still be helped if there were the means to get them out and get them treated.

It must be strange for the doctor to discover that he or she is ill, especially if the illness is severe, e.g., HAPE or pneumonia. Self-diagnosis is fairly easy, but recommending an unpleasant cure such as immediate descent just as one is about to head for the summit, must be very hard indeed.

Ken Kamler crossing the icefall on Mt Everest (photograph by Frank Fishbeck; courtesy of Ken Kamler).

Turning a climber around on a mountain is always a difficult decision. With only the most basic equipment available, diagnoses are often difficult to make. If I sent down everyone who felt tired or had a cough or a headache, no one would summit. Yet those are the early signs of pulmonary and cerebral edema. To ignore them could prove fatal. It's very hard to convince a climber to descend because I have a "feeling" he or she is too sick to continue. What I try to do is put them in the position of doctor, explaining their symptoms and then asking them what decision they would make. They always accept the decision better that way. That strategy was used on me one year. I was climbing poorly and a doctor from another expedition came to check me out. She listened to my lungs, then told me I needed to go down. I was resistant, so she said "You want a second opinion?" She left the stethoscope on my chest but put the earpieces in my ears, and said "What do you think?" Listening to my own lungs convinced me. I went down.

In the early days of a climb, it takes time to acclimate and so you would often have a difficult time breathing as you struggled upward. At one point on a very steep slope, you rested by leaning back against your jumar, which was attached to a fixed line. If the anchor had pulled out, you would have plummeted down. In rock climbing one is taught to trust the rope, but this is very different. Anchors do pull out as snow and ice conditions alter. I guess this is what differentiates the true adventurer from those who prefer to explore from the comfort of their sofas. You are willing to take big risks.

Leaning back against a jumar is a risk but it's a controlled risk. I know the ice conditions and I trust the person who put in the ice screw. People take bigger risks all the time without thinking much about it. A climber is far more likely to get killed driving to a climb than he or she is climbing.

The harsh environment one encounters in the high mountains is perhaps incomprehensible and inexplicable to those who have never ventured there. How could such a person ever believe that one may overheat at 30 below zero, real temperature? (I once did in the flatlands at 40 below!)

There are reasons why no one lives in the harsh environment of high altitude. People don't ordinarily venture there because it's incompatible with sustained life. Humans are the only animals that intentionally go to places where they don't belong. If they want to survive there, they have to be prepared to deal with environmental insults that their bodies have never experienced before.

Your descriptions are often vividly entrancing, e.g., when you were descending the high ridge in bad and slippery conditions.

Thank you. In situations like that, I know I'm going to write about it, so I try to be a careful observer of not only what I'm seeing but also what I'm hearing or even smelling. Especially, I make myself aware of what my feelings are: cold, tired, scared, wondering what I'm doing here—usually a combination of all that. I always carry a small pad and pen with me so that I can record it all, first chance I get, while it's still fresh.

I am glad that you have some positive words for Sandy Pittman. Her critics all conveniently forget that she did not have to be out on the world's highest mountains risking her life, when she had a comfortable Park Avenue apartment where she could have been watching soap operas. Whatever she did to annoy others is partially mitigated by the fact that she did climb and she did reach the high summits. Even with all of her stuff, including a satellite dish, she still slept in a sleeping bag in the cold. Indeed, she almost died.

Sandy and I climbed together on an earlier Everest attempt several years before the '96 disaster. She climbed faster than I did that year. What never got publicized was that Sandy was an experienced climber with a good climbing résumé. She was also, however, very Park Avenue. She wore matching outfits and liked to mention all her famous friends. She antagonized a lot of the climbers and when the press vilified her, she had no one to come to her support.

When the 1996 survivors came down, were you the only doctor available at base camp? I do not believe you get the credit you deserve in other accounts.

When the storm hit, I was the only doctor high up on the mountain. My team and I were at Camp Three at 24,000 feet. The disaster played out between 26 and 29,000 feet. Our team leaders, and strongest climbers, Todd Burleson and Pete Athans, went up in the storm to Camp Four to rescue whomever they could. They were later given American Alpine Club awards for their heroism. I would have been a casualty myself if I had tried to go up with them. I stayed at Camp Three, radioed medical advice to them, and, along with Jim Williams, checked on the climbers who were able to descend to us. We dispensed hot tea and oxygen, and when necessary, steroids to stabilize anyone who was confused or uncoordinated, sometimes injecting it right through their clothing. Camp Three is just a notch cut into the sheer 5,000-foot Lhotse slope, on a platform so narrow there's no room to stand up, and no way to provide definitive medical treatment. The following day, I descended to Camp Two, a flatter, more open camp where I had more supplies. A Danish doctor, Henrik Hansen, came up from base camp to help. It was there, at 21,000 feet, that I treated the two most critically injured climbers, Beck Weathers and Makalu Gau. I stayed up with them all night, and in the morning they were evacuated in the highest helicopter rescue ever.

It is 2010. Aren't there ways to protect one's extremities, especially toes and fingers? How about electric socks? Chemical hand and foot warmers? Multi-layered gloves? We have gone from strap-on to step-in crampons. Why can't manufacturers

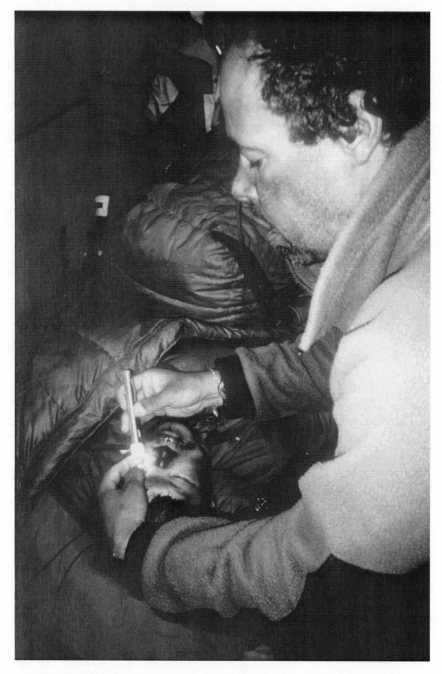

Ken Kamler examining Maklu Gau for snow blindness at 21,000 feet on Mt Everest (photograph by Frank Fishbeck; courtesy of Ken Kamler).

produce boots with clamps rather than laces? (They do this for extreme down-hill ski boots.) This small adjustment could save one from the onset of frostbitten fingers. (People who have never had the pleasure of preparing themselves on a frigid morning, could not know that even under the best circumstances, it can take ten minutes just to lace up one's inner and outer boots; more time must be allocated to crampons, and then the harness, which demands careful finger coordination to get it just right. Failure to do so can result in death.)

We have come a long way in protecting the extremities, especially the feet. The best double boots we have today really seem to do the job. Except for people caught in disastrous situations, I see very few frostbitten toes on the mountains now. Hand protection is still an unsolved problem, though. Multilayered gloves help, but real protection from extreme cold often requires triple layering, including a mitt. This results in so much bulk that climbers take the gloves off to do fine work on ropes and gear. Even the warmest gloves don't work if they're not being worn. As you suggest, it would minimize risk if equipment required less fine manipulation, such as clamp-on boots. There's the danger, though, that a misstep might pop you out of it. On a ski slope, you could walk down. On a mountain ridge, it could be fatal. Nevertheless, I think you're right. There's a lot of room for careful improvement to minimize manipulation and reduce the chance for error. People have died on Everest because their shoelaces became untied.

Ken Kamler treating Beck Weathers for hypothermia and frostbite at 21,000 feet on Mt Everest (photograph by Frank Fishbeck; courtesy of Ken Kamler).

What was it like climbing with Vern Tejas? Though even today, he is still comparatively young, in contrast, say, to Maurice Herzog, he is already legendary as the first person to do a solo winter climb of Denali.

Vern is very high spirited and fun to climb with. He brought his violin to Everest base camp and entertained us nightly with country music. He's also a consummate mountaineer. My first trip to Everest, I brought what I thought was the minimum amount of personal equipment. Vern said, "We've got to do some serious damage to that load." He eliminated half of it and I didn't miss a thing. Vern, himself, uses the same bottle for drinking and for peeing.

At one point you observe that "in the end everyone climbs Everest by himself." Sometimes this is literally true, when one's friends move out or along before you do, and leave you to fend for oneself. I have always disliked this and try to stay with my climbing partner, by speeding up or slowing down to accommodate him (or her). Occasionally, though I get left behind, which is disheartening and frightening. In extreme circumstances, it could lead to catastrophe. Shouldn't climbers, generally speaking, stick together?

Climbers should, and generally do, stick together. It's safer, and the camaraderie is part of the appeal of a climb. There are situations, though, where it's better to go alone. On Everest's narrow final summit ridge, we unhooked and climbed solo because the drop-off was so sheer. If you slipped, there would be only a small chance that your partner could belay you and a much greater chance that you'd pull him or her off the mountain with you. A very sad and poignant example of a climber who should have climbed alone is Rob Hall. In the '96 disaster he could have saved himself, but he refused to abandon his dying partner even though he knew the situation was hopeless. When the end came, Rob was too weak to move and died there himself.

No one has ever shown how the loss of oxygen harms and its reflow revitalizes.

Normal blood oxygen saturation is 97 to 100 percent. When I'm doing surgery, anesthesiologists start treating my patients if the percentage falls much below that. Yet on big mountains, I've routinely measured climbers with saturations in the 70s who are performing well. Brains are very sensitive to oxygen deprivation but studies have shown that although there is some transient loss of fine cognitive and motor skills, the changes are not permanent.

The atmosphere that Maurice Herzog creates in Annapurna *is one of tranquil harmony. This seemed so improbable that David Roberts went back and reexamined what occurred. He came to very different conclusions. I notice in your accounts that there is very little disagreement, very few fights or hassles. Everyone seems to get along. When one considers that climbing partners sometimes never speak to each other after an expedition (as depicted, for example, in Taber's* Forever on the Mountain*), your accounts are most unusual. Did you simply elide the problems or were you lucky enough to participate in innumerable harmonious expeditions?*

Maurice Herzog is my friend and I spoke to him after David Roberts's book came out. He was very upset with that version of the Annapurna climb, insisting that the conflicts were way exaggerated just to sell books. The classic tale that Maurice told was what inspired me to take up climbing and I wouldn't want to think it wasn't so. In any case, I can tell you there really was very little conflict on my expeditions. There's a popular climbing saying that "it's not the mountain, it's who you climb it with." Most climbers are thoughtful, smart, often idealistic people, who enjoy nature and enjoy challenges. I've been fortunate enough to climb with many of them.

You had a difficult but rewarding time on your first (1992) Everest climb. Many people, especially a professional with a practice and a family, would have called it quits. You are very different. Over the years, you have been on six Everest expeditions and many other excursions to some of the harshest environments on earth. Your exploratory perseverance is admirable. Has it had any negative impacts on your life?

It's always hard saying goodbye to family and friends when you're going to be away a long time. It's actually harder on them, since I'll be doing new and exciting things but they'll mostly just be feeling a hole where I used to be. Practically, it means a big loss of income and a loss of continuity for my practice. At first I thought I might not be able to maintain my practice, but it turned out that patients and doctors admired what I did, were very supportive and eager to continue our professional and personal relationships. I haven't become a prisoner of my profession; I've been able to use it to have some of the most exciting experiences I could ever imagine.

In addition to high altitude expeditions, you have participated in jungle and undersea adventures. Which of these have been most dangerous? Most satisfying?

Each one has its own danger and its own satisfaction. High altitude mountaineering exposes you to cold and low oxygen but rewards you with a sense of physical accomplishment. Every plant and animal in the jungle is out to kill each other and you, yet none of them could survive without each other. The complexity is endlessly fascinating. With my undersea work with NASA, there was always the chance of getting the bends but the work was probably the most scientific of all I've done. The extreme cold I felt in Antarctica, combined with the austere beauty of the ice and constant overhead sun made me feel as though I had left the planet. All these experiences were unique. I could never pick out just one.

Thanks so much for your wonderful accounts and for talking with me.

Thank you, Bob. I appreciate the opportunity to reflect on my experiences and to talk with you.

BIBLIOGRAPHY

Dreifus, Claudia. "A Conversation with Kenneth Kamler: Bringing Them Back, Healthy, from the Ends of the Earth." *The New York Times* (22 June 2004): F9.

Inside the 1996 Everest Disaster. Ken Kamler. Video. <www.youtube.com/watch?v=Bgqc 2m7aBzs>.

Kamler, Kenneth. *Doctor on Everest: Emergency Medicine at the Top of the World: A Personal Account Including the 1996 Disaster.* New York: The Lyons Press, 2000.

Kamler, Kenneth. *Surviving the Extremes: A Doctor's Journey to the Limits of Human Endurance.* New York: St. Martin's, 2004.

Jamling Tenzing Norgay

(April 23, 1965–)

Mountaineer, guide, author,
and philanthropist

Date of interview: January 10, 2006. *Location:* San Ramon, CA.
Interviewer: Robert Hauptman. *Method:* In person: taped and videotaped. *Videographer:* Frederic Hartemann.

Jamling Tenzing Norgay is a mountaineer and guide who specializes in
trekking in Bhutan. He lives in Darjeeling, India, but for ten years he lived
in New Jersey. He climbed Everest for spiritual reasons: His father was Tenzing
Norgay, the first person, in 1953, along with Sir Edmund Hillary, to reach the
highest summit in the world. Jamling is the narrator of David Breashear's
extraordinary IMAX Everest film.

*RH: Thank you so much for agreeing to spend some time with us. We know
that your schedule is extremely [busy]. You just arrived from India and you have
many other commitments, so we are extremely grateful and privileged that you can
spend some time with us and share your thoughts.*

JTN: It is my pleasure.

*Your father was Tenzing Norgay, the first person, along with Edmund Hillary,
to reach the summit of Mount Everest. He was internationally renowned and honored. Was it difficult to grow up in his presence? And did his profession and the
mountains exercise a strong pull on you? When you were a young child, did you think
you might like to climb?*

There was nothing difficult about growing up in the Tenzing household.
You had to live up to the reputation, just like in any big family well-known
around the world. But there was no pressure from my family or from my father
to climb mountains. Instead, he tried to move us away from the mountains,
because it was a dangerous profession. And he wanted to give us a better education so that we could continue our lives in some other careers. But I always
had this dream to climb the mountain that my father climbed. It was just a

matter of time. And I think that it was my destiny; it was my karma to climb this mountain.

When you were a young adolescent, did you do some climbing?

Yes. I started climbing when I was about six years old with my dad. I started going on a lot of treks with him in the Himalaya.

We have had many tangential accounts of what it is like for Sherpa men and women to work for or with mountaineers; and Sherry Ortner, in Life and Death on Mount Everest, *has provided a sociological perspective on Sherpa communities, but* Touching My Father's Soul, *your astounding memoir, is not only one of the few mountaineering records written from a Sherpa's point of view, it is perhaps the most spiritual climbing book ever published.*

Well, I think one of the reasons that I wrote that book was to give an insight from the Sherpa's point of view. There are hundreds of books written about Everest, mountains, and mountaineering, but there is only one book written by a Sherpa and that is my father's [*Tiger of the Snows*], and so I thought it was time to write another book from the Sherpa's point of view to let the world know who the Sherpas are, to let people know about our culture, our beliefs, our religion, the spiritual beliefs that we have which people do not know about.

Jamling Tenzing Norgay (photograph by Fred Hartemann; courtesy of Jamling Tenzing Norgay).

You indicate that as you grew up you pulled away from your Buddhist roots, but the spirit of your father and climbing drew you back, to such an extent that auguries, divinations, consultations with lamas, rituals (such as the puja), and other religious and spiritual commitments are as important as the climb itself. Indeed, the climb may depend on the correct spiritual orientation.

Yes, I think that it is very important that you climb with the right motivation. [This applies to] basically anything in life: You need to focus, you need to have the passion to climb, and you need to enjoy it. This is one of the most important things. As I said in my book, I was sort of drawn away from religion, from Buddhism. I was a Buddhist and I am still a Buddhist, but my belief grew even stronger. I started to connect with religion; I started to connect with the Sherpa people, with the spiritual aspect of the mountains and our culture. I learned a lot during this climb; it showed me a great deal.

You have met with the Dalai Lama twice. Could you indicate how these meetings affected you? Did you talk at all about Heinrich Harrer, whose White Spider *is a classic account? Coincidentally, he just passed away.*

I have met His Holiness, the Dalai Lama, actually several times. You cannot sit down and have a conversation. He is not someone you go over and have a conversation with. He is our spiritual leader, and there is only a certain amount you can talk. You cannot have a chat with him. He gives his blessing. He asks a few questions and you answer them. That's how the meetings go. When you are in his presence you immediately start to feel compassion. When you are there with him, he is so powerful. And I think people should be like that: What he teaches is very important. It is one of the basic fundamentals of life to be compassionate.

You spent 10 years living in New Jersey, where the pollution is sometimes quite bad and the mountains quite low. Were you able to do any climbing in this alien environment? Did you ever escape to New England: Vermont, New Hampshire?

Living in New Jersey was a great experience. I worked there for a couple of years. When people think about New Jersey [they think of] Newark. There are beautiful places: Northern New Jersey is very nice. I worked mostly out of north Jersey and I traveled a lot during that time climbing, climbing in Vermont, New Hampshire, North Carolina, Virginia, Maryland—up and down the East Coast, hiking on the Appalachian Trail, doing a lot of rock climbing, ice climbing, and it was a very good experience for me, something that opened my eyes to American culture because I worked with the Outdoor Experiential Education Company, so I worked a lot with kids, youth at risk, correctional facilities, corporations, the whole range [including] universities [and] high schools, and they gave me a good insight into American culture.

That's great. I live right on the Appalachian Trail in Vermont and I have climbed Stratton mountain probably 300 times, and this summer I am going to walk the Long Trail quickly. It is really nice that you have walked the Appalachian Trail.

Yes, I have walked all parts of it.

When I studied in Iceland, I discovered that Icelanders heartily detest the cultural and linguistic contamination that comes with American military bases, imports, and television programs. Do you feel, as some others do, that the Western influence and some concomitant prosperity in India and Tibet—but especially in Nepal—that has come through or with mountaineering and trekking has been detrimental to the traditional Sherpa way of life, or has it helped to truly improve things?

Well, actually, tourism (the trekking industry, mountaineering) has benefited the Sherpas; it has benefited the people of Nepal. It is one of the main [components of the] economy of Nepal, which relies on tourism. Who's to say that Sherpas are getting spoiled? We are spoiling them? They are getting too Westernized? We should leave them the way they were 50 years ago? Who's to say that they shouldn't have the opportunity to develop? Who's to say that they shouldn't have TV in their room or music or a microwave or electricity? Leave them the way they were? I think everybody has the right to grow, and tourism has brought growth to the Sherpa people. One of the greatest things is that we have Westernized, we have taken in the best of the West, but we continue to maintain our culture, our traditions, which is the most important thing; the moment you lose that, then you are nothing.

So Western prosperity has been beneficial?
Yes.

Not all people feel that way. I think all people have the right to medical help, and if they wish to have a TV.... Sometimes we overdo it a bit.

They need to have an education. I am a good example. If people think the Sherpas should live the way they did, then I would not be sitting here talking to you in English. I would be back in a village somewhere farming potatoes. I have the right to an education. I have the right to grow. But the important thing again is that you maintain your culture; you have to maintain your tradition. Like I said earlier, if you lose that then you have nothing. You just become another person with [lots of] stuff [laughter].

Would you be willing to tell us about some of the things you are doing for various Sherpa communities in Nepal and India to help?

Well, I work with the American Himalayan Foundation; I work with them in the sense that we help raise money. They have over a hundred projects in the Himalaya: in Sikkim, Bhutan, Tibet, Nepal, India. They work very closely with the Hillary Trust [and] they support a lot of the schools, hospitals, and clinics in the Khumbu area for the Sherpas. The American Himalayan

Foundation also [funds] a lot of projects [that] preserve the culture, [such as] restoration of old monasteries; [and they help] the Tibetan refugees who are still escaping from Tibet today. There is a lot of work they do and there is a lot more to be done.

I didn't know that there were Tibetans escaping from Tibet today. That still goes on?

Yes. Some people are still crossing the border and managing to get away.

And some of them are Sherpas?

Well, mostly Tibetans. Sherpas are all in Nepal now.

I guess they first came over some hundreds of years ago.

Five hundred years ago.

You were one of the members of the IMAX Everest expedition, which coincidentally was on the mountain during the great debacle of 1996. You felt that you were obligated to help members of other expeditions even though the gift of oxygen and your time endangered your own chances of making the summit. Were all members of the IMAX team in favor of helping? I know from many accounts that other expeditions were not so generous.

Yes. The IMAX team had a [group] of really good climbers. And these people were passionate about what they did. And as a true climber, as a human being, you care, you care about fellow climbers, whether they are your friends or you know them or not; it doesn't matter. You do what is right: We just dropped the camera gear and headed up this mountain to help, to help the survivors and bring them back down the mountain.

So you were instrumental in saving the lives of some of those people?

Yes. We helped (almost a dozen survivors) to bring them all the way back down to base camp.

It is always disconcerting to discover thieves among us, but on Everest and among fellow climbers, it must have been especially hurtful to have equipment stolen.

Yes, it is. To have things stolen anywhere is not good, [but] especially on mountains. There are bad people in this world, which is sad.

The Krakauer and Boukreev accounts of the 1996 tragedy are quite divergent. Could you shed some light on their points of view, because they look at what happened somewhat differently. Krakauer is very hard on Boukreev, and when I read Krakauer, I didn't like Boukreev. Then I read Boukreev's book and I liked him a lot.

First, I think there was no.... Why should you blame each other, when things have already happened? And it is nobody's fault. It was not Boukreev's fault that these people died on the mountain. He climbed the way he always climbed and maybe Krakauer is a little hard on him. What is important is instead of blaming each other, you should find solutions; see how to work things out. I don't have any negative thing to say about anybody. I think what happened on the mountain happened; you just deal with it and try to make the best of it.

I have always thought that Sandy Pittman is treated unfairly. She may have hauled a satellite dish up the mountain and been short-roped by a Sherpa near the top, but anyone who has managed to climb the Seven Summits has certainly spent some money, expended some real energy, suffered greatly, and risked her life.

Yes, definitely. I think she did not deserve most of what is said about her. There are a lot of people doing that. There are a lot of climbers even today doing exactly what she did. I mean there are a lot of people who haven't climbed in the mountains up there. At least she had climbed the other mountains on the other continents, which is pretty impressive.

Ed Viesturs recently completed the 14 8,000-meter peaks without oxygen, a feat that took him more than a decade. He is one of a mere handful of people to achieve this extraordinary triumph and the first American. Like Reinhold Messner, he is such an extremely powerful climber that he sometimes appears to be superhuman. Was it inspiring climbing with him?

Yes, definitely. Ed Viesturs is a very simple man, an extremely strong climber, very dedicated, very passionate about what he does. I mean, he is an inspiration to millions and people want to be like him. We call him Steady Ed. He is a very strong climber [and] very respectful of the mountains and the Sherpa people. I think that is important. You can be a great climber but if you have no respect, you are not a good human being.

I read Göran Kropp's Natural High *with increasing amazement. He seems to have been an authentic and caring person who was capable of almost impossible feats. Did you get to know him at all? How was he able to carry 150 pounds to base camp, and then climb unaided? Did he reach the summit?*

Yes, Göran Kropp was a really nice man, very simple. He didn't talk much; when we climbed, he climbed all by himself on the mountain and at the end he had to sort of get help [from] Ang Rita who had climbed [it] about 11 times, I think. He stayed away from everyone. He didn't let anyone touch anything. He said solo and this was the way he was going to do it. He had one tent; he cooked his own meals; he did everything himself. He went up this mountain [and] he reached the summit. We went to the summit together, actually; he was with us. When I was coming back from the summit, he was just approaching [it]. So, he finally made it.

I cannot imagine anyone so strong: to carry 150 pounds at that altitude!

He carried to base camp and then went up and down.

I am so sorry that he lost his life. Many wonderful people have lost their lives but you are affected more by some than others.

Yes, exactly.

Do you really think that earlier climbers were more respectful of the mountains? Didn't they too want to conquer, reach the summit, maybe leave garbage, and so on? I think you say in your book that the earlier climbers were more respectful.

Well, see, the earlier people, they were the pioneers; they were going into the unknown. They opened the routes for us. They opened the way for us. With the equipment they had, they dealt with these things. They went out there and made it easy for us today. They were basically explorers. There are a few who say I want to conquer this mountain, get to the top. It is like a challenge but again they did it with respect, respect for the environment. You talk about earlier climbers leaving garbage; they left garbage but not intentionally.

You speak of stress and fear. I only climb smaller peaks, but I am always anxious and fearful and therefore overly cautious. Do most people have these reactions on big expeditions or are those who choose to climb in the Himalaya inured to anxiety?

I think mountaineering is a dangerous hobby, sport—the way people do it—and I look at every mountain the same way; whether it's Everest, whether it's a 2,000-meter peak or 6,000 meters, it doesn't matter. Every mountain is dangerous. You never take any mountain for granted. You climb with utmost safety; you take precautions; you climb steadily. You never take any mountain for granted but that happens a lot; even on smaller mountains people die, but you don't hear about them. Nobody cares about what happens at a 5,000-meter peak.

Exactly. More people have died on Mount Washington than on any other American mountain.

Yes, every year people die on Mount Washington [because of] high winds and the bad weather up there, but you never hear about that.

But do you get anxious before a climb?

Well, I am always anxious. I like to get out there and climb. I'm ready. I will go back next week and I am out in the mountains again. I look forward to it very much.

Your book is most unusual because it intercalates three distinct strains: Your own experience, the Sherpa spiritual life, and the long history of Everest climbs. Somehow all of this seems to blend together, even when you switch back and forth from one subject to another. How did you manage to accomplish this?

Well, you know, I had a very good coauthor, Broughton Coburn. He lived in Nepal for almost 25 years. He knew the culture, he knew the language, he

knew the history. It was just [excellent] working with him. When I put the
book together, in the beginning, this is basically what I wanted to talk about:
the mix. This is something I had to offer that nobody [else] had: to give insight
into the stories of my father and his climb, how it related very much to my
climb, and [to] talk about the culture, the spiritual aspects of climbing, and
the spiritual aspects of what the Sherpas believe in. A lot of people do not
know anything about the Sherpas or the Himalaya. They see Everest [and
think], oh well, it's a mountain to climb, but they don't know exactly what's
going on, what the story behind it is and that's one of the reasons that I decided
it's important and time to put this down in the book and let the world know.

Thank you. I was lucky enough to see the IMAX Everest *film in a large, well-
populated New York City theater. I had just returned from climbing and was overwhelmed, so overwhelmed that I cried uncontrollably. How did you feel about the
final cut? Were the other participants happy with the final version of the film? And
when you view it again or think about the high mountains, do you want to return,
despite your promise to avoid dangerous heights?*

Yes, every time I see the film, I want to go back. Every time I am in the
mountains, I go to base camp (I go to base camp almost every year); I feel like
going back again. There's something drawing me to this mountain, not because
I want to create a record of climbing it the most times [but] just to go there
and be in the mountains; it attracts me a lot. [I] am very happy with the outcome of the film. We put in a lot of work and they did a good job putting the
film together. I couldn't be happier. It worked out very well; they covered all
the aspects, which is important.

*Yes, it's a powerful film. Trekking or climbing in the Himalaya is something
that many people aspire to do. Such an adventure would be much enhanced if they
were in the company of a world class climber. Do you sometimes join clients who use
your guiding service?*

Yes. Actually, I guide quite a bit now. I do a lot of treks; I lead a lot of
treks into the Himalaya, anywhere in the Himalaya: Nepal, Sikkim, Bhutan,
Tibet. I'm out there a lot guiding people on treks and on climbs also, [on]
some smaller mountains that we climb. I continue to do that with my company,
Tenzing Norgay Adventures.

*Did you ever experience true communion with the mountain and could you
share such a moment with us?*

We Sherpas believe mountains are sacred places, places where the gods
live, and when I climb, I climb with respect: respect the mountain because it's
a holy place. It's just like going to church or a monastery. In the mountains
you are at the mercy of the mountain; you are not there to conquer; you have
to respect the mountain and when the mountain gives you permission, then

you climb. You cannot say, well, tomorrow, I will get to the summit; the mountain will say no. I think it is very important to have respect, [to] show respect when you are climbing. But in the mountains you have that atmosphere, [a] feeling like being in the heavens, and the spiritual aspect, you feel so nice to be up there. One of the other things it makes you feel [is] like really tiny; it makes you feel smaller than an ant and it lets you know that you don't control everything. The world up there is under their control, and it gives a sense of being alive up there in the mountains. You come here into the real world and then you sit down on a couch, you have a TV, you drink, [eat] burgers. Out there you are on your own [with] nothing to depend on.

I've read that certain mountains are off limits for climbing, like Machupuchere, and others are so holy, like Kangchenjunga, that you are not allowed to step on the summit; so even Western mountaineers reach just below the summit and then they actually do not put their feet on the summit. Is that true?

Yes, that is very true. On Mount Kangchenjunga, people do not go all the way to the summit out of respect for the people of Sikkim. They go just below the summit, take photos, and come back down the mountain.

How do you feel about the current trend of getting amateur mountaineers on very high summits for large sums of money?

I don't think it's a good idea to do that. I'm not a person to say, well, you cannot climb; if you want to climb, you can go ahead and climb, but you need to think, as a climber you risk the lives of other people. When you go up without any experience, you especially risk the lives of the Sherpas, because if you get in trouble you are going to need all the Sherpas to bring you down. And then you risk their lives to bring this person, this stupid person, down the mountain. I think the most important thing is [that] whatever you do in life, you need to do an apprenticeship; you need to work towards getting up there and I think all the commercial expeditions should practice that. They should start taking clients on that basis. "Well, you want to climb Everest? Fine: what is your experience?" "I haven't climbed any mountain." "Well, start with me: I will take you on.... I will train you. I'll take you on a climbing course; you learn to climb, the basics. Then I will take you on a small mountain: Rainier. You start with Rainier. Then come to the Himalaya and climb a little higher mountain and then when I think you are fit enough to climb Everest, then we'll go. Two years, three years, work your way [up]. Then you yourself ought to feel that you have accomplished something; you work hard to get there." I think that's important.

Americans don't like to wait two or three years; they like to have it done yesterday. It is very hard for somebody who decides for some reason he wants to climb a mountain to actually train to climb. You can't run a marathon if you haven't run before. In what direction do you see mountaineering evolving in the next few years? There are all these unusual things like winter climbs, enchainments, where they do a bunch of mountains in quick succession. What do you think will happen over the next decade or so in mountaineering?

I don't know, actually. Everyone's pushing the limits, trying new things. You've climbed Everest; it's been climbed many times, maybe about 13 [hundred] or 1400 people have climbed it so far [many more now]. People want to do different things because it [makes] a name. People are looking for recognition. Whether you are skiing down [or] you paraglide [or] you skateboard. People want to do something different so that at least they have put their name up there. Luckily, my father and Hillary were the first to climb. You cannot be the first to climb again.

Do you have anything else to add?

Well, I think you did a pretty good job with all of your questions. You've covered all the aspects of climbing [and] you covered the philanthropic side.

Do you have any favorite climbing area?

Oh yes. I like to climb in Sikkim a lot. It is still unpolluted; it is basically what Nepal was 50 years ago. It still remains the same [with] no development. It is basically going out in the wilderness. [There are] no villages, just little nomadic yak traders and herders live there; its beautiful out there [with] small mountains that you are allowed to climb now.

Does it require a long trek to get to the mountains?

No. It is about five days' walk. You have to walk there; you cannot drive anywhere in the Himalaya, which is nice. I'm glad they do not make any roads. It is almost impossible to make roads up there. [If] you go to Everest on the Tibet side, you can drive all the way to base camp.

Have you been there?

No. I haven't been to the Everest base camp on the north side. I have done the Mount Kalash trek, the circumnavigation of Mount Kalash which is a beautiful trek. I really like Mount Kalash, a very, very holy mountain.

The people who participate in your treks, do you find that they acclimate okay, so they don't get sick and have to return, because you are at fifteen, sixteen, eighteen thousand feet?

I design the itineraries so that we have time to acclimate and we walk slowly.

What altitude do you begin the trek at?

We start at 5,000 feet. Then we slowly go up to 7,000. We spend a day there; then we go to 11,000, spend two days there [including] a rest day. You acclimatize slowly. Most of the treks go up to 18,000 feet.

I think Everest base camp is around 18,000. So you can actually see the Khumbu icefield from the base camp?

Yes. Most of the treks go to base camp and then to this place called Kala Patar. It's a small black rock at about 18,000 feet, actually 400 feet higher than the base camp. From there you can see really nice views of Everest, the icefall, and the base camp. From base camp you do not see Everest.

Can you see Everest as you walk in?

Yes [from] some places, but the greatest views are from Kala Patar [with] beautiful views of Everest and the South Col.

Well, that certainly sounds like something that would be very enjoyable to do. Thank you very, very much; it was a very enjoyable interview.

BIBLIOGRAPHY

"CNN's Lorraine Hahn Interviews Jamling Tenzing Norgay." *TalkAsia*. February 21, 2003. <edition.cnn.com/2003/WORLD/asiapcf/02/21/talkasia.Norgay.script>.
"In the Lap of the Gods." *The Paula Gordon Show*. May 22, 2001. <www.paulagordon. com/shows/sherpa>.
Norgay, Jamling Tenzing, with Broughton Coburn. *Touching My Father's Soul: A Sherpa's Journey to the Top of Everest*. New York: HarperSanFrancisco, 2001.

Rick Ridgeway

(August 12, 1949–)
Mountaineer, adventurer, explorer,
photographer, cinematographer, author

Date of interview: January 9, 2006. *Location:* Ventura, CA (Patagonia headquarters). *Interviewer:* Robert Hauptman. *Method:* In person: taped and videotaped. *Videographer:* Frederic Hartemann.

Rick Ridgeway is one of the last great explorer/adventurers. He has undertaken so many diverse expeditions into mountains, deserts, and jungles that it would be impossible to even enumerate them. Along with three companions, he was the first American to reach the summit of K2. He is the author of countless articles and books and the coauthor of *Seven Summits,* the modern classic by Dick Bask and Frank Wells. Ridgeway is Patagonia's Vice President for Marketing and the Environment.

RH: Thank you so much for agreeing to speak with us. Your adventures in diverse environments in most parts of the world are staggering, almost incomprehensible. Indeed, Doug Peacock calls you "one of the last great American adventurers," and I can think of no one else who rivals you.

RR: No one?

In addition to the many vocational pursuits noted above, you were also a sailor, navigator, actor, and mountaineering guide. How do you manage to squeeze so much into so little time?

Well, it's all at the risk of being a dilettante in any of those pursuits. But for whatever reason, in my career, I have never been content to just settle on one path for any real length of time but always had enough of a varied interest in an assortment of things. I have been pursuing so many of them in the course of my life, I wonder if it has been at the cost of being any good at any single one of them. Where would I be if I had just been content to write books? I would have a lot more printed and I probably would have had some that would have been very successful, but ... that would have been at the cost of these other things that I have been fortunate enough to do in my life, in my career. So in balance, I suppose, it has been a pretty good decision to try to do so many things, and I have been moderately successful in a number of them. ...

I have managed to publish six books.... All together, they have done pretty well; I think they are [reprinted] in a dozen or more languages. The total number of books that have been printed is over 400,000, counting all of the international editions. That's been pretty good. I made films for a long time as a producer and/or a director. And I was successful enough to manage to make over 30 that have actually been on TV. That was successful; I enjoyed that a lot. The film-making was an opportunity for me to really subsidize

Rick Ridgeway (photograph by Fred Hartemann).

trips to some very remote and unusual places at times when those places had seldom been visited at all by people from the outside, so the filmmaking, while I enjoyed [it], was really something that subsidized the chance to get to some really cool places, whereas writing has been a much deeper passion for me.

Well, you write very beautifully as you will hear in a few minutes: one of your sentences just blew me away.

That's where my heart and soul is.... But I love filmmaking, I love photography. I've done pretty well at it. And I have been in business off and on through all this as well. I had my own company for 15 years: licensing, reproduction rights to photography and film. And I sold that a few years ago very successfully; [I] actually got into a little bidding war with Bill Gates's group and another investment group from London competing, so that was successful. It forced me to learn a lot about business and that's serving me very well on my job here at Patagonia, which is the first real job I ever had in my life.

In 1978, you were one of the members of the first American team to successfully climb K2, the second highest mountain on earth, and the first to do so without supplementary oxygen. Since K2 is often considered one of the world's most difficult and dangerous climbs, how did you manage this feat so early, that is, at a time when most folks felt that it would be impossible to succeed without supplementary oxygen?

Well, I explained in *The Last Step,* the book I wrote about that, that success on K2 was a result of me being in the company of some climbers, especially [John] Roskelley, who were a lot better than me. I was just fortunate enough to have those guys as teammates and be able to hook into their inspiration and push myself to a place where I didn't really know I had the capability of going. And it was Lou [Reichardt's] idea to try and climb the mountain without oxygen, and he's the one who really knew that he could do it, and when he made that decision, John knew that he could do it as well.... I always had more self-doubts than those two, but then it turned out that I couldn't get my oxygen to work anyway, and then at the end I didn't have any choice but to climb it without oxygen.... I didn't want to get left behind just because.... I figured, well listen, if those guys could do it, why can't I? I am maybe not as physically, as naturally endowed as Roskelley is; he's more of a natural athlete than me, but if Reichardt can force his mind to will his body to do it, I am going to do that too. So the fact that I got to the top of K2 and that I did it without oxygen—I have to credit those guys for being teammates, to really inspire me to push myself to places where I had never been before; and without them, I doubt I would have had the wherewithal to do that on my own. I don't think I could have soloed up that mountain without oxygen without them there to encourage me along, without all of us working as a little group even though we summited in two teams of two. We were up there on our own; the rest of the team had really abandoned the mountain. And they had to. We were out of food; we were out of everything up there at the end; we had been at or above 8,000 meters for five days.

With three nights of no sleep, and no water, which is the worst of all. I don't know how you do that.

Not no water, but very little. We were really dehydrated. It was tough.

Your retelling of this climb in The Last Step *is enthralling, not just the details of the many difficult months that you spent on the mountain, but also the sometimes bickering interactions among the 14 members of the expedition. It is a superb continuation of the horrific saga of American K2 climbs begun by Charlie Houston in* K2: The Savage Mountain.

When I sat down to write that book ... at first I didn't know if I was going to write it going into the expedition. That was kind of unclear. [Jim] Whittaker wasn't sure if he wanted to write it or who was going to do it. When I finally did get agreement from everybody to do it, I just made the decision that anything less than a complete retelling of the story and all its good and bad would have glossed over and minimized the real effort; the real accomplishment was everybody's ability to overcome all of the difficulties that we had, all of the personal challenges that we faced and the arguments that we had between us and still do it at the end of the day. So I wanted to tell the whole story; I knew that it was going to be painful for probably everybody to kind of air our laundry but to do anything less than that I didn't think would have been ... it just would have reduced the accomplishment, because it really needed to be told in its entirety and as much as I could do it, the truthfulness of what transpired; and not surprisingly some of the expedition members disagreed over what was true and what didn't happen and they took exception to the way I portrayed it. And that's understandable.... I did my very best to make it as accurate as I could where I got ... especially [Jim] Wickwire's journal was so detailed and then I ... made interviews and got everyone else's notes, and I tried to collate them so that whatever I told was from the agreement of everyone's notes. But even then, some things I had to fill in from my own notes or my own memory and inevitably I had a view on it that differed from others'. And then some people were just upset that I would choose to reveal certain things. And that's inevitable too.

I think the same thing happened with Herzog's Annapurna *later on. Someone [David Roberts] wrote another book about the book; he felt that what was being said there was glossing over some of the problems because that climb was very smooth; there were no problems, but of course there have to be problems.*

But I got a note from Jim Wickwire a couple of weeks ago [and] he said all these years later, I look at the book and it's one of the best mountaineering books written, and it was a great documentation of our achievement. So, it's nice to hear back from old friends all these years later that feel that way about that book.

I have been reading adventure and climbing accounts for 50 years. Your description of expedition members looking up through a telescope waiting for Jim Wickwire to reappear on the summit is one of the most gripping and moving moments I have ever experienced. You were heading for the summit at the time and didn't experience that, but did you hear about it afterwards?

I did. I heard about it from the other teammates. I interviewed them and tried to get them to relive the emotion of that moment from base camp. It was clear from those interviews that it was deeply emotional for them.

Well, the way you articulated that had me on the [edge] of my sofa; wonderfully done: two minutes, six minutes, ten minutes; he still hasn't appeared. What's happening? I am sure that most of those people must have felt that he was finished: why would one climber go down and the other stay for 45 minutes, especially when it was getting dark. Quite amazing!

And then my attempt to reconstruct what Jim went through in his bivouac: I wanted to tell that as accurately as I could and he was so supportive of my goal in telling that as truthfully as possible in his agreement to reveal the depth of his emotional support from his family, as he reconstructed in his mind, to give him the strength to make it through that night. I'll forever be indebted to him for his openness to allow me to write that story, because I think that really does speak to what it takes to survive a situation like that, for all of us as individuals to dig into whatever toolbox or storehouse we have inside of us to pull out those things that can strengthen us to get through adversity. That's what that's about and that's his solution to it, and we all have inside of us our own sources of strength that we pull out in times of stress or distress or adversity and I hope that readers can take from that, take from the whole tale for that matter, inspiration to find in themselves what they own in their own experiences, in their own inner works, the strength that they can pull out to achieve things at the outset that seemed impossible. That's what that book's really about. It's about learning how, as I tell audiences sometimes, to eat an elephant. The only way to get a job done like that is to do it one bite at a time. It's learning what the real meaning of tenacity is. And those are the lessons that I took from that mountain back to my life at sea level and applied to my daily round and learned to do things in my family life and in my business life that seemed daunting and that seemed perhaps at the outset even something whose outcome seemed so uncertain. In our daily sea level lives we all have things like that. And the mountain, that K2 experience, really gave me a lot of strength to know how to lead my sea level life. I was hopeful in writing that book that others might be inspired to find the same kind of thing in their lives.

And it does; it sets things in perspective. If you can survive there, then the little thing that happens to you down here may not be quite as important as you think.

And it's another way of saying that there are other Annapurnas in the lives of men.* That's the idea.

I have gone for long periods without sleep and climbed for 18 straight hours with little rest, but you managed three sleepless nights, often with very little liquid nourishment (which is crucial at altitude). You were at 8,000 meters (26,240 feet) and the temperature dropped to 40 below zero with a wind chill factor of minus 115. It is a miracle that people can survive under those conditions.

Well, we lucked out with the weather. It was cold but there wasn't any wind; well, there was a little bit, but we had a beautiful high pressure day as the sun rose over the Karkorum that morning. We knew that we had that rare Indian summer moment that was going to be what we needed to pull this off.

It took you 60 days to get there.

It did. It wasn't easy.... To put it in context, looking back at it now, you have to remember that the gear was still fairly primitive, that we were just on

---

*The famous concluding sentence of Maurice Herzog's *Annapurna*.

that cusp, in '78, of mountaineering gear evolving into its current modern form, that we still had leather boots on and we still had funky old foam over-boots over that, and we had wool underwear. But we had nylon shells that had some kind of quasi-breathable membrane on it.... I had old pressed-wool Dachstein mitts with some kind of an overmitt over that. So the gear was fairly primitive. The other thing to remember is that people hadn't been up to that altitude for any length of time hardly at all; some of the early Everest guys had gotten up to 28,000 and touched on it without oxygen or even with, and [Peter] Habeler and [Reinhold] Messner had just climbed Everest without oxygen but that was only the season before us, and the reports coming down were that they had brain damage and that their short-term memory had been impaired. That was a little bit of a cloud hanging over the whole thing because you just didn't know what the results were going to be from being at 8,000 meters or above for that length of time without oxygen. The little information we had available suggested that there was going to be some brain damage and that was a little scary. So that's the context.

On Everest, Marty Hoey cut the leg straps of her harness and it slipped off; Lou Reichardt left his parka below the summit; Jim Wickwire's headlamp was in Reichardt's pack when they separated; you did not take even a short rope on your summit ascent; on two separate occasions, you had fires in tents. Some of these occur-

NASA shot of Mount Everest (NASA)

rences are very minor, but even little things can result in injury or death. Why do you suppose that even extremely knowledgeable and competent people make these poor judgments (and not just at altitude, where mental functioning is impaired), when they know the results can be disastrous. (I try to avoid these problems by following my own rules, but even then I sometimes fail and make mistakes.)

And as you well know, you especially make them at altitude. When you interview Messner you will be able to find out from him that you just have to develop an instinct; [you must] listen to your own instinct ... because your cognitive abilities are so impaired.... Roskelley is really good at that; he had been up high for so long, so many times, that it was just in his blood. Coming off the summit, we had to do that traverse back to our northeast ridge from the Abruzzi shoulder and we got into a place where we started down the slope and John goes, "Oh, no." "What's wrong?" He goes, "It doesn't feel right; something's weird; it may be avalanches." I'm nearly crawling and I go back: "Okay, what are you sensing here?" We kind of study things and we gingerly head out. He's really good like that. We are going to the summit and we are right next to each other and it's right there and he goes, "No, no. I'm going to hold onto your ankles and you belly crawl up there; it could be corniced." So he's really good at deeply imbedded instincts, and that can separate climbers who survive from those who don't.

At 28,000 feet and you're not thinking and he grabbed your ankles to protect you. That's fantastic.

But even then, things happen that you don't anticipate. You forget that the stove leaked two weeks before, when we changed canisters and we had a fire. The same thing happens again. And John did that and he's the one that had the best instincts of any of us. So things still happen. And then luck enters into it. It's not some fatal thing. You can survive it. You can figure it out.

How do you feel today, almost 30 years later, about big expeditions? You had almost 400 porters; in '77 on K2, the Japanese had almost 1,000.

Their time is gone. That was appropriate for that era; that's how it was done. Others more imaginative than us and perhaps even more skilled were able to lead out of that tradition and into the next one. Now the model for a high altitude expedition is Steve House's ascent of the Rupal Face on Nanga Parbet. You can't get any better than that.

How many people were there?

Two. Alpine style. The Rupal Face. Ask Messner about that one. Everything on their backs from the bottom to the top and down again, traversing the mountain, up one way and down another. The biggest relief of any ... high altitude wall in the world.

And they did it in just a few days?

Six days up.

Steve House, I did not know that he had done that.

It would be interesting to get Reinhold's take on that too, because to me that's the new standard; not standard; it's the new avant-garde. That is where the boundary now lies. It is ever being pushed out by new and more talented climbers, as it is in any sport that's vibrant and healthy and evolving.

Many of the problems that arise on big, complex expeditions occur because there are so many people pulling in different directions, and this is probably unavoidable. But some occur because the designated leader makes mistakes. Do you think that a more democratic system might work? For example, instead of a leader evaluating his peers based on sometimes misleading criteria and assigning people to the summit team, how about having the members vote? Then there could be little subsequent grumbling, since a majority made the decision. On the other hand, I know that some people prefer a very strong, even autocratic leader.

Yes. Who knows? What is the right model for any group of people striving toward a common theme. Right here in business, there's an infinite number of models for how you run a business either autocratically or democratically. Is the decision-making structure horizontal or vertical or is it some mix of the two? And every company's different: They answer that question in different ways, and that's what makes each of them different from the other. [It's the] same on expeditions. On our K2 climb Jim [Whittaker] really did try to be democratic but he knew that in certain circumstances he also had to be autocratic, so that [when] he saw at the beginning of the trip on the drive in a bunch of us storming off in our jeep and passing and affronting our Pakistani hosts, he had to come and do something about it. You can't call the group to have a vote: Oh, what are we going to do about this situation, or when it actually came time to choose the summit climbers: Okay this is it, the bickering's over.... He had to autocratically step in and did it. But until then, he really did try to build consensus and he did try to run it as democratically as possible. And he had to make his own decisions on where that line lay, versus somebody like Chris [Bonnington] who with a very firm hand, in a military way, [would] run his expeditions and pick people, and sign them on in advance, who were adaptable to that kind of a structure, and [were] willing to accommodate it. Even then, there were a lot of conflicts. They're inevitable.

On two occasions, once via email and once in a telephone conversation with me, Lou Reichardt downplayed his role in mountaineering generally. He said something like, I did a bit of climbing long ago but it was of little consequence. In The Last Step, *he appears to be a superhuman climber and his many accomplishments put him in the forefront of American mountaineering. Is this accurate?*

Yes, he's very, very accomplished. More than any climber I ever shared a rope or a tent with, Lou had an ability to will his body to do what he wanted it to do. I am assuming, and I don't know this for sure, because I haven't shared Lou's life at sea-level with him (I met his wife and a couple of his kids but I've never really been to his house ... and I've never been to his office and watched him work), but I have just assumed that the success he's had both as a husband and a father and the success he's had as a world's leading neurobiologist can only have been accomplished with the same sort of discipline and attitude and tenacity. He's an extraordinary person that way. He is more tenacious perhaps than any other climber I have ever spent time with....

Is he still climbing?

I don't think so, but you have to confirm that with him....

A number of crucial events stand out in the history of mountaineering: The first ascents of Mount Blanc, the Matterhorn, and Everest come immediately to mind. One that may not at first appear so obvious is Dick Bass's achievement in reaching the Seven Summits, the high point on each of the seven continents. This was certainly a stunning achievement for Bass, an out-of-shape businessman in his 50s who had had almost no high altitude experience. But there's more: By reaching his goal, he opened the Seven Summits to others including amateurs like me, who have no business on Aconcagua let alone Everest. You were along on at least three of those climbs: Vinson, Everest, and Aconcagua.

That's right. Because I wrote the book [*Seven Summits*], I was very close to them after the Seven Summits. When we finished our seven-summit year, I started writing the book even as Dick [Bass] was returning to Everest before he actually climbed it. So I was very close to both [Frank] Wells and Bass during those two years it took him to finally get to the top of Everest and me to finish the book. And he only reached the summit as I was finishing the book, hoping that I would have a great [and] successful chapter to tell at the end. He came through. He gave me the perfect ending to the book. And Dick, as you well know, has received a lot of criticism for ... trumpeting his achievement, and he's not shy in doing that. He's loquacious and he calls himself the large-mouth Bass, the Texan who's voluble and talks a lot. He's come under a lot of criticism for that, for allegedly buying his way up the mountains, but just the fact alone that he made it from the South Col to the summit unroped: think about that! [David] Breashears did not want to tie in to him. Breashears was stretching himself too; he didn't want to take that kind of risk. And Dick, not only was he not short-roped, he wasn't roped at all. The whole way up and down. And that's a great achievement. The other thing about both of those guys, especially Frank Wells, they were completely out of their comfort zone. Especially Frank had to put not only his whole business life not on hold, but he had to transition out of that. He had no idea if he was coming back to a

At 22,831 feet, Aconcagua is the highest mountain in South America. It is a fairly easy climb.

job or not; he was jeopardizing his whole family life. His wife and kids were understandably getting pretty angry at him for compromising and risking their whole security and family life as well by doing this idiotic thing that they had no understanding about at all. It was impossible for them to empathize with that; how could they? It was so beyond the pale of what their own lives were like. They had no ability to do that, understandably. They were upset. So there was enormous, not just risk, but willingness to accept and step into the complete unknown on the part of Frank. ... When they first approached me to help them out with these expeditions, I agreed only to help them ... on figuring out how to get to Antarctica and I would share with them a little bit about what I knew about Everest, but that's easy, and the other mountains were easy, they could get that information from dozens of sources. Antarctica was a lot more difficult, and I had been down there a bit and I could help them out with that. Then as I started to have meetings and exchange information and phone calls with them, then they eventually led to an invitation to join them on some of these trips. I didn't agree to do that at first, because I was still thinking, God, these are a couple of dilettantes: Do I want to hang out with these guys?

Do I really support their idea that much? I wasn't sure. But then as I got to know them better, especially Frank, I started to understand, as I said, the risk that he was willing to take and the amount he was willing to push into areas that were completely unknown for him, and as I started to understand the commitment that he had to lead as full of a life as he could and what he was doing to translate that commitment into reality, I became more and more intrigued to learn more about him. And ultimately I decided, and my wife helped me with the decision, that these guys are so fascinating ... that that's the reason my wife counseled me to go with them: Jump into this. See where it goes. See what you learn because it's going to be revelatory for you.... I eventually agreed to do that. Clearly, I'm very happy that I did. I have a richer and fuller life having known those guys....

In 1980, you were in Tibet at 19,000 feet, when you were caught in an avalanche that killed your friend Jonathan Wright. Wasn't it heartbreakingly difficult, many years later, to return to the scene with Asia, his now grown daughter? And then to recount the experience in Below Another Sky?

Yes, it was very hard; yes, that was making the last ... seeing that grave, being uncertain whether I could find it again and then as I started to close in on it realizing that this is the same place and, yes, we are going to get there, and I have no idea [about] the condition we're going to find him in, but then seeing that grave, and then arriving there and finding his remains exposed was as emotionally raw as any experience I've had in my life. If I had been there myself it would have been emotional, but it wouldn't even have been close to what I felt having his daughter there next to me. And lifting back one of those rocks and just seeing the label on his underwear, the old-fashioned, oversized label that said Patagonia, that's kind of like the one we use now, but it was a little bigger, as fresh as the day he died was startling. I describe that in the book. There's nothing I can tell you that would add or change the way I portrayed that in the book. I think I captured the emotions that both of us felt at that juncture.

A climb of Kilimanjaro takes five days; Mount Kenya is more difficult. How did you manage to do it in just a single day?

Kilimanjaro?

Kenya.

Oh, Kenya. Oh, when I climbed it with Ian Allen. He sandbagged me. We did the usual approach up to the base of the mountain and then we did a very long summit day that usually is done in two days. Usually there is an interim.... There's a camp up there, the Austrian hut, where you sleep. We bypassed it.

You just forced it all out in one day.

Well, he sandbagged me. Because he's used to that. Not only was I unacclimatized, I was jet-lagged too.

Did you suffer anything afterwards?

Coming down I started to get a little altitude sickness. I was getting dizzy and nauseous. My balance was way off. And that was dangerous. I wasn't enjoying it on the way down. I was okay until I started the rappels ... and then the worst was actually after rappelling down the regular route we had to ... traverse this talus field ... and downclimb a couple of sections. I was sketched at that point because my balance was off and I was feeling ill. I had to be really careful. But that's still one of my favorite climbs. ... I ascended the ice-window route. It's a mixed climb today, but the ice-window part of it doesn't exist anymore. The curtain that you climb behind—you actually get inside the mountain and go up this cave system—it's all gone; it's gone to global warming. And that's tragic.

On your way to climb a granite tusk near the border of Venezuela and Brazil, you hired some Yanomami porters. What was it like walking deep in the rain forest accompanied by these most unusual people? Did they watch you climb? How did you get back? Did they wait for you?

Yes. They waited for us at the base. I wrote about those guys in a little essay that was published in one of the Patagonia catalogues. Oh, you know, they printed it in a book too ... *Stories from the Field....* It's a collection of essays from the catalogues here. And in there, I remember talking about ... some of the anecdotes, what I learned from those people, those Yanomami. There were a couple of colorful little incidents that helped reveal who you are as a person from the Western world. One of them was going on our way in. We were in these little canoes and we stopped at what turned out to be the last Yanomami village before we entered wilderness where there weren't any human beings. There was a big section of the jungle there that was uninhabited and this mountain was right in the middle of this area, and so as we arrived at that last village, and we had realized by then [by] analyzing the gear that we needed to get to the base, that we were one guy short; we needed one more porter. It would just be easier with one more. So we pulled into this little village and parked our canoes on the shore of the river.... All these people would come out to greet us. We were big news. The whole group was there, maybe 30 or 40 people circled around, all naked except for some little string around them, and they had come down to greet is us with bows and arrows (they didn't know who we were [and] they carry these things with them anyway...) and we had with us a Yanomami who had been an informant for an anthropologist for years and could consequently speak Spanish; he had grown up in a mission for part of his life, so he was our translator.... So through this translator (and I can speak Spanish) we asked the village chief if there was anybody ... in his village ... that would be interested in coming along with us as a porter and we explained to him what we were going to do and we were going to be gone maybe three weeks ... back in the place where it's uninhabited and he knew the place, because they go back there on hunting expeditions sometimes, so he knew what we were talking about, and the chief says, yes, sure, and he points to a guy and says, he can go with you, and I said, great, tell him that if he can go back to his hut and get his stuff we'll wait for him. The chief looks perplexed and he talks ... to the other guy and he turns around to me, and the chief doesn't understand, because he is ready to go. He had walked down from his hut ... with everybody else to see who these people were ... probably not thinking about it but assuming that he is going to go back to his hut when we leave and his life goes on. He walks down and gets told by the chief that he's going to go with us for a month and he doesn't even go back to his hut; he just steps in the canoe with his bow and arrows and his little loincloth on, and off he goes. And he doesn't need anything else.... That is very emblematic of what it's like to be a hunter-gatherer versus somebody in our culture. The other interesting thing that happened to me walking in toward the spire through the jungle in this untracked place ... really good hunting grounds ... I saw one of them in a shaft of light ... in stealth mode.... [I was] watching him stalk these monkeys.... Then he pulls back the arrow and fires and he misses ... and he turned ... and [makes] eye contact right on me. He knew I was there the whole time.... This naked guy stalking through the jungle after this animal that gave me a glimpse of seeing a human being as an animal too.... It was a view into our ancestry that I had never had before.... And those baselines are very, very important for understanding the impact that our species has had on this planet.... My adventures and explorations have given me the privilege of being able to imagine ... those early days on this planet with the beginning of our species, and that's really deeply informed my commitment to environmentalism....

In The Big Open, *you recount a trek across Tibet. Galen Rowell accompanied you. It is very sad indeed that he was killed a few years ago in an airplane accident. Along with Vittorio Sella and Bradford Washburn, Rowell created some of the most stunning mountain photographs. Have you seen the enormous photos in his gallery in Bishop [California]? How do you react to his work? What was it like traveling with him?*

Galen is another of one of those very intense, driven people. He was the oldest guy on our trip.... He was always the first guy up and usually the last guy to go to bed. He just drove himself so hard that the accomplishments that he made as an artist are in large part due to the input of hard work that would put him in that moment at the right time with right light to get the shot that other people would miss who had a lesser dedication to hard work.... I think had Galen not died, he would have found our trip to be a bit of a watershed experience for him, because he also started to learn on that trip the limits to his own physical capabilities and he had never run into that before....

In climbing, I fear four things: avalanches, lightning, brown and grizzly bears, and big cats. How have you coped with the many animals you meet along the approach to a big peak? Even more fearsome were the thousands of large predators (lion, rhinoceros, cape buffalo, crocodile) you encountered as you walked across East Africa.

In East Africa we were armed, so we had an unfair advantage over these guys but even then we had a commitment among ourselves not to shoot them, especially if we were going to encounter any rhinos ... we would go before one of them would; we simply wouldn't shoot it even if it was at the cost of one of our lives ... because they were very endangered.... And we would not shoot an elephant unless it was our life against theirs and then we probably would because there are a lot more of them. ... Even though we were armed, there was still that tension there from being in the food chain.... When I was out in Tibet with Asia I ran into a brown bear; I was out on my own, completely unarmed, and those brown bears out there are very aggressive. [George] Schaller has commented that they're the most aggressive bears he's ever encountered in the world....

So what happened to you?

The bear never sensed me....

In The Shadow of Kilimanjaro, *you discuss at great length various environmental, ecological, and conservation issues. You are especially interested in the fate of the big African mammals. I was amazed to discover that Patagonia, which was founded by the great climber and innovator Yvon Chouinard, employs a vice president for marketing and environmental initiatives, and that person is you. This seems to be a perfect job for you. What is the connection between Patagonia's products and the environment?*

That's a long answer. Yvon and I have been climbing partners since the very early seventies; we were climbing together before Patagonia existed.... We've been able to witness the environmental degradation of so many formerly wild places in the world that we've really come to love; that has informed our own commitment to do something about it.... Yvon started to realize that he's got this company that's growing, that's very healthy ... and could perhaps be a tool to find solutions to this crisis.... The company started to support efforts to galvanize the community against development and won.... What Yvon learned from that experience was how effective a small group of activists can be when they are committed to a focused project.... So then he had this idea to start using the success of the company and its resources to support groups.... Currently we give grants to 350 environmental groups a year.... Almost all of

Rick Ridgeway high on K2, 1978 (photograph by John Roskelley; courtesy of Rick Ridgeway).

them are small grassroots groups.... So far, since we started that program, we've given away 24 million dollars.... But we do a lot of other things ... too. Every 18 months, we convene a conference that lasts a week called "Tools for Environmental Activists" ... and we teach them how to market themselves.... That's why the company exists.... He [Yvon is] able to make this company's mission not to enrich its shareholders, but to provide and implement solutions to the environmental crisis. And that's the company's mission statement....

Even though there have been a few cleaning expeditions, the Himalayan peaks are still littered with rubbish, oxygen canisters, and bodies. It is ironic that those who really do love and respect the mountains the most are responsible for their desecration. If mountaineering continues to increase in popularity, a real ecological crisis may emerge. Can you imagine any type of solution for this?

Yes. It's just increased awareness and commitment and dedication on the part of mountaineers not to be part of the problem, and it's entirely within their ability to do that. It's a lot different now than it was 35 years ago, when I was climbing in the Himalaya on the big peaks, where we really trashed them a lot more than we do now. Even then we were naive. On Everest in '76—that was only the second American expedition to ever go to that mountain—we kept all our garbage in one place, which really hadn't been done before, and then we, at great effort, dug a hole in the glacier there, through ice, mining out rocks (...Sherpas had to do most of it); we dug the biggest hole we could and we put it all in there and buried it. As soon as we left, a bunch of Tibetans came up, heard that we buried our garbage, unearthed the whole thing to see if there was anything worthwhile.... Of course they were going to do that. They shouldn't be blamed for that.... And the garbage was all over the place. So then we heard about that and we went, "oh, my God." So then we did what we should've done in the first place: we had a bunch of Sherpas go up and gather all the stuff up and we paid to bring it back down to the villages and kind of burn it, but then it all didn't burn well and had to be buried and even that wasn't good enough because it still was an impact on Namche Bazaar to have all of this garbage coming down.... So, I think that the mountaineering community is getting there; they still could do better and I think they'll continue to do better. Also having small expeditions with just two guys, like Steve's ascent of Nanga Parbet a few months ago. There's no impact there.

Toward the conclusion of Kilimanjaro, *you indicate that it is no longer necessary to hunt or to use animal parts for trinkets or various ritualistic purposes. You even state that it is no longer necessary to eat them. How do you feel about that? It sounded like you sympathized with that position.*

I do, but yet not against the reality of having a population of animals that because of man's mismanagement of an area are in ascendancy and need some sort of control. Deer in North America are a perfect example of that, because we don't have wolves around any more, and the predators have been eliminated by us. I don't have any issues with deer hunting for those reasons because it actually can benefit a restoration of an area....

You have made more than a dozen documentaries, one of which won an Emmy.

There's not a single one that I hold up with ... pride [so that] if someone came to the house and said, Oh, I want to see the film that is your favorite of all these ... that you made, that I would be able to pull [it] off the shelf and go, Oh, I got to show you this one. They were all a way to get to remote areas and see places that otherwise I wouldn't be able to get to. They were a subsidy for my passion for adventuring in wild areas. The books are another matter. The books are my attempt at my deepest levels to really tell the full story. The book format allowed me to do that. The film format and television were very limiting and still are. As television evolved and was sort of balkanized by cable into a faster and more populist medium that had less money for the same length of film that needed to be produced, it became even less effective as an honest medium for telling a full story. My interest started over time to wane and I've finally just given up on it. The passion's in the books!

You've climbed with or known a broad array of mountaineers, including Louis Reichardt, John Roskelley, Jim Whittaker, Jim Wickwire, Chris Bonington, and

Conrad Anker. Does any individual or specific event stand out that you would care to comment on?

Oh gosh, that's a tough one, because there are so many to try to pull out a single person. So many of them have been so extraordinary in their own ways. Yvon's on that list too. People who have attributes that have formed and directed my own life. Another one on the list of people that have really influenced me deeply, the guy who isn't as well known as a climber, but was an extraordinarily good climber, is Doug Tompkins. Tompkins was so focused and such a good athlete, and never really climbed for notoriety, but did some astounding ascents with Yvon (he and Yvon were the earliest of climbing partners). ... His tenacity, his ability to focus on a single project until it's done, but more than anything, his ability to really visualize and to come up with a new path to take, are attributes and qualities, that maybe more than any climbing partner I've had, really informed me.

Did you ever experience true communion with the mountain?

Yes, all the time; frequently. One of the great things about climbing is that it puts you in a situation where extraneous thought is dangerous and distraction can get you killed. Consequently, if you're going to survive, you have to evolve an ability to deeply concentrate on what you're doing in the moment. And to me those are the main ingredients of communing. ... It's a terrific pursuit for deep, deep connection to wild places, because you have to be there fully in the moment with no thoughts distracting you from being there, concentrating on what you're doing, being very fully aware also of what's going on around you. Then there are sometimes those unique moments that become transcendent: on K2 (and I wrote about it in the book) when all those butterflies floated in from the Tsing Chiao province and all of a sudden started plastering against the ice, all around us, on a day as clear and crystal as this one, then you find transcendency too....

Would you care to say a word or two about your fears and anxiety before a big climb?

Part of the art of mountaineering is the skill of containing, living with, and managing your fears. You have to be able to do it, because if you don't you shouldn't set foot on the mountain.... It will affect your performance and even more your ability to think clearly and make good, rational decisions.

Earlier, you set a reverse limit: you said you would be willing to let an animal cause harm to you rather than shoot it because the animal is valuable. Do you set opposite limits? Do you say, I am going to climb this mountain, but I will not do this? For example, I will not sacrifice another person to get to the summit. Do you have some limits that you mentally set before a climb?

No, not in a catalogued way, but I think that all climbers have to or be well advised to imagine situations in advance so when they do happen you don't have to rationalize an ethical decision about giving up one goal in order to reduce the risk to your companion who may be in some jeopardy. You need to think those things through.... But I have never ... developed any sort of catalogue of what-ifs.

But you and John Roskelley had that catalogue inbred, inherent in you when you said, "If Jim Wickwire needs help we're helping him down."

That's right. Absolutely.

That is not true of other groups of people. I think of the Koreans and the Japanese who set out a priori and say, we are willing to sacrifice one member of our team to get to the summit. It's a different attitude.

The Japanese are famous for that.... There was this famous ... well-known group of climbers that did some of the hardest ascents. Their leader was this guy who was [like a] Samurai character.... On K2, when they went to do the first ascent of the north ridge, this guy got them together at base camp and said, when you're up there everybody's on their own; you are on your own and you should not expect or depend on any of your fellow climbers here to get you out of jeopardy, if you get into trouble.... I am not going to fault them for that; it's part of their cultural background....

How do you feel about the current trend of getting amateur mountaineers on very high summits for large sums of money?

I don't agree or support the idea that people that don't have the skills should be able to pay and buy their way up to a summit, compensating for those lack of skills; they should go through the steps that are necessary to stand on their own feet. Then people say, Why do you support what Dick Bass did? I support what he did because he climbed to the top of Everest from the South Col unroped, and by the time he did that he learned enough, earned enough, and had paid enough dues to be able to do that and come back alive. And that's not buying your way up to the summit; it's different....

Where do you see mountaineering heading in the next decade or so?

The cutting edge is what Steve just did on Nanga Parbet....

Are you working on any new projects at the moment?

Right now ... I'm focused on my job at this company and I'm focused on this mission statement ... doing my best to help this company make a difference in its environmental commitment....

But you still do outdoor things?

Oh yes. I have been out in the water every day this week, because the surf's been good. I love to go mountain biking; I still love to rock climb. I can still get up an occasional 5.10 [see glossary].... I'm still in good shape, 56 and going strong.

Do you have anything else you'd like to add?

If I follow the patterns that have got me to where I am in my life right now, I'll focus on Patagonia for a while, and I'll probably in the future go back to some other effort, I don't even know what that will be yet, but I always seem to cycle through these things.... Before it's all over, I have more books in me....

Well, you write very beautifully. It's a pleasure to read your books.... Thanks so much for giving us some time and sharing much of your adventurous life with us. Thank you.

You're welcome. My pleasure.

AWARDS

An Emmy

BIBLIOGRAPHY

Rick Ridgeway's many articles for periodicals such as *Outside* and *National Geographic* and his films are not included in this listing.

Bass, Dick, and Frank Wells with Rick Ridgeway. *Seven Summits.* New York: Warner Books, 1986.

Ridgeway, Rick. *Below Another Sky: A Mountain Adventure in Search of a Lost Father.* New York: Henry Holt, 2001.

Ridgeway, Rick. *The Big Open: On Foot Across Tibet's Chang Tang.* Washington, D.C.: National Geographic, 2004.

Ridgeway, Rick. *The Last Step: The American Ascent of K2.* Seattle: The Mountaineers, 1980.

Ridgeway, Rick. *The Shadow of Kilimanjaro: On Foot Across East Africa.* New York: Henry Holt, 1998.

"Ridgeway, Rick." *Contemporary Authors* 88 (New Revision). Detroit: Gale, 2000 (356–357.)

<www.rickridgeway.com>.

John Roskelley

(December 1, 1948–)
Mountaineer, author

Date of Interview: July 8, 2006. *Location:* Spokane, WA. *Interviewer:* Robert Hauptman. *Method:* In person: taped and videotaped. *Videographer:* Frederic Hartemann.

Considered by many to be the finest American Himalayan climber of his generation, John Roskelley, with three fellow climbers, did the first American ascent of K2.

RH: You have been called "America's preeminent Himalayan climber" and "one of the world's foremost mountaineers." Long before most mountaineers gave any credence to oxygenless, Alpine-style climbs in the Himalaya, you were actually doing them. How do you feel about all of that now?

JR: I believe that mountaineers, especially American mountaineers, should be striving to reach a level of competence and extremism that fits their talent. Right now I don't see a lot of American climbers out stretching the limits. There are just a few and I read about those in *Climbing* magazine, but as far as going to Everest and higher peaks, it seems as though there are lot of climbers that still want to use oxygen and go up the normal route. I do believe that being preeminent and all of that, I think that was a little premature.... Definitely Reinhold [Messner] was setting the standards in the '70s and '80s and there's no question that other climbers came along. By far the majority of them were Europeans and Asian climbers.

Did you get started in mountaineering through rock climbing?

I started as a general mountaineer and Alpinist. I joined a club here in Spokane called the Spokane Mountaineers. I had my dad put me in the club after reading some mountaineering books that he brought home. I was 16 years old and I really enjoyed the people I was around; they were adults but they treated me like an adult, and I found that quite unusual. And then I just felt very comfortable being in the mountains and the outdoors. That's how my family has been since I was growing up. One thing led to another. I met a good climber, Chris Kopczynski ... and the two of us have continued to climb ever since.

You also care less about summits than about routes, especially first ascents.

Especially in my younger years it was more important to ascend a route, rather than just get to the summit. As a matter of fact, [on] one peak up in Canada, Mount Robson, Del Langbauer and I did the north face and we could have just walked to the summit and chose not to. It was a beautiful day, but summits at the time were not that important. It was the technical nature of the route and the difficulty....

On your first attempt of Tawoche, just a few hours up the wall, you lost your sight; you thought that you had cerebral edema. And you had a similar experience on McKinley eight years earlier. I cannot think of a more frightening experience. Despite this, you immediately returned to Tawoche after recovering. How do you get yourself to do such things?

I had enough experience from McKinley and several other expeditions to know that I was getting an altitude disease of some sort and definitely when it is affecting your eyesight, it's cerebral edema. I knew if I went back down and spent a few more days at a lower altitude, that the cerebral edema would be gone and my chances of getting it again were fairly slim. So, I went back down, reacclimatized and then continued the climb. I figured it was worth the opportunity, worth the chance. We were climbing Tawoche Alpine-style, so we were going up fairly slow; it's not like we were running up two or three thousand feet a day and camping out. We were only going maybe 600 vertical [feet] a day. I felt pretty comfortable about that decision.

At one point, you enumerate the array of horrific ailments from which you have suffered. It is difficult enough to be ill in the comfort of one's home near a medical facility, but you have had giardiasis, whipworm, dysentery, malaria, and even spinal meningitis in the mountains. How do you motivate yourself to participate in another expedition when you know you may get ill again?

It seemed like for years, I came down with quite a few parasites of some sort and other diseases. I just figured that was part of the game of climbing in the Himalaya.... **John Roskelley (photograph by Fred Hartemann).**

Tawoche in Nepal (photograph by John Roskelley).

A lot of those, I believe, were because my resistance was low after taking tincture of iodine, because as you put that in your bottled water to kill bugs, it also kills whatever is in your gut. I was susceptible to a lot of those problems toward the end of expeditions because of all of the iodine I had taken. As the years have gone by, I have had a lot less problems because I have been able to purify my water differently with purification pills and purification filters. It's worked wonders for me. The other thing is we didn't have an immunization for spinal meningitis; now you can take shots for that before you leave. ... The chances of getting ill and not making the summit are greater than being injured or anything else....

You are one of the very few people to have seen a snow leopard in the wild. Even snow leopard researchers sometimes do not see them except on the tapes that they make by triggering a camera.

Seeing that snow leopard in Tibet within fifty feet was probably the highlight of my mountaineering and outdoor career, and I've seen a lot of different types of animals and events. But I can't imagine seeing a more spectacular animal, especially the way it moved after it saw me and continued to run for 15, 20 minutes while we watched it....

In our interview with Rick Ridgeway, he discusses your intuitive approach to problems. You mention this in Last Days: *"I sixth-sensed danger. My intuition is my greatest asset as a mountaineer...."*

That's certainly true. I think it comes with experience. I was certainly a lot less safe when I was first starting out. I can't say I had much of a sixth sense back then, but as I climbed in the Himalaya, climbed with more people and experienced more mountaineering objective dangers, my sixth sense picked up more. I think, it's a trained and learned capacity and I think most climbers who have been in mountaineering situations, for instance Jim Wickwire and Rick Ridgeway, they eventually get a sixth sense of what's going on. It doesn't take much....

In Last Days, *you offer a detailed description of each of the many technical pitches that you climbed on Tawoche. Did you jot down some notes each night? If not, how could you recall all of those minute details including snow, rock, and ice conditions, leads, traverses, and anchor points?*

John Roskelley (photograph by Fred Hartemann).

I can look back through my photography. ... Also on a climb like that, when you are in such danger all the time—well, at least you feel you are in danger—it's not hard to remember every moment. ... I don't have any trouble at all remembering climbs from way back....

In the course of my life, I have traveled extensively around the world, climbed, and read many hundreds of adventure and mountaineering accounts. I cannot recall ever encountering a situation in which some people argued against evacuation for someone who was obviously dying, but this is precisely what occurred on Nanda Devi when Marty Hoey got extremely sick. I was appalled. Have you given much thought to this after the fact? What was wrong with her?

Looking back, she obviously had pretty severe AMS, acute mountain sickness, at a lower camp. I think she got that from not eating and drinking properly, and being very dehydrated. From Latta, the village, up to the next camp was, oh, about a [three to] 4,000-vertical-foot climb. [We] sweat a lot, it was hot, and I think just knowing Marty, she wasn't drinking enough. Then we had some questionable goat meat that night and she just came down with a stomach ailment and started vomit-

John Roskelley (photograph by Fred Hartemann).

ing; the next morning we moved up and it was a questionable call. Andy Harvard went to Willy [Unsoeld] and said, look, I'm sick and Marty is sick. We should probably stay behind or maybe even go down. Whatever it was, the final decision was to move up to the next camp at 11,500 or so. During that day, Marty continued to vomit and pass diarrhea and basically was severely dehydrated. When she got to the camp, she was semi-comatose. Then the next morning, I went and looked at her and knew right away by looking in her eyes, which were just blank and had no ability to focus, she had gone beyond acute mountain sickness and to possibly having cerebral edema, which as far as I could tell, was probably the case; and that's what the doctor finally diagnosed. The expedition leadership made a mistake, regrettably, but you move on....

There was an astonishing amount of disagreement, lack of cooperation, and animosity on this climb, more than on many others. And so many people decided to

*leave during the climb, again, more than on many other expeditions. Why do you
think this occurred?*

I think that the primary component was the lack of leadership. I don't
want to put blame on anybody, but on an expedition with a bunch of prima
donnas, there's always those who have climbed before who want to go one way
or two or three different ways. A strong leader will put their foot down and
take charge; who's going to put up the tents, who's going to dig the latrine,
who's in charge of watching to make sure the water is clean. Someone has to
designate procedure and there was no designation at all. It was just helter-
skelter basically. If you want to get your meal, walk over to the cook tent and
get it. Nobody was in charge of clean water or even what time to start in the
morning.... I wasn't real familiar with a lot of expeditions in 1976, but I did
know from reading [about] the 1963 Everest expedition and the Annapurna
expedition in 1950 that strong leadership was needed to pull this group together
and that's what I argued for throughout the trip. But once the disagreement
surfaced about Marty, the team was fractured at that point and it was extremely
difficult to get them all back on one page. ... I know of one leader ... who could
lead a group of people anywhere and that's Jim Morrissey. ... I don't think
there could be a better leader than Jim. He knows when to put his foot down
and when to let climbers take the lead....

*At one point you clipped into the wrong rope, which abruptly ended. Luckily,
you discovered the error. Sometimes people make these simple mistakes and do not
discover them and so they lead to tragedy.*

The scary part was while I was setting my rappel system onto that section
of the rope, I didn't realize it at the time, because normally you'll feel the weight
of a longer rope, whereas a short tail is too light to worry about. But obviously
I was done in enough that mentally I was not at my full capacity. That's the
scary part: while climbing you reach a level during the day [at which] you could
be absolutely mentally incapacitated. You're not thinking at all; I think that's
when most accidents happen. You're out 18 hours, you're working every moment.
It's like doing a triathlon every day. And you're oxygen deprived. I was a rescue
ranger on Mount McKinley for a few years. One of the climbers I picked up,
who died, fell down the west rib route; what he had done was come off the
summit late in the afternoon with two other guys and went to the lip of this
very steep crest above the route, sat down and, instead of keeping his feet underneath him, he spread his feet out, slipped on the slick ice. He never gained control and slid 4,000 feet to the bottom of the route. You just don't think....

*You have often climbed with Lou Reichardt. Do you agree with Rick Ridgeway
that he is an extraordinary mountaineer?*

I do. Lou's a very strong individual. Not only is he strong, he's very, very
intelligent. So he's always a step ahead. In some respects that's really good.

He calculates what's going to go on, on an expedition. I think he likes that better than climbing; he likes the chess game: where the players are going to be on the mountain; who's going to be where; what they're going to be doing. ... Technically, I wouldn't say he's strong, but as far as strength, brute strength, Lou can keep going and carry the heaviest loads of any person I know....

I'm quite familiar with the climbing literature, the successes and the tragedies. I do not think that I have ever read a sadder account than the death of Nanda Devi Unsoeld on her namesake peak. It is ironic that you importuned her not to continue, and the doctor also warned her, because she had been ill for many days. If she had gone down, she probably would have survived—do you think?

I hate to speculate. The problem I believe with Nanda Devi was she jumared that last section of the buttress and during that period her hernia strangulated. The difficulty of someone jumaring that section, which was very difficult: ... there was a lot of switching into gullies, avoiding sharp edges, a very heavy load, and then at the top, she got caught underneath a small cornice and she couldn't get the rope out. She wasn't experienced enough to work those jumars over the cornice, so I'm sure she damaged the hernia and that's what possibly killed her. She probably should have come down. ... The hardest thing for Willy after she died was to decide what to do with her body. Removing her from the ridge would be mentally harder for me than to just leave her where she was. But it was his choice and decision....

Reichardt and States on top of Nanda Devi, 1976 (photograph by John Roskelley).

In 2003, you and your son Jess became one of a handful of father-son pairs to reach Everest's summit and you did it together. Was this the high point in your climbing career?

I'd have to say that climbing with Jess was a pleasure and reaching the summit of Everest, of course, has to be one of my high points, if not the best. I couldn't get up it four times before that, mostly because I wouldn't use oxygen, and I would try very difficult routes. Everest is one of those peaks you can climb, given the right circumstances, good weather and, of course, if you use oxygen. I wasn't surprised that we made the summit, but for both of us to make the summit on the same day was extraordinary to me. ... It's a life-changing experience, whether you are my age or Jess's age, to climb to the summit of Everest....

I think the number has reached 2,000 human beings who have stood on the summit of Everest [the figure is higher since the interview], but as far as I know only five [actually seven] father-son pairs, and of those five, a number of them were done separately (the Hillarys were done separately and the Norgays were done separately), so you and your son and possibly two others are the only human beings to ever climb Everest together as father-son. That's a very elite group of people. Will you be taking your 16-year-old daughter up Everest in the near future?

No plans at this time. After taking her up Mount Rainier—I realize she's very strong [but never climbed before]—we did Rainier in a single push. We went up about 7:30 at night and got to Muir at midnight, kept on going, got to the summit at 7:30 in the morning, and then came on down and back to the car and I drove home. She's tough....

You are wisely careful when it comes to avalanches and lightning, two of the major hazards of high altitude climbing. Does that come of experience?

I don't see any reason to try fate with something you can't control. If it's a technical climb, then I'm willing to go the extra mile, take a fall, whatever it takes, but when I have no control over anything, I believe in reevaluating the circumstances and sometimes backing off to try another day. Carelessness just doesn't make sense. The whole idea of mountaineering is to challenge yourself, and you can't challenge yourself and show your technical skills when objective danger is going to knock you off. ... I try to select routes that avoid avalanches, rock fall, and other objective hazards.

You generally speak your mind, even when it alienates others, and yet you care inordinately about what others think. For example, you refused to put on crampons on the dangerous trail to Tengboche Monastery because you feared ridicule from American trekkers, and you would not allow Kesharsingh to beat you to Ridge Camp on Nanda Devi, although you were nearly exhausted.

I think the story on Tawoche over crampons and envying the Japanese

Ron Kauk on summit of Uli Biaho, 1979 (photograph by John Roskelley).

walking down the trail using them was more tongue-in-cheek than anything else. I think that if I had had my crampons, I might have put them on, but as it was, as we got lower, there was less ice. I do speak my mind; It's important to do so. Every time I hold my tongue something ends up happening. It doesn't make any difference whether it's in my family situation or work. I learned as a politician, too, you've got to take your vote; it doesn't matter what people are going to think of it. ... It's the same with speaking your mind. I don't try to irritate people. It's just important that everybody has a say and then you just do your thing. For what Willy was doing on Nanda Devi and what Devi did, gosh, who knows? If the positions were reversed, I might have done the same thing....

You seem to care about the environment a great deal. Do you think that it is possible to protect the mountains from mass incursions of hikers, climbers, and mountaineers, destruction of trees and flowers, sullying of waterways, and general pollution from human detritus including vast quantities of rubbish? On small Alpine ascents one can carry out one's trash, but on large expeditions what can one do?

Well, you're definitely focusing in on Asian climbs, South American climbs.... I am an environmentalist. I was elected here in Spokane County as an environmentalist, believe it or not, even though it's a very conservative area. But I believe that the Chinese and the Nepalese have finally come around, and they're doing a much better job, even charging fees to clean up garbage. They're doing garbage clean-ups all the way up to 23,000, even 25,000 feet on Everest.

And there are other climbs out there that are not getting the attention, which do have the same garbage they've had for years, but it's getting to be a lot better. Climbers are aware of the price that's paid when you go and you leave your garbage. Also, the Sherpas are becoming more aware, which is a huge change in philosophy for that area. So, things are getting better; even though there are more and more people attacking Everest, there are less climbers on other peaks. Let them beat their brains out on Everest because at least there are some controls there. If they go to Makalu or Annapurna, the controls are not as great. ... But overall, I think the environment is better off in this day and age then it was 20 years ago. ... For instance, in 1993 at the 23,000 [foot] advance base camp on the north side, there were old cans, oxygen bottles, batteries, and garbage, tons of it. It was in the rocks and strewn about in that whole area. I don't see that anymore. It's all been picked up. ... I find that if you go a mile off the trail anywhere, or even a few hundred yards off the trail, there are few people. So, you've got to police the trails. That's where the majority of the garbage is. I do find when I'm walking in on treks in Nepal or around Tibetan villages the garbage is just horrendous. The Chinese are the worst offenders. They throw their garbage right out the windows of their buildings directly into the creeks. ... They don't pay any attention to environmental clean-up at all....

On Nanda Devi, Marty Hoey got extremely ill and had to be evacuated; Nanda Devi Unsoeld also got sick and died. And on K2, you became disenchanted with Cherie Bech, which led to the following outburst: "...This is the last time I'm climbing with any of them [women]. I've seen them kill themselves trying to prove they are as strong as men. Eight of them in the Pamirs, then Devi. People always criticize me for being down on women on expeditions, but I've never yet been on a big mountain with one that's worth a damn." Ironically, you compliment the four Sherpani porters who "...worked harder than the men..." on the Tawoche approach. Have you changed your mind after considering the accomplishments of Alison Hargreaves, Stacy Allison, Christine Boskoff, and your daughter?

I have. There's no question that when I made those statements I was a little discouraged with the people I was with. Marty Hoey was a strong climber. There's no question that I would have continued to climb with Marty. Devi was very pleasant and a joy to be with; I really liked Devi. It's just that I think they were forced into situations where they were uncomfortable and it made the other team members uncomfortable. On K2, I did have some bad experiences with Cherie and [with] Jim Whittaker's wife, Dianne. It was not because of them so much as because they were put in a position of having to do something they technically weren't able to do. Cherie was a good climber, but she was abrasive and no one on the team needed that. There are enough problems on a mountain without having any kind of abrasion. Since then, I've climbed with some really strong women, mentally and physically tougher than me. I

Nanda Devi expedition, 1976 (photograph by John Roskelley).

don't have a problem with them going on expeditions and, if they get along with the guys, fine. I think my daughter is a good case in point. She's strong, capable and determined. Potentially, a great partner. I'm sure she'll go on an expedition or two with my son.

Were you on the Pamirs expedition when those eight women died?

I was. And that was another great American experiment. Marty was on that trip and she was very strong, but so was Molly Higgins, a young lady from Colorado. Molly was a good mountaineer but I think she felt out of her element in the Pamirs. That was a difficult trip. The eight Russian women who died got caught in bad weather. Their equipment didn't hold up and their tents blew away and their stoves wouldn't start. They probably should have backed off when the weather report came through that was bad. They were trying to be the first all-woman team to top Mount Lenin and there was another group of women that was trying to do the same thing. So, in other words, competition occurred between the parties. Consequently, not only did the Russian women die, a Swiss woman died in the same storm.

In Last Days, *you mention your 1980 Makalu climb. Do you recall that someone on another expedition was incapacitated, and you thought it advisable not to help?*

They came through our camp very late in the season. We gave them all the help they asked for. It was very discouraging to come home to the United States and hear that the leader of the Makalu II expedition put the blame for their incompetence on our expedition. When they came through, way too late for them to summit, they pushed it too hard and went up too fast. We had been on the west

Jeff Lowe on Tawoche, 1990 (photograph by John Roskelley).

Ron Kauk ascending Uli Biaho, 1979 (photograph by John Roskelley).

Jim States on Makalu West Ridge, 1980 (photograph by John Roskelley).

ridge of Makalu for close to a month, maybe five weeks, and we had put ourselves in position of going for the summit. We were down at base camp for a rest; they came through and went on up, and Mike Warburton came down with severe cerebral edema and went into a coma. They sent another climber, Betsy White, down; Betsy came into our camp and said, "Warburton is in a coma; my brother and my husband are with him and I need more help." So we organized all the rescue equipment for them. I even said to Betsy, "Do you want us to go up with you?," and she said, "No, we have enough people." So Chris and I headed up our route leaving Jim States, our doctor (who was supposed to go up with us) in camp. Chris and I went up on the West Ridge with a radio and kept in contact with Betsy, who was going up the next morning with the rescue crew, seven strong porters and Sherpas. She figured with her brother, her husband, and her, and the seven strong hill people, they could get this guy down. So they didn't need anybody else. We left States and said to Betsy, "Look, when he (Warburton) gets down, we'll give him oxygen and do anything we can to get help out." Mike was obviously in bad shape. Betsy and her crew got up there, but on the way up Betsy passed her brother and husband coming down; they had left Mike alone to die in the tent. I can recall being on the radio to Betsy. She's crying and saying, "We can't find him (Warburton); we don't know where he's at." I said, "You've got to keep going, you cannot

Kim Momb and John Roskelley on Everest West Ridge, 1980 (photograph by John Roskelley).

leave him, you have to get to him." She then said, "The Sherpas do not want to go any further." I said, "Put them on the radio." I got on the radio with the head guy and said, "Look, you either go or I'll make sure the Nepalese government charges you and the others with murder." Basically, I pulled the only card I could use to force them up. They get up there, package him, and set up some kind of a litter to carry him. I'm familiar with this because I helped carry a Chinese guy 11 miles down the Rongbuk, who weighed at least 300 pounds, with seven Tibetans and Sherpas just a few years later. So I knew it could be done. They put him on this litter and carried him down. He got to our camp, but the doctor couldn't wait any longer if he wanted to be on the summit attempt, so he had set off to catch us. But Kim Momb (another one of our teammates) was waiting at camp to give him oxygen and whatever he needed to bring him out of his coma, which he did. ... Armando Menocal, the leader of the expedition, never went up to help the rescue party; he stayed at our base camp. For him to condemn our expedition for not doing more was hypocritical. I can't believe how bad that is. Before they left, I told them specifically to get a helicopter and have him choppered out as soon as possible. Well, they didn't. They didn't have the money or didn't want to send someone out. Warburton was carried for days all the way out and he developed pulmonary thrombosis. A clot went into his leg and the doctors thought he was going to lose his leg. Fortunately, that didn't happen and he recovered. It was just one catastrophe after another.

I think he did survive, though.

Oh, yes, Not only did Mike survive, he came through Spokane on the bus one time and called me up and he said, "Hey, John I'm here in town, can I sit down and talk to you?" I said, "Sure, come on up. We're having a family gathering and I'll have somebody pick you up and bring you up to the farm." ... After they arrived, my dad took me aside, because he had picked him up, and said, "Did you do something to this guy?" I said, "No, I didn't do anything to him." He said, "He sure is acting funny and talking like you had left him to die or something." I thought that was odd, so I sat down with Mike and talked to him. Sure enough, since he had no idea what went on because he was in a coma, he thought that we did nothing, that we left him to die. I told him our side of the story and Jim's sacrifice. I said, "This is what we did. We took our tent poles down and gave them for litter poles, provided clothing for your Sherpas and Tibetans; we did everything we could. And we offered to go up if we were needed." That never came out in Armando's story. Betsy, after tallying all the rescue personnel, said, "No, no, you don't have to go up."

Have you ever written about this?

No. Mike continued to question our participation. It was if he was trying to find fault; for some reason, he just would not comprehend what I was telling him or chose not to. So I took him out on the deck one more time. I said,

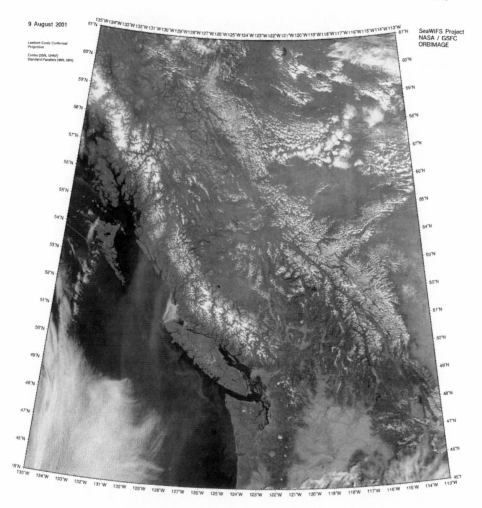

Pacific Northwest satellite image (NASA)

Look, Mike, I'm going to tell you this one more time, but if you bring it up again during your stay, I'm going to take you down to the bus and leave you. So I told him one more time what I thought transpired. We went back in (the house) and he started asking me again about it. I said, Get your stuff; you're out of here. I put him in the car; took him down to the bus, dropped him off, and I've never seen him since....

An article in The Chronicle of Higher Education *claims that we are less ethical today; I disagree, but many people did pass two helpless climbers on Everest and left them to die. I think the second guy's name is Lincoln Hall.*

I know Lincoln. Lincoln would be the first guy to tell you they should have left him. ... There are dozens and dozens of teams on Everest and they're mostly bozos. You want to stay as far away from these people as possible. They're going to kill you....

Are you doing anything exciting now? Do you have anything planned for the future? And anything you'd like to add?

I don't have anything planned right now. I'm sure my son will come up with something and I'll get hoodwinked into it. It's a fix for me. ... I love to go to Asia; I don't so much like to climb, but I sure like the travel in Asia. I love the people; I love the experience of a foreign country. I've recently been leading guided treks to Bhutan. Bhutan is my favorite destination for trekking. I think it's the ultimate trek.... As far as climbing ... I don't have the capabilities I had years ago; I have to be very careful about how stretched out I get....

Thank you so much for sharing your adventures. Thank you.

BIBLIOGRAPHY

Ridgeway, Rick. *The Last Step: The American Ascent of K2*. Seattle: The Mountaineers, 2003.

Roskelley, John. *Last Days*. Harrisburg, PA: Stackpole Books, 1991.

Roskelley, John. *Nanda Devi: The Tragic Expedition*. Harrisburg, PA: Stackpole Books, 1987.

<www.johnroskelley.com>.

Barbara Washburn

(November 10, 1914–)

Mountaineer, explorer, cartographer

Date of interview: April 19, 2007. *Location:* Lexington, MA.
Interviewer: Robert Hauptman. *Method:* In person: taped.

With no mountaineering experience whatsoever, Barbara Washburn
accompanied her husband, Bradford Washburn, on a number of early Alaskan
first ascents. She was the first woman to climb Mount McKinley. She subsequently worked with Bradford on his National Geographic Society cartographic projects including the Everest and Grand Canyon maps. She taught
the learning disabled.

━━

*RH: Thank you for sharing some of your valuable time with me. You made
your mountaineering debut by doing a first ascent of Alaska's Mount Bertha. Had
you done any preparatory climbs?*

BW: Never.

*How did you learn how to do such things as walk in crampons, belay, or self-
arrest using an ice ax?*

When I married my husband, I didn't know that I was going to climb. I
thought I would help him run the science museum; but it was obvious within
the first month or so of our marriage that he was going to go back to Alaska
in the summer and he wanted me to go with him to share all his experiences.
I thought that was pretty exciting because I was sort of adventurous but I did
not know a thing about climbing, not a thing. And so the first day, we had to
walk up a glacier, and that was all adventurous and exciting but then there
was Mount Bertha in front of us and a lot of rock climbing in the lower part
of it.... None of us was experienced in that group and so we started climbing
and we would hang on rocks and we climbed. Lowell Thomas was with us and
he was scared to death. He didn't like it. At dinner that night he said to Brad,
"What are you trying to do to Barbara? Kill her?" That was his way of showing
he didn't like it. That's how I did it. And then the time came to climb the

mountain. Brad chose me as one of the team to go to the top because he knew I could make it. I was pregnant!

I was just going to ask. After the climb, you felt a bit ill. You went to the doctor and discovered that you had summited while pregnant. Did this surprise you?

Yes. I had no idea. We didn't know that in those days.

Imagine how much stronger you might have been if you had not been pregnant.

It was in early pregnancy. But when I got down, I had a backache. I don't think it had much to do with the climbs. The doctor pointed his finger at me and said "Madame, you don't know what a chance you took." If I had a miscarriage in the wilderness, it would not have been so funny.

It surprised me that not long after your daughter was born, you left again for a first ascent of Mount Hays, also in Alaska. You did these early climbs with old-fashioned equipment. Did this make it harder? Were you cold much of the time?

Not really. We did have old-fashioned equipment and we were cold. You get used to the cold. Mostly when sleeping. We had pretty good parkas and they were heavy, old-fashioned stuff with a funny kind of lining. But I don't remember being really cold because if the weather was [bad], we spent time in our tent. We didn't stretch it; we didn't have a deadline. That's the secret; that's the secret of climbing safely: You don't have to climb when it's dangerous.

Your husband, Bradford, made the third ascent of McKinley [Denali] and then the first ascent via the West Buttress route. And you were the first woman to stand on the summit of McKinley, one of the world's great mountains. Did you realize at the time what an extraordinary feat this was? And did the media trumpet your success?

I had no idea. Climbing Mount McKinley was never on my agenda of things to do in life. It just happened that a movie company came to Brad and said, "We are publishing a book about mountain climbing, but I don't think that the American public knows anything about mountain climbing and is not very interested in it. Could you go to Mount Everest and climb Mount Everest for us?" And Brad laughed and said, "My god, you can't even get into Mount Everest these days, but I could take you to Mount McKinley. I climbed it during the war and it would be a very nice climb, with some guides and some reasonably good climbers, and we could make a movie." That's how it happened and then when the movie company heard that I had climbed in Alaska before, they said if you could persuade your wife to go, it would make a better movie— to have a girl in it. That was simply how that happened.

And then you succeeded when so many people have subsequently failed; though lots have climbed it, maybe one in two who try to climb it, fail.

Denali, the "Great One," was formerly known as Mount McKinley. At 20,320 feet, this is the highest mountain in North America.

We had time; we had time, and if you don't have to rush up Mount McKinley, anybody can climb it.

That's being very optimistic. I don't think I can. It's not an easy climb. It takes three weeks. Did you spend a lot of time?

Yes. We moved slowly up to camp. We spent two or three days in each camp. We had these professional photographers making the movie. Brad was making his own movie. We weren't in any hurry. I spent ten days at 15,000 feet, and that wasn't any fun, but we did it without any trouble.

Did any of the professional photographers make the summit?
One of them.

That's impressive. Had they climbed before?
Never. They learned with us.

Do you realize how incredible that is? Truly great mountaineers climb and die!

We stayed ten days in the tent. We were at 15,000 feet when the storm broke. Brad went up a day ahead. I and two other guys stayed in a tent; we were going to come up in the next contingent. We were going to go up the next day. The storm didn't abate. We had an igloo; we slept in the igloo and cooked in the little tent. We discussed [things].

Did the media contact you when you got back?

The day that we went to the top, I had been at 18,000 feet for probably a week by that time, so I was getting acclimatized even though I was quite miserable sleeping at night; I was feeling the altitude. But the day that we went was a lovely day. I was feeling quite strong. I had two boys on the rope with me who had headaches, so I was the strong one. When we got near the summit one of them turned to me and said (this was a guy on another rope), "Barbara, you got to go first because you are the first woman." And I said, "Don't be silly: who cares? We can go to the top together." He said, "This is important, you're the first woman." I had no thoughts of being the first woman, and so when we got back down to civilization, I was exhausted. We were up all night, doing a lot of miles every day, trying to get home.

But he took a side trip to the other peak!

Yes. It was a beautiful day, and he said, "Let's go to the North Peak. I can survey from the top." So we went up to the top. It was a beautiful day; so we did. I was in pretty good shape. But, oh, when I got back to Anchorage, the newspapers, everybody calling wanting interviews, and I said what the heck is going on? And then I suddenly realized—the first woman to climb McKinley: it means something! They asked, "Why did you climb it?" and finally I just said, "I did it to be with my husband."

Subsequently, when Hillary climbed Everest, he became one of the most famous people in the world. He then devoted himself to helping the Sherpa people.

Absolutely. And he got sick of it [the media] too. He is a very nice guy.

To climb McKinley, you had to leave your three young children behind. The stress caused you to break out in a rash. How were you able to make peace with yourself?

It took me a long time to make the decision and finally, I said, well, it is very important to Brad that I go with him.... We had four grandparents; we could not have done it without the grandparents.... So I hired a nurse and a kind of housekeeper lady, who had been taking care of friends' children in the neighborhood, so I ...knew her. And the grandparents checked in every day. I knew that there was going to be good supervision. I worried all of the time. I communicated, wrote letters to them and then the plane would come in and drop some stuff.

As you say, McKinley climbers today are on vacation, merely repeating what hundreds of others have done before them, but you were a true explorer. What was it like to be stuck in a tent with two men during a nine-day storm, while your husband was trapped above your 14,600-foot camp. Was that hard for you?

No. There were two boys, now in their eighties; it was very interesting because when Brad died, one of them called me and said, "Barbara, did you know that George and I were both in love with you all the time we were up there...? We just thought you were wonderful." I behaved like a lady: I put lipstick on, combed my hair. When I came in for a break from my tent, I tried to keep up. I didn't get sloppy. Women today are sloppy; they don't give a rip. I was an old-fashioned girl. In front of all those guys I was going to look neat. They kidded me about it. In the tent, the two guys I was with—one was the scientist, and one was a good climber but he was the most unpopular (he's dead; I'm in touch with his wife); he was an army guy. He didn't have a sense of humor. He would get angry about things. So one day we decided to discuss the things we had read. The guy who was going to count the cosmic rays, the scientist, admitted he was married to a black girl. Well that nearly finished the other guy who was from the West Coast.... So I gave a lecture on sociology, because I was taking sociology at Smith College. So I smoothed that over. We got along very well. Because of the weather (wind), we would hold hands and walk a few feet and go to sleep in the igloo. We had sleeping bags laid out there and we would play a game, ghost or something. We would get into arguments about how to spell a word. Nine days: going to sleep at night was hard because I was always cold.

The igloo didn't sweat?

No. The igloo was well-built and it was plenty cold. Inside, it was always frozen. We didn't do any cooking. We just slept there. And everything was above-board and very civilized.

How did you manage to gather the strength, the next day, to also climb the North Peak?

You have to know my husband: he was a very enthusiastic guy. It was a sunny day and he said, "Come on everybody, how about a survey from the top of the North Peak?" We carried a tripod.

How long did the climb take from the camp to the summit of the North Peak?

It wasn't bad: A few hours. We sat down and had a picnic lunch in the sun—on the summit of the North Peak. It was a gorgeous day.

When I was in Alaska a few years ago, I saw a chart that said that in July 1999, there wasn't a single day when you could see Mount McKinley.

That's right: so I was very lucky. And coming down, we had fun coming down!

You were often the only female on a climbing expedition. Was this difficult or awkward for you?

Never. When I was growing up I was always with more boys than girls. I wasn't a tomboy at all, but everything the boys were doing seemed more interesting. Two or three boys would come, even when I was in college, and say let's go and have a beer. There was always one boy especially whom I liked but he wasn't necessarily in the group. I was just a friend. That's why it was very easy; I knew how to get along with boys.

Nevertheless, some people, especially macho mountaineers, may have a bad attitude. Some of the people, young women, we have interviewed said that they do have problems with discrimination and a lack of respect.

Well, let me tell you about Grant Pearson. He had been the director of the Park Service. He went to 18,000 feet; he didn't go to the top. He said, "I promised my wife" he wouldn't do it because he had a little heart problem and he was 50 years old. Then we were sitting around in the cook tent discussing something and they got a little bawdy. There were a few little swear words. I didn't think about it. I knew how to swear... though I didn't do it. All of a sudden he banged on the table and said, "I will not have that kind of language in this tent. We have a lady in our midst and I will not have her have to listen to that." I was shocked because I thought I was a member of the group. They all stopped; they were very respectful. It was a totally different time.... We had a special system with our toilet: It had a flag and the flag was up when you were in there.... I had total privacy. It was wonderful. They really treated me like a lady.

Along with Brad, you did a great deal of cartographic field work, measuring, recording, and analyzing, which resulted in the National Geographic *McKinley, Everest, and Grand Canyon maps. Did you enjoy this onerous work? For example, you note that you made 697 helicopter landings in the Grand Canyon.*

That was fun. We walked down and then we were taken out by a helicopter. We never walked up.... There was one day at the bottom when I thought my eyeballs were going to burn. One day, I said to Brad—he always kept going and kept going and kept going—anybody who does this for fun ought to have his head examined. I muttered these things. [I enjoyed it.] It was exciting. There is a lot of work [involved in creating these maps] and of course the Swiss did a lot of the work in creating these maps and they did beautiful work. There were times when I got cross or cranky ... but I kept going. Brad was a fascinating guy to be married to. I knew that wherever Brad was, that was where the excitement was.

You mention in your memoir that the dean of Harvard Law School, and a family friend, insisted that women could not attend because they would get married and leave the profession. Did you encounter this type of discrimination later within the mountaineering community?

Never.... I encountered this only hearing it from a woman's mouth later on in Cambridge [Massachusetts]. A famous author's wife and her sister came to McKinley Park and tried to get permission to climb McKinley but they were not allowed to.... When I met her at a cocktail party she got me off in a corner and said, "You know, I hate you ... because I and my sister wanted very badly to climb Mount McKinley and we weren't allowed to." That was quite a few years before I did it.

Norman Vaughan was a good friend. He had agreed to an interview but passed away before we were able to return to Alaska. Can you tell us something about this remarkable man?

When Brad and I were first married and had to go to Mount Bertha ... Brad said we got to have some dogs to go up the glacier.... So we drove up to Norman Vaughan's place up in New Hampshire and asked if we could borrow some of his dogs, and he said yes.... We ... brought the [eight dogs] home, took them on the train, tied them up in the baggage car, then ... onto the boat. We crossed the Brady Glacier, a long way. Sometimes, I drove the dogs, and someone said, Barbara, you got to learn to swear; the dogs won't go if you don't swear. I would say some modest swear word.

Were you the only one controlling the sled?

Yes. Sometimes I stood on the runners depending on how fast the dogs were going; sometimes I ran.

I think Susan Butcher took her dogs right to the summit.

Oh, Susan Butcher was an incredible person. I did not know her personally but I knew her parents, because she came from Cambridge. And I was with Vaughan there when he got ill at a restaurant and then had a pacemaker put in.

Vaughan came so close to climbing Mount Vaughan [in Antarctica] on his 100th birthday. He was so strong. He climbed it when he was 89.

Yes. I know. I saw him after he came back.

You have been honored with many awards, including the Gold Medal of the Royal Scottish Geographical Society, the Alexander Graham Bell Award of the National Geographic Society, and two honorary doctorates. Which award has been most gratifying?

Good heavens, did I get all of those awards?

And many more.

I think the most exciting and unexpected was the medal I got from my college.... I was horrified when I got it because I thought it was for being academic. I got good marks but I didn't get academic As. And I had a funny time at that point: The telephone rang and it was my daughter telling me that she was getting a divorce, and you know what that does to a parent.... And then I went to get the mail ... and there was a letter from Smith College offering me a medal.... And I began to cry: I said I can't accept a medal with a divorced daughter, because I have been a terrible mother. But then I accepted it. I think that getting a medal from my own college was more [meaningful] than from mountaineering.

Your husband, Brad, was a great mountaineer (with many first ascents in Europe and North America), explorer, cartographer, and museum director. His black-and-white photographs, especially of McKinley, are perhaps the finest mountain images ever created. In Europe, when Brad was a boy, he climbed and made first ascents with Balmat, Georges Charlet, Alfred Couttet, and Georges Tairrez—all direct descendents of the great Chamonix guides. He did first ascents of the Aiguilles Verte and Dent. Thus, he and you connect the climbers of the 19th century with those of the 21st.

He thinks that some of those pictures that he took in Europe were the best he ever took. It is a link; it shows that life goes on. [And] women were doing things in those days, but not very many.

Do you have anything else to add?

No. I don't think so. Have you read my little book [*The Accidental Adventurer*]? ...I was sick and could not go back to work and I had nothing to do so I wrote it for my children. At the very end of the book, I said I had more satisfaction from the teaching I did of dyslexic children and seeing the improvement than from any mountain I ever got to the top of.

You have led an extraordinary life, accomplished many wonderful things, and made the world a better place. It has been an honor to visit with you. [By the way,] you are a wonderful inspiration; you don't look anywhere near 92 and you seem to be in good shape. Thank you very much.

BIBLIOGRAPHY

Alaskan Reminiscences: 60 Years of Adventure with Bradford and Barbara Washburn. Videocassette. Prd. Thomas Pollard. Williamsburg, MA: Eyes Open, 2001.

Washburn, Barbara, with Lew Freedman. *The Accidental Adventurer: Memoirs of the First Woman to Climb Mount McKinley.* Kenmore, WA: Epicenter Press, 2001.

Washburn, Bradford, and Barbara Washburn. Interview by Doug Mayer and Rebecca Oreskes. "Mountains Are Friendship: Bradford and Barbara Washburn." Appalachian Mountain Club. December 2001. <www.oudoors.org/publications/appalachia/2001/2001-washburn.cfm>.

Top: Everest North Face. *Above:* Lhotse face and climbers in the lower left (both photographs by Stacy Allison).

Above: Christine Boskoff at Everest base camp. *Below:* Christine Bokoff guiding Mountain Madness team on Mount Elbrus (both photographs courtesy Mountain Madness).

Maurice Isserman on Kala Patar (photograph by Arlene Blum; courtesy of Maurice Isserman).

Jamling Tenzing Norgay on the summit of Island Peak (photograph by Kami Sherpa; courtesy of Jamling Tenzing Norgay).

Opposite: Ridgeway and ridge on K2, 1978 (photograph by John Roskelley; courtesy of Rick Ridgeway).

Climbers below Everest North Col, 1984 (photograph by John Roskelley).

Lou Reichardt below Nanda Devi, 1976 (photograph by John Roskelley).

Jim Wickwire on K2, 1978 (photograph by John Roskelley; courtesy of Jim Wickwire).

Erik Weihenmayer

(September 23, 1968–)

Climber, mountaineer, guide, advocate for the blind

Date of interview: March 8, 2007. *Location:* Golden, CO. *Interviewer:* Robert Hauptman. *Method:* In person, taped and videotaped. *Videographer:* Frederic Hartemann.

Erik Weihenmayer is an extraordinary human being: He is an accomplished mountaineer whose résumé includes the Seven Summits; skier; paraglider; and guide. When he was a teenager he lost his sight, and is completely blind.

I'll run out of cartilage before I'll run out of mountains.

—Erik Weihenmayer

RH: Thank you for spending some time with us. We are most appreciative. You are an excellent rock and ice climber and an outstanding mountaineer. Indeed, you are one of a handful of people to have reached the high points on the seven continents, the so-called seven summits. This is a stunning achievement and many great mountaineers have died in the attempt, on Everest or Denali, for example. In addition to the normal impediments one must face, including cold, bad weather, sickness, and lack of oxygen, you are placed at a small disadvantage because you cannot see. Some people were skeptical about your ability to climb high. You certainly wished to climb and reach the summits for the same reasons that all of us do: because it is physically, emotionally, and psychologically pleasurable to do so. Chris Morris says that you are "mentally one of the strongest guys you will ever meet." This inner strength is extremely important in climbing but you are also quite strong physically. Yet Jon Krakauer and Ed Viesturs tried to dissuade you from attempting Everest. How did your react to this negativity?

EW: If somebody got hurt on the team, we would go out to get them. I remember thinking that when I came down from the summit ... if someone was hurt, I was definitely ready to go. I think there's a difference when you climb a mountain with people you know you can rely on. Your fates are linked. And because of that you're super careful, too, because you don't want to link with the wrong person. So, it's an honor when somebody links up, with you, because they are saying, basically, I'm connecting my fate with yours. That's very, very powerful. And that is what my team did. So, I have nothing against Ed. I like Ed, and he's a great guy. It did tweak me, I have to say. It tweaked me because there's a comment like, "People will have to be watching his every step; he's not going to be able to do this or that." I mean, technically he was right in many respects, but I almost felt like his perception of a blind guy was me just lying there and people putting my crampons on and doing everything for me. I'm very self-sufficient and I like to believe that I contribute to the team and that I'm not just an absolute liability. ... I'm actually part of a positive part of the equation. At least, I like to believe that. And then obviously when somebody is a big hero of yours and they say something like that about you, it kind of cuts you a little bit. So that's all. Ed's a great guy and he's had great achievements, and [his] cautiousness is a good asset.

Although you describe precisely how you proceed on a dangerous ridge, I think that it is really impossible for us to comprehend what you accomplish. I could only simulate it by closing my eyes and attempting to negotiate a precipice, but I would be too frightened to proceed. It's a pretty amazing thing, walking along a narrow ridge.

Well, I'm just careful, feeling my way; I'm feeling every step. I keep a lot of weight on my back foot, so if it gives way under my front foot, I'm still committed to my back foot, and I have my ice ax biting in with every step. Knock on wood, I just want to be cautious. Every bit of you is concentrating. I'm not using my eyes, I'm just using my sense of feel, and I'm feeling my way across. When I was doing the knife edge on Everest, for instance, I was kind of sidestepping across the left side of the ridge; I was kind of on some rock and snow; I was kicking in with every step, making sure every step was a good one; and at altitude your limiting factor is your oxygen, so I was ... in the same boat as everyone else, although I was expending probably a lot more effort, energy.

Eric Weihenmayer (photograph by Fred Hartemann).

Your rock climbing skills are equally impressive: You led some of the pitches on your ascent of the Nose route on El Capitan.

Yes, I trained all summer for climbing in Yosemite. Yosemite is really a weird place for people who haven't climbed there that much because it's like these vertical cracks; there aren't really great footholds; so everything is sort of slippery and polished; so it's very tenuous. I couldn't practice certain pitches on the Nose because they're too high up. You can't get there just in the afternoon and go practice. They call it—when you climb something for the first time ... you lead it—they call it onsighting. And so for me, my friends called it nonsighting. I led five or six pitches on the Nose and I had to lead it the first time; so I was relying on Hans, who had climbed it 50 times, to tell me vital information: Hey, the crack's going to get wider up there. He was yelling at me throughout the leads. He was giving me a lot of the play-by-play information. I remember leading the second to last pitch—they call it the Harding Roof—and coming up over the roof and belaying the team up; that was pretty cool.

You are also an excellent skier. Did your Elbrus descent go well? What speeds do you reach?

I'm really only a mediocre skier. I trained for a year with my friend Eric Alexander, my ski partner. Most of the time, he skis behind me and he's yelling out directions in a three-part command. So that's like, "Turn-a-left, turn-a-right"; and then sometimes when it's real narrow, he takes my pole and we maneuver together and I can feel through the pole what he's doing and I try to mirror his movements. If he keeps the ski pole stiff, then I can feel him moving left and right. It's sort of like what a blind person gets used to when they tap a cane or feeling through the motion of their guide dog. When we got to the top of Elbrus—you know, we had like 20 pounds of ski gear on our back and my legs were a little rubbery, and so I told Eric, I said, "I don't know if I can do this," and he slapped me in the head and he said, "You're going to do this; we've been training for a year." So, I was like, "Okay." Sometimes you do things because you don't want to let down your team. And so I clipped into my skis and wobbled my way off the summit ridge and skied that mountain. And when I got down through this area called Pastukhov Rocks, it's so wide; there's like two thousand, two and half thousand more feet to camp and Eric said, "You can ski; you can make any turns you want; you cannot hit anything." It had been snowing all day, so there's powder above the boot here. Make any turns you want, as big as you want, you can't hit anything else. I don't see any rocks; there's no trees; there's no cliffs; it's just like a blue or an easy black kind of run. Just go for it. And I just started haulin.' It was really fun. You're making such gradual turns, that, literally, you feel like you're floating in that kind of powder. I don't really know; I wouldn't have any clue how fast I'm skiing. It feels pretty darn fast to me. What I like to do on a mountain is, I like to ski in control; I like to be in control at all times. I'm conservative, so I'm probably not skiing that fast. I'm probably skiing 20 miles an hour or something like that.

In addition to climbing you also guide. Could you tell us about your guiding experience with some blind Tibetan mountaineers?

Well, after Everest, one of the things that happened was that I got this email from ... Sabria Timburke; she's a blind lady who is German, and she runs a school for the blind, a training center for the blind in Lhasa, Tibet. She fought through all sorts of bureaucracy and superstition to get the school going. She started it with a couple of blind kids and now she trains like a hundred kids a year. Kids in Tibet, blind kids, have gone from pariahs to now some of the best—leaders in the whole community. She wrote me this letter; she said sometimes in Tibet, blind kids are seen as having evil spirits inside them; they're blind because they've done something bad in a past life to deserve it. People can be cruel and people sometimes will throw rocks at them and stuff like that. And she said, "Would you ever come over for a visit? We've read your book and the kids are really inspired. At first, they didn't even believe that you'd climbed Everest, and then I convinced them that it was true." So I went over there with my Everest team, about seven members of my Everest team. She picked six kids who she thought were really highly motivated and physical and could do a climb. We trained them and then we came back in the fall and we guided them on a kind of a climbing adventure. We hiked from about 14,000 feet all the way up to base camp at 17,000 feet, base camp of Everest. And then we hiked up to advance base camp at 21,000 feet on the north face of Everest. And then we went over this little mini-crevasse field. It took us several hours to navigate this crazy crevasse field and then stood on the East Rongbuk Glacier, probably at twenty-one and a half thousand feet. And these six kids, they were struggling. They really worked hard, the hardest they ever worked, but all of them made it to advance base camp, which was really cool. Kept the team intact to 21,000 feet and, ultimately, I think that's the highest any team of blind people have ever stood in history, so that was kind of a cool accomplishment. And I was really the coordinator. When I say guide, I organized the trip, I got the sponsorships, I was the liaison, I was the communications person for all the logistics.... I was the team leader.... And that led to more experiences [with] an organization called Global Explorers, a nonprofit that does educational and leadership experiences for high school students. ... They wanted to include blind kids on one of their adventures and they asked me to do that, so I did. We had ten blind kids and ten sighted kids, teenagers. The sighted kids led the blind kids. So for the sighted kids it was a great leadership experience.... We trekked for ten days on [a path], which connects to the Inca Trail and we all wound up in Machu Picchu. ... I think it's really important for people with challenges to experience the outdoors,

Mount Everest as seen from Rongbuk

because it's a very scary, unforgiving place ... but if you can figure out how to be organized and be in control in the outdoors, it gives you a great boost in confidence....

Most of the great mountaineering accounts deal with preparation, climbing, triumphs, and tragedies. Yours is very different: Much of what you present in Touch the Top of the World *relates to the loss of your sight and the ways in which you have coped with this. This different emphasis heightens your mountaineering and climbing discussions.*

Yes, definitely. Going blind, that adversity that I faced, I guess, connects to the mountains in many ways because when you go blind there are certain things you can affect: your approach, your attitude, the skills, your training, your preparation, the kind of people you connect with, but you can't control the fact that you're blind. And in the mountains it's the same way because you can't affect the mountain, the weather, the terrain, but you can affect certain things, the same things: your attitude, your approach, your strategy, your team, your skill, your preparation, your foundation, how conservative you're going to be. You work with the rules of the mountain. And blindness has rules too. I'm not going to get in a car and drive down the road. ... Yet at the same time, those rules are kind of fuzzy. Sometimes you can even push through those rules; you can push through certain barriers. That's where new ground is broken.

It would surprise those who are unfamiliar with the travails of the disabled that it may have been more difficult for you to get a simple job (because of prejudice or fear on the part of the employer) than to reach the summit of Denali or Everest.

It's a really interesting question. It's a great issue too because blind people and disabled people struggle with this all the time. The disabled world's big criticism is, okay, this guy can climb Everest and this guy can climb Denali, and all these mountains, El Cap ... but how does that help me get a job? How does that help me support my family? Is there a translation or is it just glitz? And they have a point. A blind person who, maybe, is a phone operator or something like that—they switch over their software, they update their software, and suddenly that person's voice synthesizer that has always worked with a certain software, now doesn't work anymore. And they can't work anymore because they have no access to the tools that they need. And so, that's a bigger barrier, in a way, than Everest. But obviously a blind mountain climber gets a ton of attention because you're hanging off your fingertips from rock faces. The media love to focus on stuff they perceive as totally out there, when, really, it's the blind people that are working on very technical things—like making the Internet accessible and making books accessible and making software accessible—those are the guys who get no attention and they're doing as important or more important work than a blind guy climbing mountains.

I am familiar with much of the mountaineering literature—from its inception until today. Attempting to reach the summits of the world's high peaks is a serious business and it is unusual to encounter joking. But practical jokes seem to occur with regular frequency in your world, and you're often the butt. For example, Chris did not bother to warn you about the rocks in the melted snow on Aconcagua so that you hurt your teeth. Does this bother you? It bothers me.

I grew up with brothers; my two brothers pounded me into submission. That was a good thing because I learned humility and how to suck it up when you get teased and how to be part of a group and then how to get revenge. And, yes, my team pretty much just became an extension of my brothers. These guys would totally mess with me like anyone would. And I like it because in a way they're not doing it because I'm different; they're doing it because that's their form of how guys sometimes relate to other guys: They tease each other; they do funny jokes to each other. Yes, the rocks might have been on the extreme side but—I'll be in the middle of a snowball fight and I'll be getting pounded in the head with snowballs, but I'm fighting back. And I like it. It makes me part of the team. So, I'm fine with that.

What plans do you have for the future? And do you have anything else to add?

Guiding more. I started a nonprofit called No Barriers. Essentially, about five years ago, I went and climbed Fisher Tower, which is about a five- or six-hundred-foot rock tower in Moab, Utah, with a guy named Mark Wellman, who's a paraplegic. He climbed El Capitan, basically doing pull-ups with his arms up the rock face, and Hugh Herr, who's a double-leg amputee who is a brilliant rock climber and ice climber. He has these prosthetic legs and rubber feet that are made out of the same material climbing shoes are made out of. And so the three of us climbed this rock face together. And we all had our different styles, our different approaches, our different technologies that we implemented to do the unexpected to break through barriers. We started this nonprofit. We call it No Barriers. It's a festival that we run every year and we teach people with challenges the latest technology, the latest approaches, systems to help them shatter their own barriers whatever those may be and live full and active lives. It's basically, we bring a lot of disabled people together along with scientists, researchers, and people making really cool, innovative equipment and technologies, and we bring them all together to brainstorm and see how everyone can improve, how to improve the quality of life: nobarriersusa.org is our website. ... We have four or five hundred people coming together and all sharing ideas and hopefully benefiting from each other. And so that keeps me busy. I'd like to climb Alpamayo when I'm over in Peru this summer guiding those blind kids. I'd like to climb some more in Europe; like, I'd like to do the Grande Jorass or the north face of the Eiger. I'd like to take another crack at the north face of Les Droits. Maybe I'll try something easier this time, like Le Garde. Essentially, I'll run out of cartilage before I'll run out of mountains. I'll never get to everything on my list.

As for your No Barriers organization, it might be possible to get a grant from the National Science Foundation or the National Institutes of Health.

That's really interesting. I never thought of that. That's a really good idea. ... Well, you know, it's neat because a lot of the technologies are like the Hewlett-Packard story: the technology was built in the guy's garage. ... So that's the way a lot of the technology for disabled people is, the same way. There's a guy named Pete Rieke, who wanted to climb mountains as a paraplegic, so in his garage he built this thing; he calls it the snowpod and he cranks this little Mars-Lunar landing thing that he cranks up the mountain. And it has spikes like crampons; it's like a tractor and it goes up the mountain. He's climbed Rainier; he's climbed Shasta; he's climbed Mount Hood.

Thanks for sharing your experiences with us. Your multiple accomplishments in climbing, mountaineering, skiing, skydiving, biking, and running are extraordinary and at times incomprehensible. You are a true inspiration.

Great! Paragliding, too, though.

BIBLIOGRAPHY

"Erik Weihenmayer: Unstoppable Climber." *Outside Online*. <outside.away.com/outside/sports/200112allstars_2.html>.
Farther Than the Eye Can See. Dir. Michael Brown. DVD. [New York]: Outside Television and Outdoor Life Network, 2003.
Greenfeld, Karl Taro. "Blind to Failure." *Time* 18 June 2001. (Cover story.)
Reiman, Mark. "Erik Weihenmayer: Setting His Sights High." *Incredible People Magazine*. <www.incrediblepeople.com/people(1999–11–15).htm>.
Stolz, Paul G., and Erik Weihenmayer. *The Adversity Advantage*. New York: Fireside, 2006.
Weihenmayer, Erik. *Touch the Top of the World*. New York: Plume, 2002.
<www.climbingblind.org>.

Jim Wickwire

(June 8, 1940–)

Mountaineer, lawyer, author

Date of interview: July 7, 2006. *Location:* Seattle, WA. *Interviewer:* Robert Hauptman. *Method:* In person: taped and videotaped. *Videographer:* Frederic Hartemann.

Jim Wickwire is one of the 20th century's foremost mountaineers. He was among the group of four climbers who did the first American ascent of K2. Although he practiced law, he somehow managed to get away and go on innumerable expeditions.

———

RH: Thanks for taking time out of your busy schedule to talk with us. I know that in addition to all of your other pursuits, you are making a film in honor of Marty Hoey. So we are most appreciative that you can spend one or two hours with us.

JW: Well, I don't know about that film. ... I'm not sure whether it's really going anywhere or not. A lot of Marty's friends, those who've climbed with her, are trying to be cooperative.... Any time you make a documentary, it's a big effort finding the money and putting it all together....

In The Last Step, *Rick Ridgeway notes that he has read your journals and you too mention that they are extensive, replete, and cover an extended period of time. It is one thing for Pepys to sit comfortably at a desk and pour out thousands of pages, but you managed to write in frigid tents after extremely harsh and debilitating days. It would not surprise me to learn that you wrote during your K2 bivouac at 28,000 feet! Have you considered publishing the journals themselves?*

I actually thought about that, but there are thousands of pages and only the cognoscenti that are interested in that kind of detail would find that interesting; what I decided instead, and of course this was when I was still a full-time practicing lawyer, was to try to synthesize that writing down to a manageable number of pages. And that's what led to my book being done in 1998.

Someday, someone might go though them and garner useful information.

The problem with them is that it isn't just about climbing; it's about everything in life and some of my professional activities as a lawyer. There's a constant stream of almost daily journals, although as one gets older the energy to maintain that discipline diminishes.... I always believed that the honest thing was to write as these events occurred because if you even let a day or two go by then you're into a reflective mode about the past, and it's shaped by what's happened in the interim....

Along with the joys, we are bound to have some bad experiences, but you had four tragedies that were truly horrific. I shudder when I think of you watching Dusan Jagersky and Al Givler sliding to their deaths, your crevasse experience on Denali with Chris Kerrebrock, Marty Hoey's fall, and the murder of the Goldmark family. I would certainly understand if you prefer not to revisit any of these. But if you care to say anything, we would perhaps learn something that we do not already know.

Well, I'm happy to respond to certain questions. ... I've talked about those incidents in the context of my book and in the context of doing slide lectures. I revisit those subjects frequently. They all happened over a very short period of time, with the exception of the Goldmark tragedy which was in 1985 at Christmas. But these climbing losses, at least those that are discussed in the book, were in a period from 1977 to '82, so it's over a five-year period. There was one more tragedy that you may not be aware of that occurred on Mount Rainier four years ago in September; I was up there with Ed Homer, who was a double amputee, who was trying to become the first double amputee to reach the summit of Everest. And I was taking Ed up Rainier with two other guys. We were going up the standard Disappointment Cleaver. There had been some accidents on that route over the years, because it's the one that probably eighty percent or more of climbers who climb Rainier do.... And it was right before dawn and this one rock came flying down, about the size of a soccer ball. I was leading and it passed within about 15 feet of me. And there were two young guys. And it was their first experience on a mountain. I think one of them was a snowboarder and one of them had walked up Mount Whitney by the trail. And then Ed was fourth on the rope. And, of course, I yelled and the second guy yelled. And the rock struck Ed and killed him instantly. And it's just unbelievable that something like that could happen on Rainier on that route. ... He was a wonderful guy. He was a larger-than-life character and I had been to Everest with him in 2001. ... It was in the post-monsoon. And we were going to go back in 2003 with John Roskelley. And that was the expedition that ultimately led the Roskelleys, father and son, getting to the summit, three years ago. But obviously Ed was not around for that. ... These things happen in the mountains and it's part of the risk of going into the mountains. If we don't face up to those experiences when we have them, to some extent, it's like sticking your head in the sand.

Some mountaineers, Reinhold Messner or Christine Boskoff for example, have been on innumerable lengthy expeditions, but they earn their living from climbing or guiding. You, on the other hand, ventured into the mountains for pleasure, taking time off from your law practice. There are probably very few other people who had full-time jobs who managed to participate in so many lengthy expeditions.

Well, I think I can think of a few offhand, Glen Porzack, who is a lawyer in Colorado and who is president of the American Alpine Club, has climbed three 8,000-meter peaks and I know he has been on other expeditions. My summit companion on K2, Lou Reichardt, who is a neurobiologist at a university in San Francisco, has been on a large number of Alaskan and Himalayan expeditions. So I think there are far fewer that do climbs like the ones I've been on [who were] not professional climbers. I think the line between professional climbers and somebody who has another profession that climbs on a very serious basis—I think that distinction can get blurred. ... But even John Roskelley ... has found another life, first as a county commissioner ... and most recently ... as a kind of hearing examiner. John would certainly be viewed as a hard-core professional climber. But he's doing this other thing as he gets on in life.

When I spoke to Lou Reichardt, I think twice, he downplayed his climbing so dramatically that a person who was not at all familiar with what he had done from various accounts would say, "Oh, well, I guess he's just not a really important climber," but from what I understand, he's truly a phenomenal climber, almost superhuman, like Messner....

Well, he's understating. Lou's an interesting case because he's a brilliant scientist, and his great forte is that he's very strong and he has tremendous willpower. I think he would say that he is not a technical rock climber, but he's certainly very good on a big mountain that has both mixed rock, snow, and ice....

I enjoy climbing but I am not attracted to it because of the inherent risks. Indeed, I spend much of my time worrying! You are unusual because you admit that you are addicted to danger.

Well, that's an interesting subject. When I wrote my book, the only thing I wanted from the publisher was the right to select the title. Other than that you get the standard contract that they make you sign. And we really struggled long and hard to find a title. And we finally came up with *Addicted to Danger*. And once I picked that title, for the reasons stated in the book, that I felt there was an addictive aspect to my climbing, and I think to other climbers as well, but I wasn't planning to speak for them, I kind of wanted to change it, ... to step back away from it. But we went ahead. What I was concerned about was that it almost was a cliché. But a couple of years after my book came out, one of the climbers that I admire enormously, Reinhold Messner, wrote an essay in a book called *Voices from the Summit* that the National Geographic had published. And his essay, which was the last essay in that volume, is entirely about the addictive aspects of climbing, and in particular, he writes with great eloquence on the subject of danger in the mountains, and he writes about it much better than I did, because I wasn't trying to philosophize about it and to sort of state general principles of risk and addiction to danger in the mountains. But Messner wrote this essay, and I recommend it to you if you haven't read it, because I think it's one of the best things he's written.

On Rainier's Willis Wall you ran into a major storm and were forced to bivouac; it was so severe that you thought you might die. You even lost the will to go on. This might amaze some people who mistakenly believe that the higher peaks are more challenging and dangerous. What they probably do not know is that more people have died on New Hampshire's Mount. Washington than on any other American mountain....

That's right. I think the point that you made about Mount Washington is interesting because so many more people go up on Mount Washington, I would guess. I don't know what the statistics are. I've been up there once; I was trying to do Pinnacle Gulley in April of 1968, and had kind of an epic. We got about two-thirds of the way up. It was late in the season. April is pretty late for Pinnacle Gulley, so the ice was in terrible shape and we had to rappel off and come down in the dark to get back to Pinkham Notch. But the way the weather can turn suddenly on Mount Washington can really catch people unaware. And that's why I think there have been some really bad statistics over the years. But I think it's all relative. Reinhold Messner can climb Everest solo from the north side, and for him, yes, he's on the edge. Yes, he's in a dangerous situation. But he's always in control. Take a weekend climber who goes up Mount Rainier and tries to go up Disappointment Cleaver; that person can have the same experience that Messner had relative to his or her experience and abilities, and can get the same return out of it that Messner did, even though on an objective scale Messner's achievement is leagues beyond this weekend climber's ascent of Rainier. But one of the things Messner talks about is accountability. He kind of goes off on the whole subject of guided climbing, particularly on Everest, and how people try to buy this experience, and they buy it on the basis that this guide is going to guarantee their safety. Now the guide tells them, I can't guarantee your safety. The client is thinking, well, if I climb up there with this experienced guide, my chances of coming back down are very good. And I completely agree with Messner's view that this is getting away from the accountability that a climber should have when he or she goes into the mountains. Whether it's on Rainer, Mount Washington, K2, Everest, McKinley, or whatever it is, you get that same return relative to your capabilities, your experience.

I guess that we expect people to have individual responsibility, but when some-

thing happens, some people simply won't help; and that just occurred on Everest with those two climbers who were bypassed, and that's very sad.

And that's kind of another element of it, of the ethic that's been in climbing from the very beginning: When someone's in trouble, you go to their aid. Being up high on Everest, whether you're a guide or a client, just being able to get up and down yourself is so strenuous and you're so much on the edge that people conclude, well, I can't help that person. That person's going to die. I can't carry the person down the mountain. ... Even a guide, even an Anatoli Boukreev, could not carry somebody down the mountain.... He did some incredible things. At the time, I was the chairman of the American Alpine Club's David Sowles Memorial Award Committee, which makes awards to climbers who undertake rescues at their peril. We looked at that situation long and hard and finally concluded that Boukreev deserved the award and we made it.

You sometimes prefer to throw caution to the wind and go for it, when others might hold back. You have been lucky and survived; others have not. That is why I am particularly impressed with Ed Viesturs's attitude; he prefers to reclimb Annapurna—over and over again—rather than risk his life. He is an unusual specimen: the cautious mountaineer.

I regard myself as a cautious mountaineer. Some people would look at what I've done over the years and say, oh, he's bold, but I've always felt that I

Mount Rainier, a difficult climb, is one of the most important peaks in the contiguous United States. This Cascade mountain is 14,411 feet high, the third highest peak in the Lower 48.

was on the cautious side and I think it's evidenced by [the fact] that I've got way more failures to reach the summit of a mountain than getting to the top. I've always felt you have to know when to turn back, and Viesturs is the latest, great example for that, and Ed was just brilliant; I think it helped that he had a young family and so he was feeling the responsibility to those kids. And of course I had a young family when I was going to K2 in the '70s. I think part of that is an age thing; when you're younger, you're willing to risk it more than you are [when older]. ... But that's all relative, because as Messner says, he's looking forward to not going to the high mountains anymore but he wants to go off and explore lower mountains; he wants to cross the polar ice caps and things like that. And that's what I find appealing. Kind of gets you back to the approach that Eric Shipton took in the '30s and '40s and even into the '50s when he was doing his explorations in Patagonia, Tierra del Fuego. I mean that's what really appeals to me now, those kind of trips. I'm always thinking about somewhere to go but I'm really not interested in going back to Everest. I was there in 2003 with the two Roskelleys and Dick Bass. I got up to the North Col once. I think I could have gone higher but I just didn't want to go hang it out, to go up to 26, 27 and higher. And part of the problem was the sheer numbers of expeditions and climbers that were there. When we would

go from one camp to the next, it was like the Oklahoma land rush because you were rushing to stake out your tent space on the North Col. We got up there and staked out this area. And a large Swiss expedition came along a day later and ended up having half the expedition on one side of our tents and half ... on the other. I mean, I go to the mountains to get away from the hustle and bustle and what goes on in everyday life. And to go find hordes of people on Everest, whether it's on the South Col route or the north side, is not very appealing.

Jim Wickwire (photograph by Fred Hartemann).

Mountaineers like to reach the summit and originally that was your primary motivation, but over the years, you realized that there are many other reasons for climbing.

The expeditions that I have become the fondest about are those where I didn't succeed at getting to the top of the mountain. But it was the experience I had. One of those would be when John Roskelley and I tried to climb Everest, just the two of us, in 1993. We had two Sherpas that came along, but they were going to do cooking no higher than advanced base camp. Up on the mountain, it was just the two of us. And again we got no higher than the North Col. We had bad weather. Ed Viesturs was there trying to solo it at the same time, but he had somewhat the same experience. But coming away from that expedition and having it just been the two of us, and to be able to be with another person for a couple of months in a tent and never have an argument. It's hard to do that in a marriage. But in a marriage, you are at least off on a job. You are not with your wife all day. But on an expedition, when it's the two of you on Everest, you are with that person constantly for a couple of months. And John is a far better climber than I am, and I'm nine years older. But for some reason on the eight or nine expeditions that we were on together, we found a way to really make it work from a compatibility, from a working together standpoint. That's the good part. That's what comes out of those experiences, not just standing on the top of some mountain. And another one was the trip we had down to Tierra del Fuego in 1995, again with John, but we had with us two really world-class, outstanding climbers, Steven Venables and Tim MacCartney-Snape, [an] Australian, who had soloed Everest from the Bay of Bengal to the summit, as one of his Everest climbs. The other was the brilliant new route on the North Face of Everest in 1984, when we were there. And then the four of us, along with Charlie Porter, who was a legendary California rock climber who has been living in southern Chile for almost 20 years now, and has a sailboat. That expedition, sailing to the mountain, making the second ascent of the west peak of Sarmiento by a new route, and again just the experience we had together, this small team, close-knit, no personality clashes, no problems, [was] quite unlike some of those I've experienced on the large expeditions....

To get along with somebody day after day in those tight circumstances is really very commendable.

Well, one of the things is you have to respect the person you're with. If you really respect that person, they do not have to be necessarily a close personal friend. That goes a long way to overcoming those personal grievances that arise when you can't stand somebody, the way they eat or the way they brush their teeth.... We had problems on K2 in 1975. We thought we had a small, compatible expedition.... We had a very bad experience on that expedition. But the passage of time—people get past those things and you find yourself going back out in the mountains again with those people because they're really good guys and friendships ought to survive [the] extreme experience you have on one expedition.

Four members of the 1978 K2 expedition went for the summit: John Roskelley, Lou Reichardt, Rick Ridgeway, and you. For one reason or another, most of you decided to abjure supplemental oxygen. You succeeded. Do you think that it would have been an easier climb had you all used it?

No. In fact, I would say we were planning not to use much oxygen. We had agreed we were going to use one bottle from the high camp and part of that had to do with the fact that Jim Whittaker wanted us to use oxygen because he felt the chances for reaching the summit would be better if we did. I'd say of the four, the only person that I really believed was not going to use it was Roskelley. Lou Reichardt was with me. He started to use it and he had his mask on for quite a while, but he wasn't getting the benefit because he had a puncture in the bladder, so he finally took it off and left it behind. And Ridgeway, I think in his own book, describes trying to get this mask on his face and it's not fitting right and Roskelley has already taken off to head up the slope and he's figuring, well, if I'm going to get to the top of this mountain, I'd better get out of here and try to keep up with Roskelley. And then Rick used

Jim Wickwire in front of the Monte Burney northeast face (photograph by Jim Wickwire).

some on the way down because he had some really difficult breathing issues coming down the mountain. And I ended up getting the bottle I had—somehow it ended up being two-thirds full—so I was cut back. When I started using it I was using it at about a liter a minute and the maximum was, a couple of times I went up to two liters a minute. ... The great benefit of the oxygen for me was two things: One, it does keep you a little warmer.... And then the second thing was my experience up on the summit was I was clear-headed. I was able to enjoy it. I stayed up there too long and got into what happened on the way down....

You had a number of little accidents (fires, spilled water on equipment, loss of water bottle, lack of headlamp) each of which had a sometimes disastrous effect. I asked Rick Ridgeway this same question: Why is it that competent people often make these foolish blunders (and not necessarily because their cognitive abilities are affected by altitude), which at sea level would usually matter very little, but high in the Karakorum can easily result in tragedy?

I think to err is human, but I do think that when one is climbing on a mountain like K2 and you're up high, and you're not on oxygen, and you're dehydrated, you do make mistakes, and those mistakes can have huge consequences up there, and particularly when there's a series of them that accumulate, and for me, dropping that water bottle obviously led to much more dehydration. I think I had one sip from Lou's bottle on the way up and his was probably partially frozen, so I don't know how much benefit he really got. And then in the night, tipping over the pot and spilling water all over [your] down parka and down pants, you end up leaving for the summit with less in the way of protection than you'd want. So again, one does make mistakes. It's a constant struggle to keep those to a minimum and to keep your head about you.

Even though it occurs all of the time (even to me), I continue to be amazed that climbing partners sometimes go their separate ways even in severe conditions, where staying together would be most beneficial. You and Lou Reichardt split up on the summit of K2: He descended immediately, but you stayed for an additional 45 minutes. One of the most gripping scenarios I have ever read transpired as your fellow expedition members peered at the summit through a telescope wondering why you did not begin your descent. I imagine that they thought you were finished. When you finally did appear, they cheered and so did I.

It's always difficult to put oneself in the other person's shoes, even though you could read that that was their experience, but all I know was what I experienced and at the time I was not—didn't feel threatened at all. ... Getting to the top of that mountain was the fulfillment of a dream I had had for many, many years. ... Coming off the summit, I tried to be cautious because there is a great instinct for self-preservation and not to make a mistake, and as I came down, I knew I didn't have a headlamp. I thought the prudent thing to do was to find a spot to spend the night and there's only one place between the summit and virtually down almost to where we camped, where you could really stop. There was a place where it sort of leveled off for just a few feet and then went down again; and you're right alongside this tremendous drop down the south face. And so I thought, this is the place to do it; I had a bivouac sack; I had a stove; I had a little bit of oxygen left. And I thought, this is the smart thing to do. And throughout the night, one knows the night is going to end. I had nights like that on Rainier as a kid, as a young climber, where we got caught up there in a storm and you could be just absolutely miserable, but you knew that if you just waited and persevered that morning would come. ... I was so cold but I never went into hypothermia, interestingly, because if I had, I probably wouldn't be sitting here. I was constantly moving trying to stay warm in the shivering. The movement tends to keep you awake and alert. ... [The night] finally ended. It was hard to get going in the morning, as I've written, because I think by that time I had become somewhat hypoxic, and getting the motivation to get moving, that was difficult.

That you succeeded was a great triumph: you were the first Americans to reach the summit of K2, but you especially paid a price. You were forced to bivouac just below 28,000 feet (which very few people have ever survived) and eventually this led to some major surgery.

Well, I had some medical problems: frostbite was kind of minor; the real threat though was the combination of pneumonia and pulmonary embolus in both lungs, which I didn't feel. I had no pain at the time. I really didn't feel medically jeopardized up there at all. It was only when I started coming down, as we were working our way down the mountain, that I had this sort of odd feeling like someone was pushing in here; it was in my throat; it was on the left side, and I was thinking, that's really odd and it became more and more pronounced as I came down. The fact is, Rick was the one that was having the problems coming down the mountain. And when Rob Schaller, our doctor, came out from camp one ... I said, "Rob, you better get back up there and check Rick out because I think he needs you." So I just came in and sat down and had a cup of tea. I was there probably 45 minutes or so and now he was sort of standing there and I said, "Why don't you take a look at me?" And that's when he took me into the tent, pulled out his stethoscope, and then said, "Well, you've got pneumonia and pleurisy." I do? It was a total revelation to me. And then, of course, things went downhill a little bit after that, and the surgery later was really to remove this fluid that was becoming fibrous scar tissue. I really had to do that if I wanted to have even a normal life, let alone go back to high altitude again.

On your way down, the next morning, you soon encountered Rick and John. Had you not insisted that you were well enough to get down alone, they would have been compelled to assist you and thus forgo their summit attempt so close to completion. That was extremely considerate of you because you really were in bad shape, staggering from the lack of oxygen and freezing cold. Did you consider this?

It's a much more subtle thing than how you described it. I'm coming down under my own power. From my perspective, I'm under control and I'm making my way down the mountain and I'm convinced I'm going to get down to camp. There's no doubt in my mind. When Rick and John are coming up and we meet right on the most technical section, which is that traverse beneath the ice cliff; so you've got kind of a ramp and you've got the ice cliff here and this tremendous vertical drop there, so it's not a place to make a mistake. Their description of me is that I look—John said, "Jesus, I'm going to have to take you to ice climbing school," because he thought I was being—sort of walking like a robot almost. But it was joke; it wasn't a serious comment. And I guess I intuitively wanted to reassure them that I was fine because they were obviously coming up to climb the mountain. Now they were coming on what they described as a potential body search. They didn't expect me to get through the night. Who knows what would have happened in that event? When I encountered them, I assured them that I was fine, that I could go down under my own power, and have a great climb, you guys! Go for the top. See you down below. And that's when John kind of patted my head when I went by, which was a wonderful thing, because it was this human touch after hours of being alone up there....

Was it not devastating, both physically and psychologically, to have another fire, not far below the summit at camp six, which forced all four of you into a tiny tent?

Lou and I are in the tent and we're trying to cook and all of a sudden there's this commotion. We look out and we see these flames and [hear] yelling.... This tells you something about our state at the time because pretty soon they're standing outside: Are you guys okay? Yes, we're okay. And then they're standing outside our tent and we're failing to register the notion that they want inside our tent. It was because their tent was destroyed. It took us a while to realize that and to realize their plight. So once we did there was no debate; in they came. And, of course, this was one of those two-person omnipotent tents, which are like a little tunnel. Two people have a tough time getting inside and here are four of us. So it was understood that we would suffer. For me it was great: I had warm bodies all around the whole night. It was heavenly for me, whereas for Ridgeway, he was having great difficulty breathing, getting enough air in his lungs, and he would constantly have to stick his head outside to get air. Inside for him was claustrophobic....

Last summer, Fred and I climbed Baker; it took 18 hours. How did you manage to do this just a few months after lung surgery?

Oh, it wasn't that quickly. The surgery was in October of '78 and it wasn't until the following August; so that's 11 months. Basically, the recovery from the surgery was a slow process and I just started short runs and gradually trying to build up some endurance. And I was actually up in Alaska in June, I think it was, and I hiked up this minor hill in the Brooks Range and that was the first really good exercise I had in the mountains. So it was not that significant to go up Baker [in two days]....

You climbed Aconcagua with Frank Wells and Dick Bass (the seven summiteers) and Marty Hoey.

It was a wonderful expedition and it was sort of a warm-up for Everest. Frank and Dick were going to come with us to Everest in '82, and they really wanted to get a little expedition experience ahead of that, although Dick had just climbed McKinley the previous summer with Marty. It was one of those expeditions that went off like clockwork, except, as it turned out, Frank and Chuck Goldmark did not make the summit for different reasons. But that didn't matter. Marty and George Dunn went off on their own. It was one of the great days I've had. It was almost effortless to go to the top of Aconcagua, which I was really happy about because I was worried: Had the surgery really affected my ability to climb at altitude? and that was one of the questions I had getting ready to go on that Everest expedition.

Do you still regret not making the summit of Everest after three attempts?

How about five! One of the five, the one I went as leader with Ed Homer in 2001, I wasn't going with the idea of trying to summit, but this last time in 2003, when I went with the Roskelleys and Dick Bass, I was going with that in mind. So, do I have regrets? Not really. And the interesting thing is that I have periodic dreams about climbing Everest, and I get to the top and I usually do it without oxygen, and Everest can be like a hotel up there; it can be a real mountain. The dreams change. But when I wake up from those dreams, it's like a good feeling. Well, I don't have to do that. If I can do it in my dreams.... And Doug Scott, who I know—he's a friend; he said he had the same dreams about K2. ... Maybe we mingle our dreams and reality together in a way that we make life work for us.

Doug Scott is one of the two great escape stories from the mountains: Doug Scott on the Ogre with broken legs and the amazing story of Joe Simpson coming off Siula Grande. Touching the Void *is a stunning book and movie.*

I couldn't bring myself to read it for a long time. ... I had it in my library; I pulled it out and I read it and I just found it extraordinary. He's a great writer. ... Yates had to go through his own sort of purgatory, I guess, with the notion that he was the guy who cut the rope, but it was absolutely essential. There was no way they could have extricated themselves, either of them, from that situation.

Siula Grande is a Peruvian peak famous for being the place where Joe Simpson rescued himself, as recounted in *Touching the Void*.

Environmental pollution exacerbated by mountaineers is out of control. Do you have any thoughts on rubbish removal?

Well, I think it's a constant problem and there are periodic attempts to deal with it. In fact, [on] one of our expeditions, one of the Everest trips as well as our Menlungste expedition, we took all of our garbage out to Kathmandu. And so it went into a landfill in Kathmandu. It's more the esthetics of it. How much of that is actually doing damage, how much is toxic, I don't know. I think the impact of expeditions on the mountain environment in that part of the world, in terms of how it changes—it creates great opportunity for the Sherpa people on the one hand, but on the other they get into a kind of cash economy that's somewhat cyclical and uncertain. I think some of the impacts on the local, indigenous people are probably more serious than the environmental aspects. I don't want to understate them; I think climbers have a responsibility to clean up after themselves and there are certain countries that have less adhesion to that ethic.

You tried to pull away from climbing a number of times, but were always lured back. Have you finally broken free or do you still do serious climbs?

Well, how to define serious climbs? I am not going to Everest again. I have no desire to go, and any kind of really serious technical climb, I think, is beyond me. There are mountains that I would've loved to have climbed in my life, that I might have been able to have done 20 or 30 years ago, [but] they are out of my league today. On the other hand, I am really still intrigued about going into the mountains and mainly the kind of climbing that Eric Shipton did. That really appeals to me. There's still some exploratory climbing to be done and still places in the world that have not seen the footprints of climbers. There are places in Tibet; there are certainly places down in southern Chile—Tierra del Fuego. And curiously, going to places where the weather is terrible is appealing because it means that nobody else wants to go or very few people want to go there, so the chances of bumping into some other expedition or some other group of people are less in that part of the world than they would be if you went into any area in the United States. ... Well, at times I think, "Why not get past this? Why not in the rest of my life do some other things beside climb mountains?" And I get almost to the end of that internal rumination and then I say, "But I am who I am, I know what I know." I'm comfortable doing what I do, recognizing that I can't do the same thing at age 66 that I did at age 36, deciding that it can still be done on a basis that is not going to unduly shorten one's life. ... I think the idea is to continue to have experiences that are both challenging and satisfying. And we find ways to do that and it doesn't have to be on a mountain....

Other than your Addicted to Danger, *I can think of no other climber's memoir in which family plays such an important role. Indeed, it appears that you sometimes*

John Shipton, Jim Wickwire, and Eiho Otani at advance base camp on Monte Burney (photograph by Jim Wickwire).

saved your life by thinking carefully about your family, which inspired you during dangerous moments in the mountains.

And that's why I related so well to what Beck Weathers's experience was on Everest in '96. I can't think of any person (I'm sure there may be others out there)—how far gone he was. There was just an ember in there of life that was still flickering and it was that pull of his family that pulled him back out of the depths of wherever he was. For me, it would be anathema not to make that effort to return to the people you love. It was a great pull to get me out of some pretty bad situations. That's what love's all about, I guess.

Do you have anything else that you would like to add?

I'm delighted to participate in your project and talk about mountains and climbing....

Thanks so much for your time and comments.

I appreciate you coming. Good luck on the remainder of the project.

BIBLIOGRAPHY

Triumph and Tragedy: The Mountain Zone Interviews Jim Wickwire. <http://classic.mountainzone.com/climbing/misc/wickwire>.

Wickwire, Jim, and Dorothy Bullitt. *Addicted to Danger: A Memoir.* New York: Pocket Books, 1998.

Sharon Wood

(May 18, 1957–)
Mountaineer, guide, inspirational speaker

Date of interview: November 6, 2009. *Location:* South Burlington, VT, and Canmore, Alberta, Canada. *Interviewer:* Robert Hauptman. *Method:* Electronic mail.

Sharon Wood, "one of Canada's elite mountaineers," has summited Logan, McKinley via the difficult Cassin Ridge, Aconcagua, Huascaran Sur via a new route, despite getting hit by a rock that broke her shoulder, and countless other peaks around the world. In 1986, she became the first North American woman to climb Everest (via a new route and unassisted by Sherpas).

RH: You chose climbing and mountaineering when you were only 17 years old. Did these pursuits seem to be a real calling for you? Did you think that you could earn a living in the mountains?

SW: Yes, absolutely, climbing called to me like nothing else in my life. However, climbing was not nearly as accessible a sport as it is now. The only exposure I'd had to the mountains was the hiking and skiing I did with my dad and a Walt Disney movie about a Swiss boy, [a] goat herder who pulled off a big dangerous climb when no one thought he could. Before I even knew there was such thing as a mountain guide I wanted to make a life in the mountains—so much so that I left home when I was fifteen years old for the Canadian Rockies.

How did your experience with Outward Bound influence the course that you followed?

Initially, my Outward Bound course was a disappointment because I thought I was going to learn how to climb. Instead it was all about team dynamics and I wasn't much of a team player then—at seventeen years old it was all about me. What I did gain was some exposure to the group of Outward Bound instructors and I realized I really wanted to belong to that tribe. Laurie Skreslet was one of them and he became my lifelong friend and mentor. Following the course, despite my very unfavorable "student report," I had the audacity to ask the director for a job as an instructor. He told me something like, "All of our instructors have international expedition experience. Come back when you've got some." His reply motivated me to go out and get enough miles that by the next time I applied they would welcome me back, which they did ten years later.

You were the first woman to become both an ACMG [Association of Canadian Mountain Guides] assistant Alpine Guide and subsequently an ACMG Alpine Guide. What type of guiding do you do?

My favorite kind of guiding is multi-pitch rock, Alpine climbing, and mountaineering. My approach to guiding has really evolved from making money and wanting to bag more experience for my own résumé, to taking people places they've only dreamed of and helping them accomplish things they couldn't yet imagine. Those days end up being a monumental reference point for them. That's way more rewarding.

How old were you when you did Canada's Mount Robson? This is a difficult, time-consuming, and dangerous climb. Did you already have the necessary skills?

I was eighteen years old, and no, I did not have enough experience to climb Mount Robson. I have greatly benefited from the tutelage of friends and mentors throughout my career. In the case of Robson and early days, Chris Miller was a pivotal influence. As well, my desire often eclipsed my hesitation to take on climbs I wasn't sure I could do yet. I climbed a lot with people of an equal or lesser ability. I think that trial-by-fire approach really instilled self-reliance and confidence that in turn prepared me for the rigors of the ACMG guide's exams and set me up for a successful career.

Maria Coffey, in Where the Mountain Casts Its Shadow, *relates your experience in South America, where you were trekking alone, came across some mountains and felt the need to climb. How did these dangerous solos affect your future?*

It was less than a year before I went to Everest when I did those "dangerous solos." I was going through a period of doubt as to whether I was up to being a climber on the Everest Light team. Pulling off those solo climbs confirmed I was both worthy and incredibly passionate about my sport. That was very important for me alone to know. The outward benefit of anyone knowing was inconsequential.

Your 1977 Mount Logan expedition consisted only of women. Have you found that climbing exclusively with women (or men) changes the dynamic? Some female mountaineers have complained of gender discrimination. Has this ever been a problem for you?

I think I was so bloody-minded about climbing and getting after it that I was blind to any gender discrimination at the time. The only thing the women on the Logan team had in common was we weren't invited on the men's expeditions. The problem wasn't that apparent to me yet because I was just getting started. What we shared was not enough to go by to make a strong team. Although I'm grateful to them for giving me the opportunity to go on a high altitude climb the first time, I would not join another all-female team. I gained enough altitude experience and confidence, it seemed, to embolden me to think I could launch off and do my own thing. It also taught me that compatibility with my partner was more important to me than what I climbed. Mixed teams work best for me. If anything, I think being a woman gave me a learning advantage because men assumed I didn't know anything and were more apt to show and tell than they would with another man. It may seem that my answers are riddled with contradictions, but it is because it's not that simple. Here's one: I did experience discrimination in regard to getting on to the Everest Light team. A few members were concerned I might start something with one of the men that would mar the team dynamics. However, more than resenting that, I became more determined to prove myself, become "androgynous" and dispel any concern.

What was it like climbing Makalu and Aconcagua with the legendary Carlos Buhler?

Slow and steady. Carlos taught me it was possible to mitigate most risks with good strategy and get up nearly anything with time and patience. He gave me my first opportunity to be on a Himalayan expedition when we went to Makalu. Being with Carlos was a very conflicted and wonderful period of my life—we drove each other crazy at times. We were a couple for a very intense period of my climbing career. Carlos was and still is a very intense, committed, and talented climber.

High in the mountains, Joe Simpson broke his leg and Doug Scott broke both legs; their epic escapes are incredible stories. On Huascaran Sur, a rock hit you and broke your shoulder. How were you able to continue for eight days?

Context enabled me to continue for eight days. That season in Peru, Carlos and I had experienced a series of failures due to poor conditions. When I was hit with a rock I didn't realize I had fractured my shoulder. I feared the consequences of turning us around one more time over what would happen if I continued on. I also thought if I could keep going on Huascaran in that condition I could climb anything—I still had a need to prove myself to myself. That time was a very driven stage of my career.

You have also done both rock and ice routes, the Nose on El Capitan for example. How does technical climbing affect your mountaineering?

I would say my interest was in Alpine climbing rather than mountaineering. In my mind the primary objective in mountaineering is to bag the summit by the route of least resistance. Alpine climbing is more about how you climb the mountain, the objective is to climb it by a harder route which involves more complex problem solving, commitment, technical ability and experience. With that said, my ice climbing and rock climbing experience was very valuable in terms of my success.

What was the Cassin Ridge on McKinley like? How do you camp on this long, steep ridge? On the other side, along the West Buttress, there was undoubtedly a parade of people. Did you meet anyone on the Cassin?

I climbed the Cassin Ridge with a good friend who was as new to high altitude Alpine climbing as I was. We felt like babes in the woods and were very intimidated by both the commitment of climbing it Alpine style where it's up and over as the only way off after a certain point and the technical difficulty. There were several parties who had permits to climb it but we only saw two, one team of two who blew by us on around day two. We'd heard a few parties had been turned around by the "black ice" in the Japanese Couloir. For us, it was just like back home, easy grade three water ice with a little rocky bit.

When you did Everest, you were aware that another climber was attempting to become the first North American woman to reach the summit. Was this Stacy Allison, who became the first American woman to achieve this goal?

No. It was Annie Whitehouse.

Your Everest climb went smoothly, I think, but the descent was very problematic. What happened? How did you get separated from your partner? And how did you survive?

We both nearly died that night. I don't know how to talk about it, but I will if I write a book.

When you finally reached your tent and tried to use your stove, the cylinder blew up. How extensive was the fire? Did anyone get hurt?

No, just a few superficial burns and a hole in the roof of our tent. We lost a lot of stuff, hat, gloves, stove, pots, no food or water left.

Barbara Washburn was prouder of her work with disabled children than of her mountaineering feats. What led you to found a private school? Are you still involved with it?

The school was my best accomplishment. Far more rewarding.

Have your children followed in your footsteps? Do they climb?
Nope, thank god. They ski.

Thank you so much for taking the time to talk with us.
You're welcome.

Awards

The inaugural Tenzing Norgay Award as "Professional Mountaineer of the Year" from the American Alpine Club and the Explorers' Club of New York, 1986
Honorary doctorate of laws from the University of Calgary, 1987
Meritorious Service Medal from the Governor General of Canada, 1998

Bibliography

Martel, Lynn. *Home Is Where the Mountains Are: The Remarkable Life of Sharon Wood.* Canmore, Alberta: The Alpine Club of Canada, 2004.
<www.sharonwood.net/climbing.php>.

PART II.
HISTORIANS

Every mountaineer who ever recorded a climb in a brief report, account, article, memoir, book-length overview, or film is acting as a historian, preserving the events of the past for those who, for the most part, did not participate in the delineated occurrences. Most of these reminiscences, even if they deal primarily with an accident, derive from personal experience and are less objective than the work of a professional historian. But even those whose life's work centers on history (rather than physics, biology, medicine, law, construction, or guiding) deal with the events in very different ways.

Elizabeth Hawley did study history and historical methodology, but even according to her own interpretation, she is merely a chronicler. She interviews climbers and records the results in files. She attempts to get at the truth, but she avoids interpretation, judgment, and synthesis. All of her information, data, and statistics are now codified in a database, but it is up to researchers and scholars to draw useful information or specific and general conclusions from them.

Maurice Isserman is a professional historian, a college professor, with an interest in social events. He is also a climber and so it is natural that he decided to write an overview of Himalayan mountaineering. He did this by consulting papers and manuscripts, individual periodical and monographic accounts as well as previous full-length histories supplemented by interviews. His 2008 *Fallen Giants* (with Stewart Weaver) is a massive, comprehensive, and detailed overview from the beginnings of climbing up to 1996. It is, for the most part, a noninterpretive, nonjudgmental, objective history of the many expeditions that have climbed in the Himalaya.

Finally, Audrey Salkeld offers a slightly different perspective. She too is a historian and like Isserman she writes about the experiences of others; she can thus be more objective. Unlike Hawley, whose files cover mountains or specific expeditions or Isserman, who presents the big picture, Salkeld often homes in on specific issues—the discovery of Mallory's body, for example.

Additionally, Salkeld is also a translator responsible for bringing many of Reinhold Messner's works to an English-speaking audience.

Both Hawley in Nepal and Salkeld in Great Britain have extensive private archives, and both Isserman and Salkeld are intimately connected to their subjects, since they both also climb.

Elizabeth Hawley

(November 9, 1923–)
Chronicler, historian

Date of interview: December 26, 2009. *Location:* South Burlington, VT, and Kathmandu, Nepal. *Interviewer:* Robert Hauptman. *Method:* Electronic mail.

Elizabeth Hawley is an American expatriate who has lived in Kathmandu for 50 years. She is the unofficial recorder and historian of all Himalayan mountaineering expeditions and climbs except those of some of the lower mountains termed "trekking peaks." The vast information and data that she has gathered are invaluable.

"No one has a wider knowledge of Himalayan mountaineering."
—Sir Edmund Hillary

RH: Thank you so much for taking the time to talk with us. We are well aware of how busy you are, especially during the climbing season. How did you come to live in Kathmandu and to take an interest in recording the details of Himalayan climbing expeditions?

EH: I visited Nepal in early 1959, when Nepal was in an interesting stage of just having joined the rest of the world after having spent many decades in almost total isolation. I had a BA with honors (one of the courses I took was in historiography) and an MA in history from the University of Michigan, and this development fascinated me. I returned to the States to earn some more money, and came back to Kathmandu in the fall of 1960. My work in the U.S. had been for *Fortune* magazine as an editorial researcher, and not very long after I arrived in Kathmandu, Reuters news agency asked me to be their part-time correspondent. In the 1960s and onwards for quite a while, mountaineering accomplishments in the Himalaya were big news, so I started meeting expeditions, and have been doing so ever since. (There now are so many teams that I have two assistants helping me to meet them all.)

Have you done any trekking or climbing?

I did some trekking in the hills north of Kathmandu and in the Everest region years ago.

Can you explain the difference between a historian and the chronicler you claim to be?

A chronicler tries to be impartial. An historian evaluates people and events. Thus, I seldom evaluate expeditions. I don't authenticate expeditions, but I try to learn the truth. Any authentication is done by the Nepalese tourism ministry or by the China Tibet Mountaineering Association in Lhasa.

You document [and evaluate] the details of each expedition. How do you accomplish this?

My assistants and I take detailed notes as we interview teams, whom we meet twice: on their arrival in Kathmandu and their return from their climb. Then the notes we have taken come to me and are entered in my computer and eventually Richard Salisbury, who devised my database, receives the information.

You contact expedition leaders as soon as they arrive at their hotels both before and after the climb. Do they all cooperate? Has anyone ever refused to speak with you?

A very few leaders have refused to see us; one thought his unsuccessful climb wasn't worth talking about; another has had periods of talking and not talking over the years; another has been unhappy about my recording his statement to me that he wasn't sure that he'd gotten to his summit, that perhaps he had stopped 50–100 meters below it.

Have you ever had an altercation with a climber?

I don't remember any altercation with a leader, but I did walk out of a meeting on his arrival in Nepal when he was being unpleasantly rude about a previous expedition he had been on; when he returned to Kathmandu, he apologized, having realized that his unhappiness was not my fault.

Do expeditions still keep in touch with you as the climbs progress (via runner or phone)?

Only very occasionally do I now receive reports from expeditions while they are still climbing.

About how many expeditions have you recorded and analyzed?

I have no idea how many expeditions I/we have recorded. Obviously thousands, perhaps tens of thousands.

Do any one or two stand out for any reason?

A lot of climbs stand out since I started meeting teams—not just one or two.

Among the many hundreds of well-known climbers you have worked with, do you have a favorite or two?

I wouldn't call them favorites, but there certainly are some mountaineers whom I am glad to be seeing again, and some of whose deaths in the mountains make me very sad.

You once allowed Carlos Buhler to carry away your Annapurna file in order to copy it. Have you done this often? It seems like a very dangerous thing to do, since it could have gotten lost or destroyed.

I don't remember letting Carlos Buhler borrow my file. I agree it is a rather risky thing to do.

Why did the ministry of tourism ban you in 1974 from reporting on expeditions?

The tourism ministry banned me from reporting on climbing because of a scoop I'd had that angered some Nepalese reporters for other international wire services, and they prevailed on the ministry to take such action.

Have you had an opportunity to look at Fallen Giants, *Isserman and Weaver's massive and exhaustive history of Himalayan mountaineering? It is, for the most part, nonjudgmental, recording the events as they occurred, and in complete detail. One of the things that they do that other authors of a comprehensive history might have elided is to name not only Western members of expeditions, but also to enumerate the names of each Sherpa accompanying the climbers. Do you think that the Sherpa community has gotten adequate recognition for its role in the history of Himalayan mountaineering?*

No, I do not know about *Fallen Giants*. Our database reports on climbs, gives the names, and, in recent years, biographical data about all Sherpa summiters and about any others named in our reports. When I was reporting to Reuters, I always gave their names; it was the editors who didn't publish them. It is probably true that the Sherpas and other Nepalese who assist foreign climbers do not get the recognition they deserve. Actually I'm not sure they get it in their own country.

What do you think is special about Bonington and Messner?

Reinhold Messner was special for climbing all the 8,000-meter mountains and doing so without supplemental oxygen; he and Peter Habeler proved to the world that summiting Everest itself would not make a climber turn into a vegetable mentally; they were quite brave to make the test. Messner conceived increasingly difficult methods of climbing: summiting 8,000'ers—including Everest—completely solo, and doing it by what he called fair means (a minimum of hardware, Sherpas, camps), and summiting two 8,000'ers in a single season. Chris Bonington was an excellent expedition organizer, including choosing the right members and handling the logistics of the climbs. In addition, he is very articulate and good at explaining climbing to the general public.

Do you think Breashears is unfair when he accuses you of concentrating on big names and being hypercritical of lesser lights?

I don't know the details of David Breashears's criticism. If what you say is his view, I would say that while reporting for Reuters I may have concentrated on the big names because they are the newsmakers, but for the database, we certainly meet everyone, big or not, and record their activities.

One of the most incisive comments I have encountered is your belief that a climb cannot really be considered a success if all the people die on the descent. And yet, if it turns out that Mallory and Irvine did summit Everest, people will have a very different attitude toward them. It would make a difference. This is why summiting should be only part of the picture. Do you agree?

I don't hold the view that a person has not been successful if he or she reaches the summit and dies in descent; they have succeeded in getting to the top, but not on making the full round trip. I know Hillary thought a climb was unsuccessful if the summiter died before reaching the foot of the mountain. I don't think people will have a different attitude about George Mallory and Andrew Irvine if it turns out that they summited in 1924. I think they are already greatly admired for what is known that they accomplished with the high altitude clothing and equipment they had in those days, and the pioneering they bravely set out to do. But in the case of the thousands of people who have trudged up the huge mountains, I think many of them have not such admirable motives—such as bragging rights when they get back home.

Do you still believe that women merely follow the men? Have things changed in the last five years?

Women are still not doing pioneering climbs, not determining new routes, climbing unclimbed peaks, even seldom—but now not always—organizing expeditions themselves without men's participation in the planning and even climbing.

In 2006, Isserman wrote an essay in The Chronicle of Higher Education, *in which he claims that contemporary climbers do not treat the mountains with the respect they did in the distant past: Their ethical commitment is tainted. Is this fair? You seem to disrespect the average person who nevertheless wishes to climb? Is this true?*

I do not disrespect the "average" person who wishes to climb; I think the mountains should be open to anyone who is capable. The "average" person is simply following in other climbers' footsteps, but that is his right, I believe. I don't think highly of a team who asked me on their arrival in Nepal about what is the route on the mountain they have chosen. Contemporary climbers vary in their attitudes towards littering the mountain they are climbing. We Westerners tend to be more conscious of the maxim "take nothing but pictures, leave nothing but footprints." But others are catching on.

Are too many people climbing in the Himalaya? Should the government protect the environment by severely limiting the number of expeditions each year?

Which government is going to deprive itself of the income for its treasury and their citizens who win their livelihood from climbing? The Chinese government? The Indian or Nepalese government? The Nepalese government did try imposing restrictions on the numbers on its mountains, but it created such a strong reaction from Nepalese trekking agents, hoteliers, Sherpas, and others that the experiment didn't long survive. In a sense, there are too many on some routes on some mountains, especially on the standard routes on Everest, Cho Oyu, and Ama Dablam. They are too many in the sense that there is dangerous crowding at some bottlenecks, such as the Khumbu Icefall and

Lhotse lies perpendicular to Mount Everest. At 27,939 feet, it is the fourth tallest peak in the world.

the Hillary Step on Nepal's side of Everest. The Nepalese government tries to encourage climbers to go to more widely scattered, but lower, peaks. But most people have never heard of these mountains and have no interest in doing something different.

What role do you play in Sir Edmund Hillary's Himalayan Trust, the organization that builds schools and hospitals for the Sherpa people?

I am on the Kathmandu staff of the Himalayan Trust, which has built schools and hospitals in the Solukhumbu District of Nepal that benefit all the people who live in the district, not just the Sherpas. Furthermore, it adds to the structures already built and regularly sends large amounts of supplies to them. (It is not building any new ones.)

Recently, a peak has been named for you. Was this a welcome surprise?

Fortunately almost no one knows about the French team's naming a peak after me—and surely no one including the Nepalese government takes it seriously if they do know. But it was a compliment to me for the climbing records I have built up over the years. It certainly was a surprise.

All of your files are now available on a disk. How might this information and data benefit climbers and scholars?

The database was initially intended as a means to preserve my records. But it is used by climbers wanting information about the climbing history of a mountain they're interested in or wanting to know the times that most successes take place on particular mountains; by researchers who want facts about numbers and circumstances surrounding cases of high altitude sickness; perhaps by people who are just curious about Himalayan mountaineering facts. I am often thanked by interviewees for this work.

Do you have anything else to add?

Nothing to add, thanks.

We would like to sincerely thank you for your comments: Thank you!

Awards

Literary Award from the American Alpine Club, 1994
King Albert Medal of Merit, 1998
Sagarmatha National Award from the Nepal Ministry of Tourism, 2003
Honourary Queen's Service Medal, awarded by the Queen of New Zealand, Queen Elizabeth, 2003.
Honourary consul of New Zealand; this is a title for someone who represents New Zealand where there is no embassy, and who is not a member of its foreign service.

BIBLIOGRAPHY

Hawley, Elizabeth, and Richard Salisbury. *The Himalayan Database: The Expedition Archives of Elizabeth Hawley.* (CD). Golden, CO: The American Alpine Club, 2004.

McDonald, Bernadette. *I'll Call You in Kathmandu: The Elizabeth Hawley Story.* Seattle: The Mountaineers Books, 2005.

<http://www.himalayandatabase.com/index.html>.

<http://www.k2news.com/mak1129.htm>.

Maurice Isserman

(March 12, 1951–)

Historian, professor, lover and
admirer of mountains

Date of interview: December 8, 2009. *Location:* South Burlington, VT,
and Clinton, NY. *Interviewer:* Robert Hauptman. *Method:* Electronic
mail.

Maurice Isserman is a professor of history at Hamilton College. He has
written extensively about American radical movements, and the history of the
1960s, and more recently has shifted his research to the history of mountaineering and exploration. His massive book *Fallen Giants* (with Stewart
Weaver) is the most current and comprehensive overview of Himalayan climbing to date; it covers the entire period up to 1996, the year of the great debacle
on Everest. *Fallen Giants* won the 2008 Banff Prize for best mountaineering
history and the National Outdoor Book Award for best mountaineering book.
Isserman is currently writing a history of American mountaineering.

━━━

*RH: Thank you for agreeing to answer some questions regarding the historian's
role in recording mountaineering events. Many climbers and mountaineers write
accounts of their climbs, but a professional historian will, of necessity, approach the
task differently. Why did you decide to write* Fallen Giants *and how did you go
about it?*

MI: Stewart and I have been friends for many years, and occasional climbing partners in the Adirondacks (he teaches at the University of Rochester and
I at Hamilton College, so we are both based in upstate New York). At the start
of the 21st century we were both at a point in our scholarly careers where we
were casting around for a new focus for our research (I, for one, had decided
if there was anything left to say about the 1960s, after having written several
books on the topic, then someone else was going to have to say it) when we
noticed that the last comprehensive history of Himalayan mountaineering,
Kenneth Mason's *Abode of Snow*, had been published a half century earlier. It
seemed time for a new look, both because a lot of mountaineering history had

been made in the Himalaya since Mason's book came out, and because there had never before been a book on the topic by professional historians. Our idea was that it would be interesting to tell the story of mountaineering "from the bottom up," which is to say by combining an account of mountaineering achievements with an attempt to describe the mountaineers in terms of their distinctive national, cultural, and historical roots—thus the subtitle of the book, *A History of Himalayan Mountaineering from the Age of Empire to the Age of Extremes.*

You are a hiker and mountaineer; have you done some climbing in the Himalaya and did this influence what you did in Fallen Giants?

Well, you are very kind in calling me a mountaineer, but what I have done in the Himalaya amounts to trekking, not climbing, and having spent some time in the company of real mountaineers while writing this book—mountaineers of the caliber of Charlie Houston and Tom Hornbein—I would hesitate to claim that title for myself. But the kind of small-scale mountain climbing that I did in the Cascades, while I was a student at Reed College in Oregon, certainly helped me imagine what it was like to climb at much higher elevation and on much more difficult terrain in the Himalaya. The gear is similar, the techniques are somewhat similar, and you can get killed by falling into a crevasse on Mount Hood just as you can on Everest. And when I did the basic Everest base camp trek while researching *Fallen Giants*, I was self-consciously following in the footsteps of Charlie Houston and Bill Tilman on their famous 1950 reconnaissance of the south side of Everest. Climbing 18,150-foot Kala Patar, as they did, and, after catching my breath, looking across the Khumbu glacier towards Everest, as they did, gave me a vicarious sense of the excitement they must have felt at that important moment in the history of Himalayan mountaineering. And also looking up at the mountain and tracing the various routes that present themselves from that perspective—West Ridge, North Face, Northeast Ridge, as well as the South Col and Southeast Ridge—helped me make that leap of imagination that always helps when you are trying to set down someone else's history. Stewart, by the way, has stronger ties to the Himalaya, because he lived for several years in India as a teenager, and was a frequent visitor to the mountains, including an Annapurna trek he made in the 1970s.

Much of your work is, of necessity, based on secondary sources: accounts, monographs, and articles. Did primary source material—your own experiences, interviews, discussions—play a role here?

We made extensive use of expedition accounts, in books and in the various Alpine club and climbing journals—which historians would call primary sources, since they are written by the participants. But we also found a lot of new and interesting unpublished material, especially correspondence, in archives ranging from the American Alpine Club library in Golden, Colorado, to the Royal Geographic Society library in London, to the German Alpine Club archives in Munich, which helped us tell the story of mountaineering "from the bottom up." One example, illustrating the social exclusivity of American mountaineering in the 1940s, was a 1946 letter I found in the AAC library from Robert Underhill to Henry Hall (two prominent figures in the climbing establishment in those days), in which Underhill denounces mountaineering writer James Ramsey Ullman as a Jewish "mongrel" with low-class manners (Ullman, the product of a prep school education and a Princeton graduate, was half Jewish). Finding that kind of material allowed us to tell a more complicated and hopefully more interesting story than just rehearsing the long narrative of mountaineering achievements and tragedies. We also benefited greatly from our conversations with a number of Himalayan mountaineers, who generously shared their time—and sometimes their artifacts. I'll never forget the afternoon Stewart and I spent with Charlie Houston in his Burlington, Vermont, home, when he told us the story of the 1953 K2 expedition, including the red umbrella that they carried up the mountainside (in lieu of the flag that they left behind in base camp), which they intended to open ceremonially once they reached the summit. Of course, they didn't get to the summit at all, and had to abandon the umbrella, and much of the rest of their gear, on the mountainside in their epic retreat off the mountain trying to get Art Gilkey to safety—something else, unfortunately, they were unable to do. The following year the Italians attempted and succeeded in climbing K2— and found Charlie's umbrella, which they later returned to him at a ceremony in Genoa. So the story was very interesting, but then, after telling us the story, Charlie asked if we would like to see the very same red umbrella, and we said "yes," naturally, and he took us to the closet under his front staircase where he kept it with the other umbrellas, and showed it to us. That was quite a thrill—to see and touch that K2 expedition umbrella, which had lain for a year high on top of the mountain before returning to Charlie's possession. Things like that you just can't get out of books....

Mountaineering is perhaps the only sport that raises pressing epistemological questions. This is why Elizabeth Hawley is so demanding and precise in her interviews with expedition leaders. How do we know that a person is telling the truth? How do we know that even if he or she is, the perspective is not skewed?

Historians often face those kinds of questions. Well, your question was about sports, so maybe not baseball historians, because the stats don't lie. But historians of most other human activities, from politics to war to mountaineering, should know they need to maintain a critical perspective when they weigh the evidence provided by fallible human beings. People's memories of the past tend to be as unreliable and self-serving at sea level as they are at 8,000 meters. It's always going to prove to be a judgment call to decide who is a reliable nar-

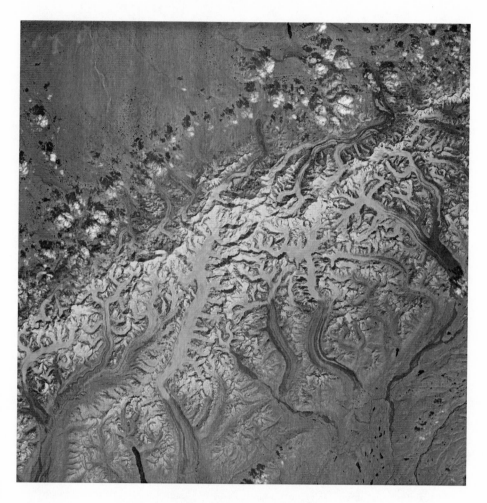

Landsat photo of Denali (NASA)

rator, and whose memories need to be taken with the proverbial grain of salt. Dr. Frederick Cook, who made distinctly dubious claims to have both been the first to climb Mount McKinley and the first to have reached the North Pole, falls into that latter category.

Do you think that reliability and validity in the mountaineering literature is often questionable, especially when two accounts of the same expedition conflict with each other? Consider the Herzog controversy, if you like.

There are many examples of those kinds of conflicting accounts in Himalayan expeditionary history—K2 in 1939, Annapurna in 1950, K2 again in 1954, among others. And the pendulum of opinion as to who to believe in those conflicts tends to swing back and forth. For example, for a long time Fritz Weissner was seen (in published accounts and in the opinion of the mountaineering community) as the villain in the 1939 debacle on K2 that led to the deaths of one American and three Sherpa climbers—then he was exonerated, then found guilty again, then re–exonerated, so I don't think that one will ever be resolved. David Roberts's reexamination of the 1950 Annapurna expedition turned Herzog, at least in the eyes of some readers, from hero to villain—but I suspect the pendulum will swing again in that case. The only major controversy that I can think of that has apparently been put to rest after many years of acrimonious charges and counter–charges is K2 in 1954, because Lino Lacedelli finally came out and admitted, shortly before his death, that his fellow summiter Achille Compagnoni had indeed conspired to keep Walter Bonatti from finding their high camp, just as Bonatti had always argued. Except in the very rare instances where one of the principals in such controversies decides to change his story, we can't have any final assurance as to who is telling the truth and who is not.

How are both the history of cartography and the desire to advance scientific knowledge generally intimately related to the history of mountaineering? Do they still play an important role today?

As you suggest, the history of expeditionary mountaineering and the history of mapmaking are intimately bound together, not only in the Himalaya but in many regions (Alaska comes to mind—with Brad Washburn as a key figure in both endeavors.) Mountaineers have good reason to value cartography, because without it they would have a hard time finding their way to the mountains (one of the things that makes the ascent of Annapurna in 1950 so impressive is that Herzog and company had only skimpy and inaccurate maps to guide them, and made a heroic effort to find their way to the mountainside even before they made their heroic effort to climb it). However, in the Himalaya, "science" in a more general sense—glaciology, high altitude physiology, and so forth—was often tacked on by expedition organizers as a fundraising gimmick to attract well-heeled sponsors to pay for their mountaineering, as was certainly the case of Norman Dyhrenfurth's fund-raising efforts for the 1963 American Everest expedition.

Hiking, climbing, mountaineering (and even skiing) are enticing, enthralling, and life-affirming activities. (I would be a very different person indeed had I not avidly pursued all of these.) But, as I have previously noted, the history of mountaineering is littered with dead bodies. Given what we know about potential harm or death, do you think we would be better off avoiding the big mountains?

I almost always get asked that question when I give talks about *Fallen Giants* to non–mountaineering audiences. And I usually stammer out some version of the Mallory justification for climbing Everest (and feel a little ashamed of myself afterwards, since I haven't really earned the right to do Mallory impersonations). When I talk to mountaineering audiences (at the

AAC library, for instance, and at Banff), they never ask that question—such things are just taken as givens—which is one of the reasons I like to talk to mountaineers.

Do you agree that many of the tragedies that have occurred during mountaineering's now long history almost always derive from poor decisions on the part of participants? I think that this is even true for those debacles caused by objective dangers such as extreme cold, avalanche, or lightning, all of which can be protected against or avoided. But very few mountaineers (who are courageous and fearless by nature) are willing to abort a climb or turn back just below the summit. Perhaps this is why Boukreev is dead, whereas Ed Viesturs, known for his excessive caution, is not.

There is a historical dimension to that whole issue. The fourteen 8,000-meter peaks were climbed in the 1950s, instead of in the 1930s, because of many factors (including better gear and, probably, better mountaineers). But also because by then mountaineers were willing to assume greater levels of risk than had previously been thought appropriate. If Maurice Herzog had held to the standards of the 1930s British Everest expeditions, for example, where safety was the paramount virtue, he would likely have turned back short of the summit of Annapurna in 1950. The same for Hermann Buhl on Nanga Parbat in 1953, and for Herbert Tichy on Cho Oyu in 1954. Thanks to their risk-taking, they all got their summits and they all survived (although it was a near thing for Herzog). The point is that what is a "poor decision" for one generation of climbers has proven to be within the spectrum of acceptable risk for later generations. Of course, the equation changes when people who are unqualified to take on or make informed judgments about those kinds of risks are being led to the summit of dangerous peaks by professionals, as was the case in 1996 on Everest. There the rule should be always to err on the side of caution—which is, as *Into Thin Air* suggests, a difficult rule to adhere to when competitive business pressures plus hypoxia are factors in a guide's decision-making.

Men have sometimes given women a hard time as they attempted to participate in expeditions. For example, John Roskelley, among others, has had some harsh things to say about female mountaineers. Do you think that this is why they have mounted all-women expeditions?

Absolutely. Attitudes towards women climbers varied by nation (Polish men, for instance, proved not nearly as hostile as many American male climbers to the concept that women could hold their own in high altitude mountaineering). And, I think, attitudes in U.S. climbing circles today are quite different than they were in the 1970s and 1980s. Arlene Blum was a lightning rod for a lot of that hostility, and deserves a lot of credit for standing up to it.

Do you think that the history of Himalayan mountaineering reflects mountaineering in general?

In some ways. In the Himalaya, as in the Alps, the ridges got climbed first, then the faces. In the Himalaya, as in the Alps, the impossible (the Matterhorn, Everest) has a way of becoming routine; once a mountain has been climbed, it (or at least certain routes on it) become domesticated (an "easy day for a lady" as was said in the Alps in the Victorian era, "the yak route" as began to be said of Everest's southeast ridge after it had been climbed a few times). On the other hand, the sheer scale of Himalayan mountaineering, the remote locations of the peaks, and the objective dangers of climbing at such high altitude, set the region apart from the Alps. You can climb Mount Blanc in the early morning, and enjoy a good dinner and a soft bed in Chamonix that night, an experience that has no equivalent on an Everest climb, never mind K2. The other distinct feature of Himalayan climbing, of course, is the extremely important role played by the Sherpas, at first as porters, and later as fellow climbers.

Those who chronicle an expedition may at times offer sanitized versions. Herzog apparently covered up some controversial issues and the Italian conquerors of K2 distorted what they did. These unpleasantries occurred long ago. But in Fallen Giants *as well as in your* Chronicle of Higher Education *essay you insist that things have changed: "In the final decades of the twentieth century that sense of duty and obligation to others waned." But don't you think that just as there are also caring, committed, environmentally conscious mountaineers today, there were [concomitantly] uncaring, selfish, and polluting climbers in the distant past (when ethical commitment was ostensibly stronger)?*

Of course. The point is, from the 1920s through the 1960s, a powerful norm, what philosophers would call a categorical imperative, prevailed in mountaineering—often described as a "brotherhood of the rope." Plenty of expeditions fell short of living up to that ideal, but they all aspired to it (and, as you say, sanitized the record if they violated its principles). When we think of great climbers in that era, we tend to think of them in terms of partnerships—Shipton and Tilman, Houston and Bates, Hornbein and Unsoeld. What's changed in recent decades is that, increasingly, the world's best climbers do not subscribe to the romance of the brotherhood of the rope—Messner, Roskelley, and others made it quite clear that they preferred to climb mountains unroped (literally and figuratively) to others. And then in commercial climbing, nothing but the cash nexus bound together the participants. That doesn't mean that there aren't plenty of caring, committed, environmentally conscious mountaineers out there today—just that the norm, the imperative has shifted.

Would you care to venture an opinion on who is the greatest mountaineer of all time?

Nope. But I do have some candidates for the greatest climbs of all time, including the first ascent of Nanda Devi in 1936, of Cho Oyu in 1954, and the first ascent of Everest via the West Ridge in 1963. Each of these climbs

Maurice Isserman on Gokyo Ri (photograph by Arlene Blum; courtesy of Maurice Isserman).

were accomplished by small groups (or in the case of Everest, a small grouping within a larger expedition). Each overcame formidable challenges, in good style and in good feeling.

Do you have anything else to add?

Just how much fun it was to write *Fallen Giants*.

We sincerely thank you for your time and responses.

AWARDS

Banff Prize, for best mountaineering history, 2008
National Outdoor Book Award, 2008

BIBLIOGRAPHY

Isserman, Maurice. "The Ethics of Mountaineering, Brought Low." *The Chronicle of Higher Education*, 5 May 2006: B15.
Isserman, Maurice, and Stewart Weaver. *Fallen Giants: A History of Himalayan Mountaineering from the Age of Empire to the Age of Extremes*. New Haven: Yale University Press, 2008.

Audrey Salkeld

(March 11, 1936–)

Mountaineering historian, editor,
translator, scriptwriter, mountaineer

Date of interview: January 27, 2010. *Location:* South Burlington, VT, and Ashford, Kent, Great Britain. *Interviewer:* Robert Hauptman. *Method:* Electronic mail.

Audrey Salkeld is a mountaineering historian and editor; her books include biographies of George Mallory and Leni Riefenstahl and studies of the world's mountains and major epic climbs. She also has translated writings by Reinhold Messner and Kurt Diemburger into English. In the course of her work, Salkeld has built up a large private climbing archive.

RH: We know that you are busy so we thank you very much for agreeing to participate in our project. A good place to begin is with George Mallory, a man to whom you have devoted at least five books. They are all quite different and have different audiences, but they do cover the same ground. Why are people so infatuated with this early twentieth century climber?

AS: I thought it was three books "devoted" to George Mallory and his contemporaries, though he has had a habit of creeping into other aspects of my life and writings. I first heard of the early Mount Everest pioneers when I was eleven or twelve and Frank Smythe, a climber who had carried on the struggle to climb the peak in the 1930s, came to lecture at our school. Then, it was the seeming audacity of the adventure and the tragic outcome that caught my imagination. Everest was still unclimbed at that point—and so far as we young girls were concerned, seemed set to stay that way. It's harder to know what so fascinates people about the Mallory and Irvine story these days when each year sees hundreds of men and women clambering over Mount Everest and scores of them making it to the summit, and when more than 200 victims have joined the pair who never returned in 1924. I think the romance of a lost age has something to do with it, and the intriguing mix of high moral intentions and human fallibility. And of course the sheer pathos of the out-

198

come, of what might have been if they had survived to live out their full lives. Above all, I think it is through his writings that George Mallory remains a very real presence to us today.

Photographs of Mallory and his climbs are often included in mountaineering histories, but they are invariably reduced in size, which diminishes their [power]. In your photobiography of Mallory, the images are enormous; extraordinary clarity and detail lacking in other versions shine forth here and alter the way in which one perceives and considers the issues. Do you select the images and oversee their production?

Images have always been very important to me. In fact picture research, I would say, is a fundamental part of factual research. I would hate to produce any book with which I hadn't been deeply involved in the picture research. It's always a bonus when a publisher commissions a "picture-led" book and is prepared to guarantee quality reproduction. In a narrative-led book, pictures are necessarily restricted to a few groups of pages and the temptation is to pack in as many as you can at the expense of doing them justice. The scale of the pictures in *Mystery on Everest*, the photobiography I think you refer to, was a hallmark of the series it formed part of, which was aimed at younger readers. I remember David Breashears and I were thrilled when we were commissioned to produce *Last Climb*. With a year's lead-in we thought we could enjoy the luxury of visiting the families of all the old Everesters and pore over their photo albums and diaries, do a truly thorough job. We weren't banking on Conrad Anker finding Mallory's body high on Everest within a couple of months of us signing the contract. The publishers then had a change of heart and wanted the book delivered in six weeks! Even so, we managed to turn up a few pictures that hadn't been aired before.

You have participated in at least three major expeditions: one that sought Mallory's remains as well as those that made IMAX films on Everest and Kilimanjaro. Were you able to ascend, to some degree, both Everest's north and south sides? Did you climb Kilimanjaro?

Well, as you know, my expeditioning career started rather late in life. I was 50 years old the first time I was invited to Everest, to the North side in 1986. My role was as a historian. So the highest I reached was advanced base camp, 21,300 feet. Thrilling for me, of course, to even get that far. Ten years later, in 1996, my job was to send back dispatches, so I had to follow the dramas of that year from base camp on the Nepalese side. And in 2000, when at 64 I took part in the IMAX Kilimanjaro trip, my participation was specifically to demonstrate that even old ladies could reach the top! Actually, a few months later, we had to go back and do it all again to get extra summit footage, and that was even more enjoyable. We camped several nights in the crater on that occasion.

What was it like being on Everest during the 1996 tragedy?

What can one say? From the elation of hearing the first climbers were on the summit in the early afternoon of May 10, to the gnawing worry that evening when at base we learned that as many as 20 climbers were strung out along the southeast struggling to get back to the South Col. A fierce storm had blown in and as darkness fell, they were being lashed by fierce winds and horizontal sleet and snow. It was already clear that Rob Hall and his slowest client, Doug Hanson, were in trouble. They had gotten down the Hillary Step and were in the vicinity of the South Summit, but were out of oxygen and in poor shape. They could go no further that night. Members from all the expeditions joined the vigil at Hall's New Zealand Base Camp, where the radio lines stayed open. Nothing more was heard from Hall until 4:45 on the 11th, when the gravity of the situation was borne in on us all. With frantic rescue attempts going on higher up the mountain all that day, there was a sense of helplessness at base. Those caught up in the fight for life could have been on the moon, they were so far from us. Everyone sat around Rob's tent listening to the news as that dreadful day went on and we learned the scale and details of the tragedy, and in the evening many of us heard the heartbreaking last messages from Rob, patched through to his wife back home in New Zealand.

Did you interact often with David Breashears while on the mountains?

That's a difficult question. Apart from Kili, during an expedition, the climbers were mostly out of the lower camps to which I was confined. But there was a lot of filming on all three of those expeditions, and on much of that I worked very closely with David. When the team did come down for periods, of course we all did a lot together. In 1986, particularly, when we had the long journey through Tibet at the beginning and end of the expedition, we were a pretty tight bunch. I still think of them all fondly as "family." David and I saw quite a bit of each other off the mountains, too, despite living on different continents—what with the film editing, and researching a number of projects together.

Were you somewhere on Everest when Mallory's body was discovered?

No, I was moving house in Cumbria at the time the news broke—sitting on the floor in a bare room amid a pile of boxes, when I got a call from a press man asking if he could bike over some photographs for me to look at and comment upon. Funnily enough, I would have known it was Mallory's body in the pictures, even if I hadn't been told. There was just the half-buried back view, but it was the hands with their lean fingers that gave him away. I recognized them from an earlier Everest photograph.

How do your mountaineering experiences affect your writings?

Professionally, most of my writing has been about mountains or mountaineering, so I can't answer that one. I wish I had written more on other subjects, but I just got swept along with what I was doing. These days most of the research and writing I find myself immersed in is related to family history—and I haven't managed to find any explorers or mountaineers among my ancestors.

In The Mystery of Mallory and Irvine, *you use letters as a basic primary source and then cite them at great length, which allows you to present the issues in exquisite detail. Is such extreme citation usual in historical accounts?*

I think I was just blown away by the detail contained in these early Everest papers, which hadn't had the exposure back then in the 1980s that they have now. Mallory and his contemporaries simply leapt off the page to me through their personal thoughts and assessments. I think Mallory's, in particular, is a very modern voice. We can understand his preoccupations and sympathize with him. Whether it's usual to quote so much, I'm not sure. This was one of my first books and I suppose if I sat down to write it now, I might edit it differently. There is so much material and so many different ways to come at it. And of course there are always more intriguing tidbits leaking into the mix as time passes. I've certainly evolved a little in the way I interpret it all, I think.

Your co-author Tom Holzel insists that we now view Mallory and Irvine quite differently than the way they were presented in the earlier biographies. What are the major differences?

I think we haven't changed our opinion in so far as Mallory's character is concerned. He was an idealist, with the urge to "make a difference"—and he had a strong sense of duty. I think he retained an air of boyishness and impish fun well into maturity. He could consciously charm, which with his innate modesty led some to rather underestimate his talents. For instance, the prevalent idea that he was dreamy and mechanically impractical is clearly nonsense when you consider he was put in charge of a large gun in a siege battery as soon as he arrived on the front line in WWI and he served throughout the Battle of the Somme. Maybe he could be absent-minded, but it was unfair of [Tom] Longstaff [contemporary of Mallory], even in jest, to call him a big baby who shouldn't be put in charge of anyone, including himself.

During his life, Mallory's climbing and mountaineering skills were highly praised. Would he be considered in the same light as climbers such as Reinhold Messner or Steve House today?

Quite obviously he wouldn't. Compared to today's "career mountaineers"—the time he actually spent climbing was episodic. That's not to say he wasn't brilliant on rock, nor that he didn't derive intense spiritual sustenance from the hills and from the friendships he made among them. But you couldn't say Mallory "lived for mountains" when there was so much else in his life.

Do you think that we now have an accurate account of what happened to Mallory and Irvine?

We still don't know what happened to them. We know more about their intentions, and more about their preparations; we know where Mallory ended up and we have some idea where to look for Irvine. But every clue we discover throws up as many questions as answers. We are nowhere near discovering whether they made it to the top of the mountain.

Do you continue to believe that they did not reach the summit or have you altered your opinion?

I have never held the opinion that they either did or they did not reach the summit. I have seen nothing to influence that conclusion either way. Like most people I have always hoped they did, that they had earned it. But proof is not an act of faith; it needs evidence. We do not know what time the pair set out, nor how much oxygen they took on that day, nor indeed which way they went. We do know Mallory was optimistic in his assessment of an attainable climbing speed, and that he probably underestimated the lateral distance ahead of them. Their chances of getting back from summit to their high camp that day would always have been slim, if not impossible—let alone getting all the way down to the North Col, as he hoped. We can be sure they both had the motivation to go for it, and that Mallory had spent more time studying tactics than anyone else. He fully appreciated the help oxygen could give, including sleeping on it the night before the attempt. Beliefs that the presence of sunglasses in his pocket or the absence of a photo of [his wife] Ruth are pointers to success shouldn't be seen as definitive, even if they are of considerable comfort to his family.

Have you, by chance, seen The Wildest Dream, *the new film on the 1924 attempt, which will be released to the general public in April 2010? If yes, does it capture the magic of Mallory and his obsessive need to reach the summit of Everest?*

Yes, I did catch it at the Kendal Film Festival last November, although I would wish to see it again before commenting in any detail. There were points I would take issue with, largely along the lines I've already mentioned about the conclusions to be drawn from what we know so far. I think a lot of people will love the film and—since it is presented as a drama-documentary—will believe that is how it really happened. For myself, I am satisfied for the outcome to remain a mystery until we really know.

Early climbers argued about the ethics of using oxygen. This same business reoccurred more recently and now many people refuse to use it. Do you think that using oxygen is unethical, that it changes the interaction between the climber and the mountain? If yes, then can't the same be said of crampons, ice screws, or Kevlar ropes? The only way to fully avoid all censure would be to climb naked!

It will always be a personal decision over how much "technical" assistance one is prepared to accept. As you suggest there can't be a universal right and wrong about these matters—the line was crossed when we invented climbing boots and first took along a rope.

Another controversial issue is expeditionary climbing with its many hundreds of porters, mules, yaks, and so on. Do you feel that expeditionary climbing was unethical in the past? How about today for smaller expeditions?

Of course a small party achieving a high and/or difficult climb with minimum aid warrants more acclamation and credibility than a monstrous expedition with unlimited resources—especially in today's environmentally concerned climate. But you can't backdate ethics and attitudes. And there are different ways of approaching the mountains even today. I hope that climbers and trekkers will always employ local guides and porters—or they will miss out on a lot—and so will the local economy of these remote areas.

At one point, you discuss the habit of leaving people behind. In my own climbing, this has always struck me as an extremely dangerous thing to do. Unroped mountaineers may leave a starting point at different times or one races ahead of the other. When danger strikes—an accident, fall into a crevasse, avalanche—an unnecessary tragedy may ensue. Does this occur because it is inherent in mountaineering culture or because people just act foolishly?

I'm sure you will never find anyone who advocates "leaving people behind" on mountains. It goes against all natural ethics. I think the point Tom Holzel was making was that despite holding this view, there are times when by accident or design parties do become separated, or someone strikes out on their own. It is because the concept of abandonment is such a big no-no, that one is so shocked to hear of it happening anywhere—high on Everest, or as in the cutting of the rope in *Touching the Void.*

Your enormous and beautiful World Mountaineering *is a truly extraordinary achievement. Was it very difficult to coordinate all of the contributors and to get them to present the material in the precise and complex format that you required?*

A large compilation like this is infinitely harder work than writing a personal narrative. And there are numerous pitfalls completely beyond your control. One of the hardest things is that with illustrations on every page the designer has control of the master copy from quite early in the process. Words can be taken out or inserted to fit text around the pictures and maps with no reference to the editor. Or one day you may be told that all the foreign co-publishers will only take the book if it is trimmed by a third, or that all names are to be reduced to initials and surnames—but not to worry because somebody has been employed to do that for you. Only nobody tells that person that many Asian names have the surname first, and that Spanish-speaking climbers often have their mother's surname tacked on at the end of their family name. One of my big regrets about *World Mountaineering* is that a recognizable picture of the top of Everest had to be flipped on the title pages as that suited the design better! So there's a lot of frustration, and you certainly don't win all the arguments, but on the positive side is the satisfaction of working with so many international climbers and photographers.

The many hundreds of color images, marked routes, and maps help the reader to understand and empathize with the mountains, multiple routes, and potential pitfalls involved in climbing the world's great peaks. As a professional historian, were you satisfied with the work of the contributing mountaineers, some of whom are extremely well-known?

I selected the various contributors and had confidence in them—it was a fairly tight structure requiring certain facts and figures. There wasn't much room for personal expression—sadly, you might say. Of course, you inevitably end up with the odd typo, and or occasions where routes are not drawn quite accurately. You can never be completely satisfied you have everything right—and certain facts, particularly with regard to access and travel, can quickly change.

Aerial photo of Bhutan (NASA)

Does a professional historian's method and published accounts differ from the work produced by mountaineers whose historical and literary training may be deficient or non-existent?

You may be making too much of "the professional historian" and whether or not there are accepted methods. Writing up the history of particular climbs is fundamentally dependent on the accounts written by those who were there. Whenever I follow up a story for an article or book or film, it's always the same: read every published account you can find and wherever possible speak to the individuals concerned. As time passes, there may have been peer criticisms or praise for certain events or characters, and that gives another thread in the story. The "job" is really to get as rounded and human a picture as possible. It's not the dry facts that carry weight for me, but the people and their experiences.

As a historian of mountaineering exploits, an area notorious for deceptive claims, how do you validate what is said or published? Is it sometimes difficult or impossible to get at the truth?

I can't remember ever having to validate a potentially false claim. Where I know of controversy I report it. Historically there are claimed climbs that are now regarded as hoaxes, but I'm glad I haven't had to be the one to prove it. I'd always be thinking, "What if I was wrong?!"

Do you agree with Maurice Isserman's contention that contemporary mountaineers are generally less ethical than their forbears, that the brotherhood of the rope has been replaced by a selfish indulgence that favors individual achievement over cooperation?

Certainly you hear more about it nowadays, but that could be down to more reporting. There are generations that seem to be more selfish than others, whatever they do, but I doubt if people are really so much different than they've always been. I do think it's no longer fashionable to conceal your ambitions or to be modest about your achievements.

Recently, Achille Compagnoni followed by Lino Lacedelli passed away. Walter Bonatti accused these conquerors of K2 of subverting his attempt on the mountain, something they denied until 2004, when Lacedelli admitted that Bonatti was right. This subversion occurred more than half a century ago and is the type of action I would take to be truly unethical (rather than the current trend of, say, solo mountaineering—which Charles Houston condemned). Do you agree?

What a nasty taste this all leaves—and such a tragedy, really, this story. Whatever the reason Bonatti could not find the top camp on the crucial day to deliver oxygen to Compagnoni and Lacadelli, his gagging and subsequent ostracization tainted the Italian team's first ascent and the reputation of all the other climbers, who should have enjoyed a lifetime of comradeship as John

Hunt's 1953 Everest team did. It is almost unbelievable that it got as far as a libel suit; and that it took more than 50 years for the truth to come out. Thank goodness Lacedelli found the courage to set the matter straight before he died. Solo mountaineering has always been deplored by the establishment, though to practice it is down to personal choice and rarely affects other climbers. Whether the most celebrated solo climbers are natural loners, or whether they feel themselves driven by events to climb alone would be worth more exploration.

It seems to me that two major ethical alterations in Himalayan and Karakorum mountaineering are positive: Today, Sherpa and Balti porters and climbers are treated with more respect and remunerated with a fairer wage, and many Westerners refuse to litter the mountain environment with their detritus as the large expeditions of the past were wont to do. How do you feel about this?

Of course in this day and age it is only right that Sherpas, Baltis, and any other local porters should be paid fairly for the dangerous job they do. Life would be fairer still if they had a choice of occupation, and only took to working in mountains if they felt a personal call to do so. But I expect economically that choice is still a long way off for most of them.

When translating Reinhold Messner and Kurt Diemberger from German into English, do you ever consult with the authors? Do you enjoy translating as much as writing?

That's an interesting question—and the answer is no, and yes, respectively. I didn't meet or correspond with Messner until I had worked on several of his books, and there was no contact during the translation, and no feedback afterwards. No reason for that, beyond that it was all done through publishers and agents. Kurt Diemberger, on the other hand, I did know before I began working with him, and his climbing partner Julie Tullis had been a friend of mine for more than 20 years. Kurt's English is good, and often he would make the first stab at a chapter translation before I had the chance to tinker with it. We would exchange tapes and notes, and eventually get together to read through the whole manuscript. Those were brilliant times, lots of very late nights—I at the computer, Kurt reading eloquently and waving his arms, a bottle of Scotch whisky to keep things flowing—lots of jokes and laughter. We were both conscious that we were writing for a different audience than his German and Austrian fans. Things would be adjusted, tailored, new asides would go in; the finished work was no straight translation, as anyone comparing it with the original would soon know. It was a different composition altogether, and I have to say that sort of "translation" is a joy. Otherwise it could be a bit of a chore, and I only took it on because I was pressed to.

Do you wish to add anything?

I think we've more or less covered everything, haven't we? If you wanted more on how one looks at material differently over time, I attach a copy of an article I wrote a few years ago for the Cambridge University MC [Mountaineering Club] journal. I don't know if it was ever published, but feel free to extract some points if you wish. In the absence of more hard facts, in recent years I have been exploring Mallory's motivations and thinking which I think is as valid in the situation as much of the other speculation. The other piece I wrote, but more about analyzing the information gained from the finds, was in *Voices from the Summit*, edited by Bernadette McDonald and John Amatt in Banff.

Thank you so very much for your contribution to the climbing literature generally and for your time and help here.

AWARDS

Boardman-Tasker Award, 1996
Grand Prize, Banff Mountain Literature Festival, 1994 and 1998
American Alpine Club Literary Award 1999

BIBLIOGRAPHY

Breashears, David, and Audrey Salkeld. *Last Climb: The Legendary Everest Expeditions of George Mallory*. Washington, D.C.: National Geographic, 1999.
Holzel, Tom, and Audrey Salkeld. *The Mystery of Mallory and Irvine*. (Fully revised ed.) Seattle: The Mountaineers, 1999. [1986].
Salkeld, Audrey. *Kilimanjaro: To the Roof of Africa*. Washington, D.C.: National Geographic, 2002.
Salkeld, Audrey. *Mystery on Everest: A Photobiography of George Mallory*. Washington, D.C.: National Geographic Society, 2000.
Salkeld, Audrey. *People in High Places*. London: Jonathan Cape, 1991.
Salkeld, Audrey. *A Portrait of Leni Riefenstahl*. London: Jonathan Cape, 1996.
Salkeld, Audrey, ed. *World Mountaineering: The World's Great Mountains by the World's Great Mountaineers*. Boston: Bullfinch, 1998.
"Salkeld, Audrey." Contemporary Authors 220. Farmington Hills, MI: Thompson Gale, 2004 (307–309).

Conclusion

Climbing is a very serious business, even for those who do it purely for pleasure. If someone climbs rock faces or big mountains often enough, he or she will certainly encounter accidents, illness, and fatalities. It is surprising that so many otherwise ordinary people engage in what can only be considered an extremely dangerous pursuit. Even the overly cautious run into problems because bacterial and viral infections, dehydration, hypothermia, hypoxia, avalanches, lightning, and other hazards are sometimes very difficult to avoid—especially in the high and distant Andes, Karakorum, or Himalaya. But as the foregoing interviews show, the lure of encountering, ascending, and perhaps summiting in some of the most exquisitely beautiful environments on earth is very hard to abjure. Indeed, many amateurs who participate in commercial guided climbs pay in physical deterioration and loss of body parts as well as in burdensome financial terms. It costs some $60,000 to climb in the Himalaya. Even a simple trip to central Mexico from the U.S., which is very inexpensive if one drives there on one's own, can cost almost $3,000 just for the guiding fee.

The interviewees in this collection are all well known and for good reason: their accomplishments are legendary. Their experiences indicate that although they are highly motivated, extremely strong, able to go for long periods without food, water, or warmth and withstand extreme pain and suffering, they too are human and may succumb to bad thoughts or divisiveness with colleagues. But what we learn here is that these people do not give up—on their dreams or in their pursuit. No matter what happens, in occurrences that would certainly deter an ordinary person, these superhuman mountaineers persevere, suffer, return home to privation and surgery, but then begin to dream of the next expedition. They never give in or give up. That's what differentiates them from the timorous who prefer their outdoor pleasures in a more moderate form. We can do little more than admire in awe those who risk their lives to engage and preserve the world's great peaks.

Glossary

This is not meant to be a comprehensive listing of terms related to mountaineering. Rather, it includes only the specialized terminology used by the editors or interviewees that might be unknown to someone unfamiliar with climbing.

acclimatize (acclimate)   To allow the body to get used to higher altitude by producing more red blood cells. This is accomplished by slowly climbing higher, and, when possible, sleeping lower. For the very high peaks in the Himalaya, which rise to 26, 27, 28, and 29,000 feet, this process takes many weeks. Indigenous peoples in the high Andes, in La Paz, for example, or in the Himalaya, in high Nepalese villages, can climb higher with less acclimatization because their anatomy and physiology are inherently better suited for the higher altitudes—which does not mean that they are not susceptible to acute mountain sickness (q.v.).

acute mountain sickness (AMS)   Formerly called altitude sickness, this is an unpleasant malady that strikes many people as they ascend and especially if they go up too quickly. It is unusual for this to occur below 10,000 feet. Children are more susceptible than adults. Symptoms include headache, stomach pain, nausea, and coughing.

aid climbing   In rock climbing, using artificial materials, such as pitons (q.v.) or slings, rather than just the rock face, to help me ascend.

aiguille   A towering, sharp rock needle in the environs of Chamonix (France); there are many of them.

Alpine-style   In mountaineering, to ascend a peak (even in the Himalaya) in a simple, speedy fashion, without the use of porters (q.v.) or intermediate camps. Sometimes the climbers bivouac (q.v.) along the way. *See* **expedition**.

altitude   Height above sea level.

anchor   Anything to which a rope can be tied, including a tree, piton, or ice screw (qq.v.).

aphasia   Loss of the ability to use language.

ataxia   Loss of muscle coordination.

avalanche   Any material can avalanche, but here we almost exclusively mean a sudden release of snow, which pours down at hundreds of miles an hour inundating and destroying anything in its path. Many types exist, including slab and loose snow.

belay To protect a fellow climber by holding a taut rope attached to both people and often also to an anchor (q.v.) such as a piton or an ice ax (qq.v.).

bivouac One is said to bivouac when one is caught out in darkness, a storm, or a whiteout and is forced to sleep high on the mountain because camp cannot be reached. Some Alpine-style climbs include purposeful bivouacs. People sometimes carry foreshortened sleeping bags called bivy bags.

carabiner A small metal device with a spring-loaded door; it is used to connect ropes to harnesses, slings, belay points, and anchors (qq.v.). It often includes a locking device so that it does not accidentally spring open, which could result in a disaster. Sometimes called biner (pronounced beener).

cerebral edema *see* **high altitude cerebral edema**

climbing This is a general term used for any type of ascent on boulders, rock, rock faces, ice, volcanoes, indoor climbing walls, buildings, and so on. It also connotes ascending rock and rock faces as opposed to mountaineering (q.v.).

col A pass, for instance the South Col on Everest.

cornice A cornice is formed when the wind blows snow over the edge of a ridge (q.v.) and it slowly builds up and cantilevers outward. It is extremely dangerous because the climber may not realize that the solid ridge has ended and step out onto the cornice, which can disintegrate, thus causing the climber to fall many thousands of feet.

coulier A steep gorge between slopes or faces (q.v.). Couliers often provide efficient and enjoyable climbing, but they can be extremely dangerous because both rock and snow avalanches (qq.v.) can pour down, sometimes relentlessly.

crampons Metal devices that are strapped or, more recently, clamped onto one's boots. They contain 10 razor-sharp points that face downward and two that stick out in front. They help stabilize a climber on an icy slope. Crampons are an impediment when snow (q.v.) is soft and deep. They are also used to ascend vertical ice walls, for example, a frozen waterfall.

crevasse A cleft in a glacier (q.v.); it occurs when the sun's heat melts the snow; the glacier splits apart and an opening develops. As the years pass this gap can get wider and deeper. Some crevasses are so enormous that a large locomotive, as someone so colorfully put it, would disappear in its depths. Crevasses are extremely dangerous to those who walk on the glacier because new snow builds up over them, creating a bridge which may collapse under stress.

crux The most difficult point in a climb.

dexamethasone One of a group of powerful drugs that alleviate the symptoms of acute mountain sickness (q.v.).

8,000-meter peaks The 14 mountains that rise above this altitude (26,247 feet).

eight-thousanders Abbreviated nomenclature for the mountains described directly above.

enchainment (enchaînement) The sport of climbing a series of peaks very quickly without returning to camp, sometimes with the help of a helicopter for transport.

expedition Usually, a large complicated business, wherein a group descends upon a distant country, sets up a base camp, and stays for many months. Some expeditions have as many as 20 members and employ many hundreds of porters and climbing Sherpas.

face The broad expanse of a mountain, as opposed to a ridge, which is the point at which two faces come together. A small vertical ridge on a face is often called a rib.

first ascent The first time anyone reaches the summit of a mountain (or rock climb). First ascents are also designated for different routes on the same mountain. Second ascents are also important.

5.10. This is an example of the Yosemite Decimal System, used in the United States to rank the difficulty of a rock climb: 5 through 5.3 are easy maneuvering on variously inclined surfaces. Simple climbing begins at 5.4; 5.5 is substantially more difficult, and so on. At one time, perhaps 40 years ago, 5.10 was the hardest climb possible. Today, very infrequently, someone manages a 5.15. After 5.10, climbs are additionally delineated by the letters a, b, c, and d thus: 5.11a or 5.11b. France, the United Kingdom, and Australia have their own systems. Additionally, variations exist for aid and ice climbing (qq.v.).

fixed rope A rope (q.v.) that is attached to the mountain either permanently or for the season. It makes both ongoing ascents and descents easier and safer.

fourteeners Abbreviated nomenclature for the mountains described directly below.

14,000-foot peaks Those mountains that reach an altitude of at least 14,000 feet. Colorado has at least 54 such mountains, and the highest peak in the 48 continental states is California's Mount Whitney, at 14,494.

free In rock climbing, to ascend a route without the aid of artificial devices such as pitons, slings, ropes, and so on. (qq.v.) These technical aids are used only to protect against a fall.

glacier Permanent snow or ice that covers a large and sometimes enormous area usually in a valley between two mountains. Glaciers are active and move downhill continuously. Many types exist, including hanging glaciers, which are permanently suspended on the side of a face (q.v.).

guide A professional mountaineer who helps amateurs climb bigger mountains. A guide from Chamonix (France) or Alaska who has never been to Peru can still act as a guide there.

harness A device that is belted around the stomach and looped around the thighs, and to which a rope (q.v.) is attached. It allows hard falls without constricting and thus seriously harming the body's midsection, which is what occurs if the rope is simply wound around the abdomen.

high altitude cerebral edema (HACE) This occurs when liquid builds up in the brain. It is the worst possible effect of high altitude on the body, and unless one descends immediately, HACE is fatal.

high altitude pulmonary edema (HAPE) Much worse than acute mountain sickness (q.v.) , this malady occurs when liquid builds up in the lungs. If one does not descend immediately, death will follow.

hypothermia The body's reaction to a loss of body temperature. It leads very quickly to death.

hypoxia The body's reaction to a lack of oxygen, which includes a deterioration in mental abilities and physical well-being.

ice Frozen water or snow (q.v.). Many types exist. Black ice is especially harmful and dangerous because it is very difficult to get one's crampons or ice ax (qq.v.) to penetrate it.

ice ax An implement or tool (q.v.) used for protection and chopping in mountaineering and, in pairs, for climbing vertical ice (q.v.). The former are considerably longer than the latter. The top often consists of an adze and a serrated pick; the bottom ends in a sharp point. They come in many shapes. They are often tethered to the harness (q.v.) or wrist.

ice climbing The ascent of vertical ice (q.v.) such as that which one often finds on quarry or cliff walls. It is a specialized sport that requires crampons and two small ice axes. Climbers either lead and place ice screws for protection or they top-rope, that is, they first go to the top and drop a rope down, which eliminates the need to place protection.

ice screw A small device with a hole at its top that is screwed into ice. To it are attached carabiners (q.v.) to which are attached rope (q.v.).This anchor (q.v.) is created in order to protect against a potential fall.

jumar A mechanical device that allows one to ascend a rope (q.v.) safely and securely but which jams when pulled downward by the hand. The English term is ascender, but jumar (derived from the Swiss manufacturer) is preferred. To jumar is to climb a fixed rope (q.v.) using this device. Jumars may also be used in pairs with attached stirrups for the feet when ascending vertically.

lead In all types of climbing, to go first. To take the lead is often more onerous and dangerous than following. Leaders must place protection, be wary of hidden dangers such as crevasses and cornices (qq.v.), and trudge through very deep, unbroken snow.

mixed climbing In mountaineering, climbing on or over ground, boulders, talus, acute rock, snow, ice, and vertical rock and ice.

moraine The rocky detritus left after a glacier scours a valley or the upper portions of a mountain. Lateral moraine can be found at the sides of a glacier, medial where two glaciers meet, and terminal at the end.

mountaineering Climbing a mountain as opposed to a vertical rock or ice face (qq.v.), although both of these pursuits are often necessary in mountaineering.

oxygen, supplemental Mountaineers carry supplemental oxygen in canisters on their backs. Having an additional source of oxygen once one gets up to 26,000 feet serves two purposes: It offers more air to breathe in a place where the available ambient air is one-third as plentiful as it is at sea level. This obviously makes it easier to climb, and, additionally, it is much easier to sleep when infused with a small amount of extra oxygen.

piton A small metal pin with a hole at its top; it is pounded into a crack in a rock face (qq..v.); a rope (q.v.) is then attached to it via a carabiner (q.v.). This allows one to belay (q.v.) a fellow climber while attached to the wall.

porter In some countries, Nepal and Pakistan, for example, a local person hired to carry goods and equipment to the base of the mountain. These treks can take weeks if the ground conditions are bad. High altitude porters do some low-level climbing. A limited number of Sherpas (q.v.) with mountaineering skills climb high in the Himalaya and often summit. Expeditions may have anywhere between 20 and 1,000 porters. Sometimes yaks are also used for hauling.

puja A religious ceremony or ritual that often occurs at the base of the mountain and is controlled by the sherpas. Incense is burned and the climbers and equipment are blessed.

pulmonary edema *see* **high altitude pulmonary edema**

rappel To lower oneself on an anchored rope (qq.v.). The rope is subsequently pulled down.

ridge The point at which two faces (q.v.) come together. They often lead to the summit (q.v.) Ridges are easier to climb than faces.

rock or technical climbing This is a diverse sport with many variations, but the primary objective is to climb a rock wall or face (qq.v.); an artificial, indoor wall; or a boulder. Some cliffs are just 100 feet high. Others, such as El Capitan, can soar upward for thousands of vertical feet.

rope Cord that is used for protection and to help in an ascent of a steep mountain slope (see **fixed rope**), when it is permanently attached to the face. Static rope does not stretch. Dynamic rope does, and it is this type that must be used when a long fall—into a deep crevasse (q.v.)—is possible; otherwise when the person at the end of the rope is brought up short, he or she will be severely hurt by the accompanying jerk. Ropes are designated in millimeters, and the 11 mm ropes of the past are being replaced by much thinner (9 mm) models made of newer, stronger substances such as Kevlar.

self-arrest In mountaineering, using one's ice ax (q.v.) to stop a slide or tumble on a steeply inclined snow or ice slope by first flipping over onto one's stomach, getting the head to the uphill side of the slope and then sliding or digging an ice ax into the surface. If the ice is too hard this does not work well.

serac An often enormous block of ice, sometimes precariously balanced among its brothers. If one falls as a climber passes under or among them, severe harm or death may result.

seven summits The highest point on each of the seven continents. Some people try to climb all seven in emulation of Dick Bass, the first person to accomplish this feat.

Sherpa An ethnic group of some 35,000 or more people, originally from Tibet, who moved down into Nepal and India about 500 years ago. (Sherpa was originally a family name.) Because they live high in the mountains, they are acclimatized to extreme altitude (q.v.) and therefore make excellent expedition porters (qq.v.) and fellow climbers.

short-rope When a mountain climber is very tired, weak, or ill, he or she can be tethered to a much stronger person and coaxed or hauled up the mountain. Some people accuse Sandy Pittman of being short-roped up Everest.

skins Even today, when cross-country skis may have specialized surfaces that allow climbing uphill with ease, people still tie skins (originally animal hide; now synthetic materials are also used) to the bottom of their skis in order to ascend. At their high points, they remove the skins and ski down. To skin-up is to apply these accouterments to the skis.

snow Precipitation that occurs when the temperature is below freezing. The many different types of snow and snow surfaces are extremely important to the mountaineer.

solo To solo is to climb alone, but this does not mean that the climber or mountaineer is unprotected. When necessary the person can belay (q.v.) him- or herself. Climbing alone and unprotected is called free-soloing.

summit The top of the mountain. To summit is to reach the top. Most mountaineers desperately wish to stand here as the culmination of the climb, and they sometimes are willing to sacrifice fingers, toes, and even lives in their attempts. A smaller group of aficionados care more about the route, the challenge, and the joy of climbing; for them the summit is of secondary or little importance.

technical climbing *see* **rock or technical climbing**

téléférique An aerial tramway that usually carries 30 or 40 people at once up or down a mountain. They are more common in Europe than in the U.S., where smaller gondolas that hold about 10 people are the norm.

tools The handheld implements that rock, ice, and mountain climbers use. They include the long-handled ice ax (q.v.): the short and often curvilinear ice ax (used in pairs to ascend vertical ice); and the hammer, which is used to pound pitons (q.v.) into rock cracks. This latter activity is slowly being replaced by nuts and caming devices, which are placed in cracks, but subsequently removed so as to maintain the pristine quality of the rock face (q.v.).

traverse To move horizontally or diagonally across a slope or face (q.v.) rather than moving directly upward. Traversing is extremely dangerous because instead of facing directly up or down the slope, one is disbalanced and any slip is hard to counter. It also means to ascend a peak on one side and descend on another.

trek To walk sometimes long distances, especially in the Himalaya and Karkorum and at altitudes as high as 18,000 feet. It is a popular diversion for those who prefer not to climb the surrounding high peaks.

whiteout A whiteout occurs when snow (q.v.) is violently blown around; it is difficult or impossible to navigate in these conditions. Fog produces the same effect.

Index

Numbers in **_bold italics_** indicate pages with photographs.
_C_ followed by a number indicates pages in color insert.

219